35€

Whither EU-Israeli Relations?
Common and Divergent Interests

ETHNIEN · RELIGIONEN · KONFLIKTE

Herausgegeben von Abraham Ashkenasi

Band 5

PETER LANG
Frankfurt am Main · Berlin · Bern · New York · Paris · Wien

Ephraim Ahiram
Alfred Tovias (Eds.)
with Paul Pasch
in cooperation with the
Leonard Davis Institute

Whither EU-Israeli Relations?

Common and Divergent Interests

PETER LANG
Frankfurt am Main · Berlin · Bern · New York · Paris · Wien

Die Deutsche Bibliothek - CIP-Einheitsaufnahme

Whither EU-Israeli relations? : Common and divergent interests / Ephraim Ahiram ... In Cooperation with the Leonard Davis Institute. - Frankfurt am Main ; Berlin ; Bern ; New York ; Paris ; Wien : Lang, 1995
(Ethnien, Regionen, Konflikte ; Bd. 6)
ISBN 3-631-47549-7

NE: Ahiram, Ephraim [Hrsg.]; GT

ISSN 0934-0343
ISBN 3-631-47549-7

Printed in Germany 1 2 3 4 6 7

Contents

Preface

This book grew out of research on the topic of "Israel and Europe: Common and Divergent Interests." The book encompasses a wide spectrum of relations between Israel and the European Union: political, economic, scientific, cultural, as well as human rights issues. On each of these aspects more than one chapter was contributed by different authors from a large number of countries: in addition to Israel, these include the United Kingdom, France, The Netherlands, Germany, Switzerland, Italy, Spain, Greece, Turkey, Ireland, as well as the EU Commission. The book provides a perspective on the development of European-Israeli relations: their ups and downs, present situation, and future possibilities.

The initiators of the research were: the Leonard Davis Institute for International Relations, Hebrew University; the Friedrich Ebert Stiftung; and B'nai B'rith-Europe. The studies, and a workshop that was held in Jerusalem to discuss them, were made possible by the funding of the Friedrich Ebert Stiftung and of the Leonard Davis Institute.

Our gratitude is extended first and foremost to Dr. Anke Martiny, head of the Friedrich Ebert Stiftung in Tel Aviv; without her interest and generosity, most likely neither the studies nor this volume would have materialized. Also, the State of North Rhine Westphalia generously financed the publication. Thanks are also due to Mr. Ernst Ludwig Ehrlich of B'nai B'rith-Europe and to the Otto Herz Foundation in Vienna. The head of the Delegation of the EU Commission, Ambassador Albert Maes, took strong interest in the work of the groups, participated actively in the workshop, and arranged the participation of some members of the EU Commission. Otto von der Gablentz, ambassador to Israel of the German Federal Republic, also participated actively in the workshop. Our thanks go also to the administrative staff of the Ebert Stiftung, of the Delegation of the EU, and of the Davis Institute. The manuscript editing was done by David Hornik of the Davis Institute.

Our hope is that this volume will contribute to enhanced mutual understanding and the overall strengthening of European-Israeli relations.

Introduction

EPHRAIM AHIRAM AND ALFRED TOVIAS

Political Aspects[1]

Since the establishment of the state of Israel, the policy toward Israel of the EC and of Europe in general has been enacted according to the real or imagined interests of Europe in the Middle East. In the 1950s and 1960s, Europe, and especially France and Britain, had an interest in securing free passage through the Suez Canal; Britain, in particular, was concerned about maintaining its foothold in Egypt so as to enable easy contact with its still-existing empire in Africa and Asia.

Also, both France and Britain wanted to prevent the dictatorial regime in Egypt under President Nasser from becoming the leader of the Middle East as well as the Third World, and to prevent the Soviet Union, as well, from gaining decisive influence in those countries. These were also, very much, the interests of Israel.

France had a special interest in augmenting Israel's might through supply of armaments and a nuclear reactor, thereby deterring Egyptian and other Arab forces from reinforcing the Algerian revolt against French control—which was an Israeli interest as well.

In the same period, Germany provided Israel with considerable restitution payments. Germany's international image thereby improved, and also, in accordance with agreements, Israel made considerable purchases from West Berlin, which helped in the economic restoration of this city.

Thus, overall in this period, between Europe and Israel common interests prevailed over divergent ones. The common interests indeed culminated in the joint invasion of Egypt in 1956 by France, Britain, and Israel.

The only success in this invasion, however, was the military success of the Israeli army, which in three days occupied the Gaza Strip as well as the whole of the Sinai up to the shore of the Suez Canal. The economic intervention of the United States, which mainly threatened the U.K., prevented the achievement of the goals of the invasion: the French and British troops were forced to leave Egyptian soil, and Israel was forced to retreat from all the territories it had taken including the Gaza Strip. Thus, Nasser's position was strengthened both within Egypt and at the international level, in particular in the eyes of Third World countries—much in contrast to the aims of the invading countries. Israel's military might, however, was established in the eyes of both foes and friends, and this contributed to the prevention of another war for a decade; also, Israel's military ties with France were strengthened. This decade of relative peace allowed Israel not only to build its military power but to strengthen its economy and its democracy.

Nevertheless, in the eyes of the Arab states and some of the Third World countries, Israel's collusion with France and Britain constituted convincing proof that Israel was actually a stooge of the colonial powers, as they had always claimed.

This period of common interests concluded with the end of the war in Algeria and the establishment of the Algerian state. Common interests faded, and a change transpired in Europe's relations with Israel that culminated in de Gaulle's famous proclamation following the Six Day War in which he declared a total arms embargo on Israel, in which some other European countries followed suit.

In the long run, however, this change proved a boon for Israel insofar as the United States gradually adopted the role of providing Israel with the necessary armaments and the financial means to pay for them. On the whole, these armaments were technologically superior to their European and Soviet counterparts. The European embargo also led to the acceleration of the establishment of Israel's military industry and through it, its high-technology industry.

Toward 1973, following the increase in world economic development in the 1960s, world demands for oil increased. Furthermore, many oil fields in the United States dried out. In accordance with this change in the oil market, in 1973 the Organization of Petroleum Exporting Countries (OPEC) decided on a dramatic increase in oil prices, and an embargo on countries supplying oil to Israel. The European countries and others, because they were then dependent on oil from the Middle East and North Africa, complied with the embargo. Indeed, Arab countries supplied 50% of Western Europe's demand for oil; only Japan had a larger dependence, importing 80% of its oil from the Middle East.

The period of oil scarcity and high oil prices intensified the fears in Europe, Japan, the United States, and other countries that the Soviet Union might take advantage of the West's preferential policy toward Israel, its relative neglect of Arab interests, to gain a strong foothold in the Middle East and thereby also a major influence on the oil policy of the Gulf states, as well as on the international markets. Such a development could have had a considerable impact on the course of the Cold War. These fears were probably exaggerated, however, insofar as, after all, the West remained the main oil user and importer. However, it is arguable that the Soviet Union's involvement in the Middle Eastern sphere, its forging ties with and arming the Arab countries and distancing itself from Israel, was one more aspect of the Cold War between the superpowers.

In order to maintain and increase their own influence in the Middle East, the European countries supported the Palestinian cause, which was dear to all of the Arab countries, by providing various Arab countries with conventional arms and ingredients for the development of weapons—chemical, biological, and nuclear—of mass destruction.

The peak of European anti-Israeli policy was reached by the then-nine members of the EC in the Venice Declaration of 1980. The main motive force behind the Venice Declaration was France. From Israel's point of view, the main problems with the Declaration were: (1) it did not condemn Palestinian and Arab terrorism—indeed, it did not mention terrorism at all; (2) it preempted future negotiations by recognizing "the legitimate rights of the Palestinian People . . . to exercise fully its right to self-determination"; and (3) it did not mention that the territorial occupation by Israel was the result of a war instigated by the Arab countries—in particular, Jordan, which had been warned not to join Egypt and Syria, had entered the conflict by bombarding Jerusalem, and thus lost its West Bank territory.

Then in 1982, with the outbreak of the Lebanon War, almost all the European countries declared an arms embargo on Israel. During most of the period since the establishment of the state of Israel, most European countries did almost nothing, whether legislatively or diplomatically, to diminish the harsh impact of the secondary and tertiary economic boycott on Israel. U.S. policy in this respect, though not very definite, was nonetheless more active and constructive in both domains.

Gradually, however, almost all the European countries lifted their arms embargo on Israel. But France, and particularly the United Kingdom, retained their embargoes for a long period; indeed, the U.K. lifted its embargo only in 1994. Although Israel has not been dependent on arms supply from Europe, it has been eager to sell its own high-technology arms to European countries, and the embargo made this difficult.

For a long period, European policy toward Israel was to a large extent a function of the oil market. It took about a dozen years, i.e., until 1986, before the supply of oil from new sources such as the North Sea (Britain, Norway, the Netherlands), Mexico, Nigeria, and some Middle Eastern countries, together with oil-saving devices and the establishment of nuclear reactors, particularly in France and Japan, brought about, after several fluctuations, a decline in oil prices to the real 1973 prices and lower.

Then, toward the end of 1987, the Palestinian uprising broke out. Among its manifestations were basic human rights violations, including murder and torture of both Israelis and Palestinians; reasons for intra-Palestinian murder or mayhem were often private quarrels or violations of "family honor." Gradually Israeli reactions also became more violent, including mass arrests and other violations of the Palestinians' human rights.

The European countries (through the European Parliament) took new measures to "punish" Israel, in the economic domain and by imposing an embargo on relations with its scientific community. The European countries did not, however, react to the Palestinians' violations of human rights against both Israelis and their own people.

This approach proved costly when, because of an Israeli veto, neither the EC nor any European country was invited to cosponsor, with the United States and the Soviet Union, the Madrid Peace Conference. Only after Europe more or less ended its anti-Israeli policy, as the new Labor government assumed office in Israel and began to take the peace negotiations seriously, did Israel give its consent for the Europeans to join some of the multilateral negotiation forums, thereby involving the Europeans in the peace process. This is based on common interest: Israel is aware that the Palestinian entity, as well as some other Middle Eastern countries, will be in need of large investments; and, more generally, that without serious economic development the peace, if it materializes, will be endangered. Thus the positions of Israel and the EU have been reversed: Israel is now the one encouraging the EU to help the Palestinians.

Since the peace talks became serious in 1993, overall the relations between Israel and what is now the European Union have moved to a focus on common rather than divergent interests. Significantly, the EU has opened its markets to Israeli products, though more so in the agricultural than in the industrial domain. Europe is a major export market for Israel, and the source of Israel's largest share of import. Thus, Israel's largest trade deficit is with Europe, and most of Israel's overall trade deficit results from the one with Europe. Reducing this deficit is now the main objective in terms of improving Israel-EU relations.

Eberhard Rhein, in his chapter on "European and Israeli Common and Conflicting Interests in the Middle East and the Mediterranean," emphasizes that Europe and Israel have strong common interests concerning the Mediterranean and Middle Eastern regions, such as the establishment of peace with an optimum of social stability and a minimum of upheaval. He advocates that Israel and its neighbors establish a free trade area, which would increase intraregional trade and the economic development of the area in general. This should include projects for infrastructural links, management of the scarce water resources, tourism, and a large-scale youth exchange program. Europe would be prepared to support such efforts with advice, finance, and technology.

In "Common and Conflicting Interests of Mediterranean Europe and Nonmember Mediterranean Countries," Charalambos Tsardanidis argues that the southern European states have both common and divergent interests with the northern Mediterranean states. Creation of a security community would depend on many factors belonging to the security, political, and economic fields. An eastern Mediterranean regional cooperation, similar to the forum of the Ten in the western Mediterranean, could be established, and could play a major role in laying the groundwork for a security community in the Mediterranean area. Tsardanidis concludes that it is questionable whether promotion of cooperation can alleviate rivalries and decrease the growing economic gap between the northern and southern Mediterranean.

The Economic Perspective

Israel has understood at least since the early 1960s that being small, it needs to keep export markets open for sheer economic survival. An obsession with market access has long dominated trade policy. Of course, supporting the GATT-system was part of Israel's overall strategy. But in the aftermath of the two world energy crises and ensuing economic recessions, it was felt that the GATT's liberalization exercises would not procure substantial market access for Israel and that the fate of any GATT round would in any case not be decided in Jerusalem. Clearly, being a "pariah" state in the UN system for much of the last three decades did not augur any good for Israel in case the GATT-system should break down. Some policymakers felt that it was not effective enough, or capable of imposing discipline on or restraining, Israel's major trading partners (the EC and the United States). It should not be forgotten here that Most Favored Nation status guaranteed to Israel under the GATT was without consequence in those Contracting Parties' markets that applied de jure or de facto a boycott on Israeli goods. The lack of diplomatic relations with a large number of UN members was a critical barrier to trade with them, much more than tariffs or QRs. That is why attention naturally turned toward OECD markets and particularly to the EC and U.S. markets.

Having market access in mind, some liberal-minded public officials at the Ministries of Finance and Trade and at the Bank of Israel thought already in the 1970s that they could kill two birds with one stone by concluding bilateral agreements with Israel's major trading partners (first the EC, then the U.S.) that would have disciplining effects on a corporatist economy dominated by public and private monopolies and oligopolies and by an all-encompassing labor union. In times of turbulence this strategy can pay off, and already has in some circumstances. For instance, in spite of being regarded in GATT as a developing country, Israel has never been submitted to the rigors of the MFA and has never been restrained by MFA quotas, for example, in the EC. The explanation lies in agreements that are based on reciprocity. Already today, 70%-75% of Israel's exports can enter duty- and quota-free under preferential treatment given by the EC, the U.S., and EFTA provided they conform with the origin rules included in the different agreements.

As far as the EC is concerned, is that enough reason for satisfaction? Is the future of Israel's formally privileged relations in the economic sphere a given? Certainly not. The EC is a nation-in-the-making, and Israel is not a part of this process. This is a challenge, which nowadays takes the form of the further deepening of the EC to become the EU, but which could reappear no less forcefully when the new EU proceeds with a further enlargement in early 1995 to four EFTA countries and later on to East European countries. In 1990 Eastern Germany was absorbed into the EC as well. With an eye to further enlargements of the EU early in the next century, the Twelve have applied all the directives for the completion of the Internal Market. The Maastricht treaty has been finally ratified; thus the final economic goal of the new "European Union" is the creation of an Economic and Monetary Union by the end of this century.

Israel cannot remain passive in view of these developments (the one probably linked to the other), given its trade interdependence with the EU. The larger the area of geographic discrimination in international trade, the more nonmembers in the periphery suffer from exclusion. One does not need to develop sophisticated analytical models to accept this point. The movement toward regionalism and the creation of huge trading entities will continue, because of lack of traditional U.S. opposition to the idea—on the contrary, the U.S. is joining in the trend (e.g., with the emergence of NAFTA).

But which, then, is "the natural trading bloc" in the case of Israel? Economically and culturally it makes more sense for Israel to link up with the European bloc than the U.S.-led one. First, economically speaking Israel has more overlapping features with an average European country than with one in the Western Hemisphere. Second, Israel has more to offer to the European bloc than to any other (apart from a hypothetical Middle East Common Market). Third, Israel has more to gain from membership in a European bloc than in an American one. Fourth, it is not clear how Israel would obtain membership in a regional trading bloc that is not in its natural neighborhood. Joining a Middle East Common Market is not an alternative to EU association for Israel. Its economic size is currently about 1% that of the EU or the U.S., but larger already than all its neighbors combined! Technologically and scientifically the two regional entities cannot be compared. Israel should not make any move that would lead to loss of the "North" of its compass, and Israel's "North" is the European Union.

The main reason is economic geography. In distribution activities what counts is the time of delivery and economic distance, and this is valid for Israel too. The short geographic distance (Israel and Western Europe are only one hour apart in terms of time zones) facilitates real-time commercial intercourse (e.g., opening and closing times are practically the same; there is no "jet lag" when traveling to Europe; quick feedback from markets is possible; highly perishable products are tradable). Also connected to geography, Israel and parts of Western Europe share the same maritime and meteorological factors, enabling easy knowledge of the natural conditions prevailing in the trading partner. Moreover, Israel's consumption and cultural patterns and standards largely overlap with European ones; and its climate is similar to that of southern Europe.

Israel has, of course, other neighbors than Europe, but there are limited possibilities for Israel to direct its exports to them, not only because of the state of war with some of them but also due to their limited absorption capacities; unfortunately, this will not change if peace materializes.

Numbers speak for themselves. In 1992, 34.5% of Israel's exports were to the EC, rising from 30% in 1986, and the share of the U.S. in Israel's exports reached 30.5%. Half of Israeli imports originated in the EC-12 in recent years (e.g., 50.2% in 1992), which contrasts with a U.S. share of less than 20% (e.g., 17.2% in 1992).

However, in spite of the fact that there is a Free Trade Agreement between Israel and the EC, Israel is already in a much worse position than Finland or Norway. From the Israeli exporter's viewpoint, the elimination of duplication of testing and certification procedures in intra-EEA (European Economic Area) trade as from 1994 by application of the principle of mutual recognition accords an advantage to EEA-based exporters in relation to Israeli ones. There is no mutual recognition of laboratories and tests. Another example is government procurement. If EEA preference becomes the rule, instead of the more liberal system of open tendering, any present exports of goods or services by Israel to the EEA are entirely endangered. Thus it is the creation of a Single European Market including 17 countries that is behind the willingness by successive Israeli governments to negotiate with the EC since 1988. Not for nothing did past and present Israeli governments seek a status similar to those EFTA countries joining the EEA. Barring this, the aim has been to review the 1975 EC-Israel agreement so as to eliminate some of the NTBs on mutual trade. The idea from the start has been that Israel should negotiate EC concession of some of the advantages that EFTA countries benefited from, such as participation in European Standards Institutes (e.g., CEN, CENELEC), free trade in services, participation in some of the EC's technological programs (e.g., ESPRIT II, RACE), introduction of the SAD (Single

Administrative Document) in trade between Israel and both the EC and EFTA, participation in ERASMUS, a liberalization of origin rules, and so on.

It was only at the 1992 Cooperation Council that matters began to take shape. The EC spoke of ameliorating the existing agreement; Israel desired anchorage in the EEA. The EC insisted on a double-track approach. Israel had first to deepen its relations with its neighbors, and only then with the EC. Anchoring Israel only in the EC would do a disservice to Israel if it brought with it being detached economically from its region. Israel would then become a Western garrison in the Middle East. Israel could not be part of the EEA because the EC could not discriminate positively in the face of other Mediterranean nonmember countries, even if this could be justified in economic terms.

Exploratory talks were conducted from mid-1992 until the summer of 1993. The Commission received a formal mandate from the Council of Ministers in late December 1993. Negotiations and conclusion of the new agreement are scheduled to culminate in 1994, so that the new agreement enters into force in 1995. According to informed sources it will not contain much more than the present agreement does in the domain of trade in goods. The most significant improvement will come in the domain of R&D. Although participation in ESPRIT is not to be expected, Israel will be able to take part in other programs. In the area of services, less than what was scheduled initially will likely be agreed upon. In financial services, the goal is to liberalize slowly on a reciprocal basis. Air and sea transport will probably not be covered. To sum up, in the best of cases, Israel will still be very far from obtaining the status of an EFTA country regarding its relations with the EU.

In conceiving this book, the editors had the present negotiations in mind and asked a number of the authors to address specific economic issues affecting Israel-EC relations. For instance, what will be the implications of the completion of the EC's Internal Market for Israeli firms? In their chapter on "The Effect of Europe 1992 on Outsider Firms: Theoretical Considerations and Empirical Evidence—The Case of Israel," Seev Hirsch and Tamar Almor show theoretically that EC-92 will benefit insiders more than outsiders. Therefore they conclude that outsiders' firms have an interest in becoming insiders by investing directly in the EC. Predictions pertaining to variations in investment patterns by sector, by region, and over time are tested on empirical data concerning Israeli firms.

Jacob Kol, in "Trade Liberalization Under GATT and by the EC: Implications for Israel," looks first at the wider economic implications of the current liberalization drives taking place within the EC. He draws an interesting parallel between mercantilism and EC-92. Since January 1, 1994, the program has been extended to practically all EFTA countries by creating a European Economic Area, of which Israel is not part. Given Israel's high profile in international trade and revealed comparative advantages (which he calculates), Kol suggests that Israel should from now on try to diversify the geographic distribution of its foreign trade.

It appears, therefore, that the implications of the creation of the EEA for the Israeli economy cannot be neglected. This is the conclusion arrived at in Victoria Curzon Price's chapter on "The European Economic Area: Implications for Non-members in General and Mediterranean Countries in Particular." She first systematically studies the different items to be found in the EEA agreement (e.g., services, people, capital) and concludes that, Israel apart, other Mediterranean nonmember countries will not be heavily affected by the creation of the EEA, except for the case of some agricultural products covered in special bilateral dealings between EFTA countries and some southern European EC members.

Taking a longer-term perspective, Alfred Tovias, in his chapter on "The Shape of the EC's Pyramid of Privilege in the Year 2000: What Is in Store for Israel?," explores the wider economic implications for Israel of further EC enlargements or association dealings with third countries outside the EFTA area. To give a foretaste, the main focus of research is on a particular case study, namely, the progressive economic and political integration of Turkey and Cyprus into the EC. Tovias shows that the adoption of the EC agreements with Israel by non-EEA European countries would have a very positive influence on Israel's trade with those that do not have preferential relations with Israel whatsoever such as the Visegrad countries, Turkey, and Cyprus.

How could Israel react to the different moves made by non-EC countries so as to come closer to the EC? In particular, given that Israel's acceptance into the EC is not on the agenda in the foreseeable future, should "association to the EC" be considered? J. Redmond considers "The EC's Approach to Association" from an economic perspective and looks into its applicability to the Israeli case. He attempts—succesfully, we think—to formulate an operational definition of association, something that cannot be found in previously published research. Interestingly, he concludes that the association model as understood in Europe would not serve well the interests of Israel.

Is that, then, cause for despair? Not if one accepts the conclusions reached in the chapter by Luis de Sebastián on "Trading Blocs and the Stranded Countries." De Sebastián's topic is the fate reserved for outsiders in a world of trading blocs. After defining what a trading bloc is and identifying the existing blocs, he reviews the GATT's doctrine on the subject. De Sebastián shows that Israel, as an outsider, has in fact followed the best strategy available to outsiders for the moment, namely, concluding free trade agreements with different countries/blocs (the EC, the U.S., and EFTA), without relying too much on a succesful outcome of the GATT's Uruguay Round of Multilateral Trade Negotiations. He calls this original strategy "polilateralism."

An exploration of possible Israeli responses to the European challenge would be incomplete without an in-depth analysis of monetary developments in the EC affecting Israel's economic posture. The chapter by Elise S. Brezis on "Europe and Israel: The Effects of EMU on Development and Growth" deals with the consequences of a monetary union for European countries first and shows that it will affect the specialization of countries and the technological race, increasing growth prospects in Europe but also in Israel. But for Israel to reap the benefits, barriers on EU trade must be totally eliminated rather quickly. In the words of Brezis, "to become a satellite of Europe is possible when the mass of Europe is not yet in high density. . . . However, if Europe already has a huge mass, then satellites are not viable as such."

Leora Rubin Meridor, in "Should Israel Enter the EMS?," presents a short empirical note on the lessons to be drawn by Israel from the functioning of the European Monetary System (EMS). She concludes that Israel was fortunate not to try, in recent years, to adjust itself unilaterally to EMS members' macroeconomic strategies in view of the different external shocks it had to cope with (such as the absorption of new immigrants). Israel did much better in this regard than Germany after unification.

Finally, opening a larger and unfinished debate that could greatly affect peripheral countries such as Israel, Emilio Fontela considers "The Futures of Europe." He draws different scenarios for Europe and for its periphery based on a model tried before (i.e., CADMOS, adopted in the context of the EC's FAST program), opening a real agenda for research. It emerges clearly that Europe constitutes "unfinished business" and that Israel will have to deal for a while with a moving target in a changing environment. Given the past record of EC-Israeli institutionalized relations, there is reason to expect that a new modus vivendi will be found sooner or later.

European-Israeli Cultural Relations

The Jewish population of Israel has come from about 100 different countries. Therefore the culture of Israel is combined from dozens of different cultural heritages—often with no common denominator other than the Jewish religion. During the latter nineteenth century and the first third of the twentieth century the bulk of the immigrants came from Eastern Europe, mainly Russia and Poland. Although their cultural heritage was to a large degree the Jewish religious culture, many of them had emancipated themselves from this heritage. However, they brought with them cultural heritages from the nations among which they had lived for centuries, such as the famous Russian theatrical tradition together with Russian folkdances and folksongs, which influenced Israeli song until about the 1950s. These immigrants also developed an original sociocultural phenomenon, the kibbutzim, which contributed greatly to many spheres of the development of Israel, as well as the notion of nationalism.

The 1930s brought a large immigration from Germany as well as small infusions from other European countries such as Austria, Britain, and Czechoslovakia. Immigrants from Germany, as well as from countries such as Poland and Austria, introduced some of the great European musical culture including classical and operatic music, and contributed considerably to the establishment of the Israel Philharmonic, which has achieved worldwide fame. They also introduced the Bauhaus School in architecture and painting, as well as the streams of German expressionism and the abstract and French schools. The creations of these immigrants in these categories are still among the highlights of Israeli cultural achievements. The European immigrants, together with young Israeli actors, also succeeded in revolutionizing, after the establishment of the state, the then-prevailing theatrical culture and prevented its stagnation in Russian modalities.

The European immigrants also contributed enormously to the development of the Israeli universities in almost all disciplines: physics, chemistry, biology, mathematics, demography, medicine, as well as in the humanistic studies such as philosophy, literature, Judaism, archeology, psychology, juristic studies, and economics. Overall, the impact of European intellectual life on Israel is immeasurable; it is difficult to imagine the cultural and intellectual life of Israel today if this foundation had not been laid.

The country's civic culture (defined as the behavior of citizens in relation to society and the state), including democracy and the observance of human rights, "clean" administration, the rule of law, disinterested jurisdiction, and so on, were largely adopted by the state of Israel from the British Mandate.

It should also be noted, however, that in Europe the Jews, over the centuries, contributed to most areas of culture in their host countries. The Old Testament itself was, of course, a major cultural contribution, a source of ideas and inspiration both in the arts and in civic culture. Thus, in the Diaspora there gradually developed a fertile cultural symbiosis between parts of the Jewish and the non-Jewish population. Furthermore, as the Jews were often forced (for a variety of reasons including persecution, discrimination, and economic difficulties) to wander, they also disseminated cultural aspects of their former countries of residence. When large numbers of Jews eventually emigrated to Israel, they brought with them cultural heritages to which they themselves had contributed and of which they often felt a part. Following the establishment of the state of Israel came the massive immigration that was comprised of Holocaust survivors and of immigrants from Arab countries, mainly Iraq, Morocco, Algeria, Tunisia, and Egypt. The latter immigrants also included a small minority of professionals, particularly the Iraqis but also the North Africans among whom were people who had received an excellent French education. All of these immigrations brought with them a rich Arab musical heritage as well as a distinctive Jewish music considerably influenced by oriental sources. It should also be noted that among the immigrants from Muslim countries, various aspects of civic culture had a very different meaning than for the immigrants from Russia who had exerted such a formative influence over Israeli life.

Now that several generations of immigration to Israel have transpired, some questions arise as to the nature of the cultural developments that have crystallized in the country:

1. Has Israel become a cultural melting pot?
2. Which cultural heritages have prevailed in the country?
3. To what extent has an original Israeli culture evolved?

In music, particularly from the 1920s to the 1950s, there were several attempts to synthesize European and oriental music, but these did not really strike roots among the Israeli public, except for the music of one group called Habreira Hativit (the Natural Choice), which has its admirers among Israelis both of Western and Middle Eastern backgrounds. Otherwise, in music, immigrants and their descendants have remained faithful to their own musical heritages, and even their new compositions tend to maintain the style of their culture of origin. Israel's eclectic musical culture has, however, produced many performers who have achieved worldwide fame.

Young Israelis tend to be drawn to two kinds of music: Israeli-composed songs connected with Israel—its nature, its experiences in love and war, and so on; and music mainly of American origin: rock, disco, and so on, which are embraced by almost all young people all over the world, bridging gaps between cultural backgrounds and sometimes even generations. There are also original Israeli contributions to these popular genres. Classical music, too, still has its devotees among youngsters in Israel, though it does not bridge cultural gaps in the way that the popular music does.

Thus, so far as music is concerned, over several generations the cultural heritage of most of the countries of origin has prevailed, and very little successful synthesis of the various musical cultures has occurred; the melting-pot characterization does not apply. More recently, both the audience and the number of performers of classical music have been considerably enhanced by the immigration from the former Soviet Union.

In dance, there has been more synthesis between the Western and oriental heritages, but in this area as well new creations have mainly been influenced by American dance culture.

As for theater in Israel, in terms both of composition of plays and performance it is now almost totally Western in nature, with almost no oriental influences. A considerable number of original Israeli plays have, however, been written, some of which have also been performed in Europe and been well received there. In addition, plays, often classical, from European and other countries are staged.

Pantomime, based mainly on the French school, has also developed in Israel. There are also satirical groups, highly original and successful, especially when poking fun at Israeli politics and politicians as well as the various immigrant ethnicities.

So far Israel has not been very successful in film making, although a few films of international quality have been produced. In general the world of cinema and of television in Israel, as in most European countries, is flooded with American productions, although good British, French, Italian, and Swedish films often achieve great success as well. Overall, though, this area of cultural life is undeniably very Americanized, and exerts an Americanizing influence on many other spheres of life.

The world of Israeli literature shows only scant West European influence. In the East European diaspora and particularly Russia, Jewish literature, some of it of very high quality, was written mainly in Yiddish and Hebrew and was largely based on Jewish life in the *shtetl*. The literature written by Palestinian Jews in the early decades of the twentieth century was still influenced by this body of work, but a new kind of literature was beginning to appear that was based mainly on life in the Promised Land. After the establishment of the state, Israeli literature gradually developed in original directions, and today is increasingly flourishing in both quantitative and qualitative terms. Relatively large numbers of Israeli works have been translated into other languages, and some authors have achieved fame abroad. Most of the literature draws on present-day Israeli life, including in wartime, although there is also a trend of looking backward to Jewish life in Palestine during the World War I era and earlier.

Most of the writers from the West European diaspora who settled in Israel, particularly in the 1930s, were unable to express themselves fluently in Hebrew, and their writings in their original language could not find a large audience either in Israel or in Europe during World War II and its aftermath. Thus these writers, unrecognized and depressed, faded from the scene. Also tragic was the fate of East European writers who produced their best works in the Diaspora in Hebrew, whereas in Israel the works they wrote were generally of far lesser quality.

In contrast to immigrant writers for many of whom Israel was the end of their career, for many painters, whether they came from the Bauhaus school or other ones, there was less trouble in adjusting their techniques to Israel's variegated landscapes and human subjects; the land with its beautiful lights and colors was for them like an enchanting, God-given present. Some of the painters and sculptors, as well as some of the creations of the Bauhaus architects, became world-famous. Despite being able to express themselves, however, these artists often had serious financial difficulties because of the small and rather poor market available for their work. Overall, the new generations of Israeli painters, sculptors, and architects broke away from the European schools, but have been influenced by American and French modern and postmodern schools while often showing marked originality.

Since the end of the Second World War, academic life in Israel has been considerably Americanized. The stress on academic studies that was "imported" to Israel by the European immigration has prevailed and even strengthened, as the early Zionist inclinations of return to the land and manual labor have receded and the need for highly educated people in many professions has grown. Unfortunately, so far only a small percentage of Israelis of Middle Eastern background have achieved university educations, so that in some regards the gap between them and Israelis of Western background as well as new immigrants from Eastern Europe has widened. However, the seeds of cultural heritage, of academic education and freedom, have been sown by the immigrants from Europe; and Israeli academic life, with a considerable American influence, has been able to develop from this foundation.

Overall, then, parts of the Israeli population have preserved the cultural heritage of the countries from which they emigrated. On the other hand, Israelis have made original contributions in many cultural spheres. What has almost not occurred at all has been the synthesis of different cultures, i.e., the melting pot.

The Western and Middle Eastern cultural tendencies, however, exist side by side, in spite of the deliberate effort, during the first two decades of statehood, to make the immigrants from Third World countries relinquish their cultural heritage and embrace the Israeli culture.

In most spheres of cultural life in Israel, European influences have laid the foundation. However, as has occurred in Europe itself since World War II, also in Israel cultural life has changed, regenerated itself, and incorporated considerable American influences. Technological advances in communication—such as television, video cassettes, satellite communication, and so on—are greatly expanding the dissemination of culture and changing the world, for better or worse, to some extent into a "global village." Thus, new ideas and new schools have been adopted in Israel more rapidly than in the past. Still, even though Israel has become a part of this changing world, many cultural aspects of the European heritage have been preserved, particularly in music, theater, dance, and academic studies both in the humanities and sciences.

So far as language is concerned, the second generation in Israel has often, at least to some degree, retained the language of their parents; but much less is retained by the third generation. The first generation acquires the Hebrew language to varying degrees of competence; but overall, by now, Hebrew is the main language of communication in Israel, which was not the case three to four decades ago. Although for the Israeli-born generations Hebrew is the first language, those who study abroad, or have professional connections there, speak at least one foreign language, most often English but also French, Russian, or other European or Latino-American languages.

Close cultural relations between Europe and Israel find expression in, for example, visits of theatrical groups from Germany, the United Kingdom, France, Italy, Austria, and other countries who participate in the annual Jerusalem Festival and other festivals in Israel. Conversely, Israeli theatrical groups perform in some of the same countries, such as in the Edinburgh Festival. Several European countries have opened cultural institutions in Israel, such as the British Council, the Cultural Center of France, and the German Goethe Institute. Recently Israel has also joined various European sport organizations, through which Israel participates in European sport events. Thus, Israel's relations and ability to communicate with various European cultures continue, probably more so than for some other countries.

It should be mentioned that there are two communities in Israel that, for the most part, do not take part in its cultural life: the ultra-Orthodox Jews, who maintain separation because of their strong religious beliefs, and the Arab minority in Israel (within the Green Line).

In his chapter "Symbiosis, Misrepresentations, and Pitfalls," Abraham Ashkenasi considers implications for Europe of some cultural developments in Israel. Jews contributed much to the arts, philosophy, and science in Europe; and the Jewish community in Israel was influenced in these fields by immigrating European and particularly German Jews. Israel's European attributes, however, are gradually being diluted by the large non-European immigration, an increase in religious fundamentalism, and difficulties and conflicts in dealing with the Arabs both within and outside Israel's borders. Israel has, however, coped well in integrating Jews of many ethnicities into its society. Therein lies a fund of experience that has much to offer today's Europe, through cultural and intellectual exchange and analysis.

Anke Martiny, in "The Cultural Dimension of a Unified Europe: Implications for Israel," notes that a common European culture has not yet emerged, though the beginnings of cooperation are evident in the areas of cinema and media. Cultural traditions of various European countries have, however, entered Israeli culture through immigrations from those countries, though Israeli culture on the whole shows a stronger affinity for American models. The pluralism of European culture, however, which shows the unmistakable characteristics of the respective states and allows for multinationality within states, could potentially serve as a model for regions such as the Middle East that are beset by fundamentalism and dogmatism.

EC-Israel Cooperation in Scientific Research

The roots of Israeli natural science are European and go back to the 1920s and particularly the 1930s, when Jewish scientists from Germany, Hungary, Britain, and other European countries were emigrating to Palestine and often joining the Haifa Technological Institute and the Hebrew University in Jerusalem, both of which were then very young institutions. Thus the formative influence on Israeli scientific attitudes was European—mainly German, and to some extent also British, as, in that period, many Israeli students did their graduate work at British universities.

During World War II and its aftermath, science developed much more rapidly in the United States than in Europe because of the large number of immigrant European scientists as well as the much greater funds available for scientific research, which affected, among other things, the quality of laboratories and the availability of scholarships. Thus, after the war, and particularly after the establishment of the state of Israel, most Israeli science students or postdoctorates preferred to carry out their studies or research in the U.S. rather than Europe. Other factors were the memories of Germany's deeds in the war, as well as the comparatively widespread knowledge of the English language among Israeli students and scientists. Overall, interaction and cooperation between Israeli and U.S. science became intensive.

In the past few decades, Israeli science and technology have contributed to developed as well as developing countries. Cooperation with European countries, particularly Germany and to a lesser extent France and Britain, is on the increase. In addition, EC programs are open to Israeli scientists and students. Israel has not been included, however, in the prestigious COST program, but in 1993 it was accepted as a member of EUREKA.

The emergence of European scientific cooperation with Israel has probably been influenced by the successful U.S.-Israeli cooperation. There have, however, been difficulties in developing Israeli-European scientific relations associated with the EC's political attitudes toward Israel. It is to be hoped that in the wake of the current peace process between Israel, the Palestinians, and the Arab countries, further development of EU-Israeli scientific cooperation can be expected; and, particularly, that the notion of a European Science and Technology Community will not eventually become an aspect of a "Fortress Europe."

M. Macioti, in "How Can EC-Israeli Scientific Research Be Expanded?," points out that Israel is a recognized and impressive technological power by relevant indicators. Hence, there is a sound basis for scientific cooperation between Israel and Europe. The main areas of Israeli-European scientific cooperation are in: advanced structural and functional materials, biotechnology, optoelectronics, nanoelectronics, and desertification. Beyond R&D, other Mediterranean programs link Israel and the EC in valuable cooperation, such as protection of the environment and of natural habitats. In science and technology, some areas of cooperation that are better represented in Israel than in Europe include aerospace engineering and technology as well as horticulture. EC-Israeli scientific cooperation could also benefit the Third World.

In her chapter on "International and European Cooperation in Scientific Research: A German Viewpoint," Beate Kohler-Koch describes from a German point of view the internationalization of scientific communities, the multifaceted situation of European scientific cooperation, and recent trends in scientific research. Reflecting the current dominance of the intra-European attitude toward scientific research, Israel, as noted, was initially excluded from some European-initiated programs in international scientific cooperation. However, Israel's cooperative projects with individual European countries, particularly Germany, are well institutionalized; indeed, if measured in terms of funds raised in relation to GNP per capita, Israel ranks first among Germany's scientific cooperation partners.

In "The State of Cooperation in Scientific Research: Israel and the EC," Alex Keynan discusses basic concepts of international scientific cooperation, the trends in Israel's international cooperation including the shifting balance between Europe and the United States, and Israel's scientific cooperation with individual European countries and with West European regional organizations. Regarding the EC, he notes that Israel's cooperation with it developed much later than with other European organizations, since the EC's bureaucratic structure makes it easier for industry to deal with it on projects than for individual scientists. He also discusses the problems in EC-Israeli scientific cooperation arising from EC political attitudes.

The Human Rights Issue

The issue of human rights has been taken up mainly in the postwar era by the United States and West European countries. Apparently, this was a result of the atrocities of the war and of a repugnance toward dictatorial regimes that had no respect for human rights.

The human rights issue is an offshoot of the Western democratic culture and values; hence the definition and application of human rights were molded accordingly. These have been the human rights of mostly affluent, rational, well-educated, well-cared-for societies, which are, however, still a minority among humankind. In the latter half of the 20th century these countries have almost completely decolonized, granting former colonies the right of self-determination; the treatment of the black and other minorities in the United States has considerably improved, though there is still more to be accomplished; capital punishment has nearly been abolished (though not in the U.S.), as well as torture by government agencies and unlawful detainment. Also, women have achieved a vast improvement in their human rights.

Nevertheless, the definition as well as application of human rights by this minority of humankind have been highly egocentric. They have applied human rights mainly to their original populations, but only partially—at best—to immigrants and foreign workers, and have not extended these rights to the Basques in Spain, the Irish in Ulster, or the Gypsies everywhere. Thus the affluent societies have been able to comply only partially with their own notion of human rights; yet they preach their gospel to other countries that have different problems and different cultural origins.

One of the most serious mistakes of the affluent countries is the failure to include the standard of living in their definition of human rights, even though most of humankind still lives in dismal conditions. In the less developed countries, poverty not only constitutes in itself a deprivation of human rights, but is associated with poor health care and relatively low life expectancy, hunger, scant education, and unemployment.

The affluent Western countries attempt, by extortion, to impose their own notion of human rights on many of these societies. This seldom succeeds, for several reasons. To begin with, the affluent countries have done very little—in some cases nothing—to help improve the living standards of the poor ones, as evidenced by the persistent huge gap between North and South. The affluent countries only worsen the situation by preventing immigration from the South, though such immigration would alleviate unemployment there and enable transfer of earnings to the families at home. The Northern countries have even contributed to the creation of dictatorships and abuse of human rights in the South.

Second, as already mentioned, in many cases the human rights that the affluent countries try to impose on the South have not been implemented at home, so that the affluent countries are in a position both hypocritical and of dubious efficacy.

Third, the affluent countries use their human rights pressures differentially, according to their own political interests. For example, the NATO countries do not threaten Turkey with human rights sanctions, even though Turkey has violated human rights in its conflict with the Kurds; yet the NATO countries have taken harsh measures against Iraq in part because of its own behavior toward the Kurds. Even toward Iraq, however, NATO did not take strong measures immediately after the Gulf War because of its political interest in preventing Iraq's disintegration. Western countries have taken no serious measures against Saudi Arabia, where women have almost no human rights to speak of, and capital punishment and maiming of the body are used even for minor violations of the law. In this and similar cases, because of their political-economic interests the affluent countries have made no attempt to alter grave situations.

A most serious miscalculation was made by the EC when, because of human rights violations in Yugoslavia, it recognized the self-determination of Slovenia and Croatia, but thereby provoked the bloodiest war and worst human rights violations in Europe since World War II, the toll of which involves hundreds of thousands dead and injured, thousands of women raped, and hundreds of thousands of people forcibly expelled from their homes in the infamous "ethnic cleansing."

The relations between the EC and Israel have long been hampered by the deprivation of the human rights of the Palestinians in the occupied territories. In this respect, Israel is in a very similar situation to that of France in Algeria until the 1960s and Britain in Ulster to this day: these countries have introduced considerable human rights at home (Israel being the most advanced country in the Middle East in terms of human rights) but not in the various occupied domains. The EC has time and again penalized Israel by boycotting some of its agricultural exports and suspending scientific relations, through decisions taken by the European Parliament or by EC officials. No such measures, however, were ever remotely imposed on France or the United Kingdom—or, for that matter, on Spain in regard to the human rights of the Basques.

The aim here is not in any way to excuse Israel's human rights violations in the occupied territories, but to point out the EC's inconsistency and double standards with respect to this issue.

In "The Role of Human Rights in the Design of the Community's European Political Cooperation: Application to the Middle East," Gianni Bonvicini notes that the European Political Cooperation (EPC) now plays an increasingly prominent role in the field of human rights. This recent achievement, particularly with respect to the Middle East, may play a key part in building an autonomous role for the Community in the region. Although in other areas EPC declarations are traditionally felt to carry little weight, this is not the case regarding human rights, where even a simple EPC condemnation puts a country on the defensive. When made against Middle Eastern countries, declarations of this kind tend to isolate and create difficulties for the accused country. The nervousness with which third countries usually react to such initiatives attests to their effectiveness.

David Coombes, in his chapter "The European Community and Democracy in the Mediterranean," points out that the EC has progressively enlarged both its perspective and capacity as an independent power in international affairs. So far its policy regarding the accession of new members, and thus also toward developments in southeastern Europe, seems to be determined mainly by economic and strategic considerations, with commitment to democracy remaining a secondary concern. The prevailing trend seems to favor a system in which a core of mainly larger states in effect determine the welfare and security both of smaller powers in the core itself and of a wider periphery of satellite dependencies. The further development of relations between European states on those lines cannot bode well for democracy in any part of the world; in the newly unstable conditions of world politics today it is most unlikely, on the other hand, to restore significant power of independent action to European states, acting individually or collectively.

Notes

1. This section is by Ephraim Ahiram. The subsequent section, "The Economic Perspective," is by Alfred Tovias; the remaining three sections are by Ephraim Ahiram.

PART I

POLITICAL ASPECTS

Chapter 1

Common and Conflicting Interests of Israel and Europe in the Middle East and the Mediterranean

EBERHARD RHEIN

It is clear that between Europe and Israel there is a convergence of interests in the Mediterranean. Indeed, the Mediterranean is as much a European sea as it is a Middle Eastern one, and Europe has the same concerns as Israel or Turkey—for example, regarding a secure energy supply from the Gulf countries.

Without being exhaustive, I shall try to specify some basic interests that Israel and Europe share.

First, they would both wish the Mediterranean to be a zone of peace, with an optimum of social stability and a minimum of social upheaval.

Second, they would both wish that such a zone of peace would mean that all the countries around the Mediterranean can live in secure, recognized borders and that peace and security can be achieved with as low a level of defense expenditure as possible. At present, of course, the Middle East is very far from that latter goal; defense expenditure in the major countries in the region is about four to five times as high in relation to GNP as it is in Europe.

Third, Israel and Europe would both prefer that the Mediterranean become a zone of relatively high economic prosperity, with disparities in income levels between Mediterranean countries (e.g., Israel and its neighbors) and between Europe and Mediterranean countries being much lower than they are at present. This economic point is underlined by the presumably shared perception that there is a close interrelationship between the economic and the political well-being of a region. If the basic economic needs of populations for housing, food, clothing, and education are not being met, sooner or later those populations will revolt against their own leadership and/or against neighboring countries.

Fourth, Europe and Israel should both strive to make the Mediterranean a zone of ecological stability. Both must resist, as much as possible, existing pressures toward environmental degradation. Israel and the European Community are pioneers in this area, even if neither is free from ecological sins.

All these are interests that Israel and Europe share not only with each other but also with their common neighbors, the Arab countries and Turkey, who are no less interested in the goals of peace and social and economic stability.

So long as common interests are expressed in terms of basic political goals, it will be easy to achieve harmony between Europe and Israel. When we look at the details, however—in particular, the way in which Europe on the one hand, and Israel on the other, have in the past tried to realize those fundamental aims of peace and prosperity—we find differences; differences that, over the past two decades, have sometimes led parts of Israeli public opinion to believe that Europe was anti-Israeli and segments of European public opinion to believe that Israel and Europe were no longer adhering to the same set of basic political and humanitarian values. Indeed, sometimes in the past there has been a perception in Europe that Israel was pursuing a vision of peace that did not seem tenable since it implied retaining Palestinian and other Arab land that had been occupied or even annexed, in the wake of military confrontations.

Today, however, those reciprocal doubts in Israeli and European public opinion seem to belong to the past. In light of the peace process being pursued by the Israeli government, Israel and Europe have regained the conviction that they are thinking on the same wavelength, in terms not only of grand designs but also of ways of implementing such designs. Thus, not only is there now a close and fertile interchange of ideas between the two sides, but their parallel thinking has developed in such a way that sometimes papers on the region's future drafted by one side could well have been drafted by the other. This fundamental change of psychological and political climate is manifested by the way in which both Israelis and Europeans regard the long-term future of the region Europeans call the Near East, which comprises Israel and its immediate neighbors Lebanon, Jordan, Syria, Palestine, and Egypt.

First, and most important, the prospects for peace have become real. Israel is closer than ever before in its short history to attaining its long-pursued goal of being fully accepted as a country and, more important for the future, as a partner for the region. The days when Israel's Arab neighbors spoke of "the Zionist entity" and contemplated the destruction of Israel have passed.

In parallel, the prospects for establishment of a Palestinian state, most probably in federation or at least confederation with Jordan, are more real now than ever. In other words, a process has begun of drawing border lines between Israel and Palestine.

One of the points of contention and mutual mistrust between Europe and Israel had been the Venice Declaration of 1980, in which the Community asserted that all the countries in the region should live in secure borders and that the right of the Palestinian people for self-determination, including statehood, should be recognized. Today, however, the principle of such a state no longer seems in doubt, only its delimitation.

The prospects for normal diplomatic and commercial relations between Israel and all its Arab neighbors have also become encouraging, in terms of the not too distant future. The establishment of formal peace does not by itself, of course, entail a "warm peace"; this requires the establishment of links of interdependence between Israel and its neighbors. That, of course, is the objective of the multilateral peace talks, in which Israel and its main neighbors (so far with the notable exceptions of Syria and Lebanon) are participating, as well as Europe, the United States, Russia, and Japan.

In some regards, there are special European perspectives on how peace can be achieved. The European experience of economic and, increasingly, political integration may have much to offer, though it is also understood there that the European experience cannot simply be transferred to the Middle East. Underlying the European course has been the conviction that if joint interests between neighboring countries are created, it will be much more difficult for disputes to harden into conflicts as these would seriously harm the interests of each of the countries involved.

To give weight and expression to the commonality of interests, Europeans have thought it useful to set up common institutions such as the Commission, Council of Ministers, Court of Justice, joint research centers, and so on. It is widely believed in Europe that Israel and its neighbors, too, need to create joint interests that bind them together, although European observers are aware that this requires greater caution in the Middle Eastern context. It will indeed take some time to overcome many years of mutual distrust before Israelis and Arabs can work together on joint projects.

How can joint interests be created? The best and probably most direct and efficient means is to encourage trade between the countries. Skeptics may focus on the lack of complementarity between the countries of the region; yet, undoubtedly, the potential for intraregional trade remains largely untapped. To exploit it more fully, two bold, parallel steps should be taken: (1) the red tape at customs and borders that hinders the rapid movement of goods should be drastically reduced; and (2) customs and customslike fees on imported goods from neighboring countries should be cut back dramatically. Ideally, a free trade area should be established between Israel and its neighbors as soon as possible, with Israel dismantling its tariff protections immediately and its much less developed neighbors following suit over a 10- to 12-year transition period, much in the way that Europe and Israel have accomplished their free trade area since 1975 (with the Community abolishing all duties) and 1989 (with Israel fulfilling its part of the deal).

To encourage trade, it will be necessary to establish basic infrastructural links. Some of these are of vital interest: if, for example, all the countries in the region were to interconnect their electricity grids, or if the region or part of it were to be linked by a network of gas pipelines, for example, from Egypt to Israel and Jordan. Cooperation in the field of tourism would also be an essential asset in terms of creating common interests. Indeed, the region is one of the most attractive worldwide for historical tourism; however, each of the countries is so small that only by pooling their resources and setting up regional tourist itineraries could the potential for attracting tourists from Europe, the United States, and Japan be fully tapped.

Joint management of scarce water resources is essential if the region is to survive and to maintain peace. Water has been—and will become even more so—the gravest source of potential conflict; hence, the countries of the region must jointly harness this scarce and irreplaceable resource, for example, by setting up a Jordan Valley Water Authority or by jointly building and managing desalination plants.

In the fields of energy or transport, a joint Jordanian-Palestinian-Israeli hydropower station on the Dead Sea is a possible project of common economic and technical interest. Another might be a jointly run solar power plant in the Sinai or the Negev.

There are at least two long-term challenges facing all the countries in the region that require them to work together on research and development: to make the desert bloom by using new innovative methods of vegetation and using brackish water for minimizing irrigation needs; and to develop solar energy as a long-term substitute in light of the phasing out of the fossil energy age.

Last but not least, the Israelis, Palestinians, and other Arabs should follow the Franco-German example by setting up a vast youth exchange program in order to foster reconciliation for future generations.

Europe can contribute much to realizing such visions. It is prepared to become the advocate of regional cooperation in the Middle East, to help as a go-between and catalyst. Progress toward Arab-Israeli peace will not always be easy, and the services of an honest broker may be necessary for some time to come. Europe has indeed been playing this role for the past two years, not with very high visibility but at an increasing pace. As a few examples, Europe has been financing Israeli-Palestinian cooperation between social scientists as well as between women's groups, summer camps for youngsters from Israel and Palestine, and is in the process of financing prefeasibility studies for regional interconnection of the electricity grids, future road links, and a hydropower plant on the Dead Sea; and, of course, Europeans have been considering ways in which trade barriers between the Middle Eastern countries could be abolished.

Once peace has become tangible, Europe will also be more than willing to invest massively in the region, mainly through private but also through public funds, and this will involve looking beyond Israel and its immediate neighbors to the countries of the Gulf. Indeed, these harbor the largest concentrations of mineral (and thus also financial) wealth in the world. It does not seem extravagant to envisage that by the early twenty-first century, Europe, Israel, the Mashreq, and the Gulf will form part of one great Euro-Mediterranean industrial free trade area, in which Israel might play an important role as one of the suppliers of high-tech products.

To conclude, then, Europe and Israel clearly have common interests in the region. It is our joint responsibility to convert the Middle East from a region beset by conflict and mutual distrust, fraught with highly dangerous military hardware, into a region of mutual cooperation and prosperity.

Chapter 2

Common and Conflicting Interests of Mediterranean EU Member States and Third Mediterranean Countries

CHARALAMBOS TSARDANIDIS

Introduction

The Mediterranean region is very important to the European Union in economic and political terms. It is the Union's third-largest trading partner after EFTA and the United States, and provides it with regular trading surpluses. It is vital for the EU's current and future energy supplies, and the Union shares with its neighbors responsibility for the fate of the Mediterranean Sea insofar as the threat to its ecological balance calls for joint efforts. Its economic welfare is also dependent on the availability of cheap labor from the Mediterranean region for certain kinds of menial work in the EU itself.[1]

During the 1980s, three countries on the northern rim of the Mediterranean basin became full members of the EU: Greece in 1981, Spain and Portugal in 1986; and three others, Turkey, Malta, and Cyprus, have applied for membership. Undoubtedly, with the second and third enlargements the Mediterranean area's weight in the EU increased.

It is of great importance for the EU, and particularly its Mediterranean member states, to have a stable policy toward the Third Mediterranean countries and to maintain good relations with them in the future.

The EU countries of Southern Europe (Portugal, Spain, France, Italy, and Greece), though they share the sense of a common cultural identity, do not necessarily constitute a permanent bloc. Nevertheless, they do have common interests and perceptions and sometimes manage to coalesce on specific issues.[2] More particularly, southern EU countries have the same major options in security policy. They are all members of NATO, participants in the CSCE, and members of the

WEU (Greek membership is subject to ratification by the parliaments of the member states). Yet even though fundamental security options seem to coincide, this is not reflected in similar defense positions.[3]

On the other hand, the Third Mediterranean countries—excluding former Yugoslavia—naturally fall into three subregional groups: the Mashreq, consisting of Egypt, Syria, Jordan, and Lebanon; the Maghreb, consisting of Algeria, Morocco, Tunisia, and Libya; and the non-Arab countries of Israel, Cyprus, Malta, and Turkey. Each of these groups has certain key characteristics.

Several considerations impel the Mediterranean member states of the EU to maintain the keenest interest in their "backyard" Mediterranean Sea area. First, the Mediterranean states' economies are deteriorating. Most of the Third Mediterranean countries face serious development problems: inadequate export earnings and large foreign debts (with implications for employment and food self-sufficiency) as well as general deterioration of the environment (the effects of urbanization, marine pollution, desertification, etc.).

Second, demographic pressures are growing. The effects of the "population bomb" are quite evident on the southern Mediterranean shores. If present birth rates continue, it is estimated that by the year 2025, 75% of the Mediterranean population will be of Middle Eastern and Maghreb origin.

Third, the region is marked by ongoing, "traditional" crises—the Arab-Israeli conflict, clashes in the Western Sahara, the Cyprus problem and the Greek-Turkish dispute generally, and so on. Since the 1980s these elements of instability have been compounded by another factor arising directly from the deterioration of politico-economic conditions in the Mediterranean, namely, radical Islamism.[4]

Fourth, on Europe's own northern Mediterranean rim, the implosion of Yugoslavia threatens the other fledgling democracies of the Balkans and could rekindle the peninsula's tinderbox, thereby intensifying the Greco-Turkish dispute, of which the divided status of Cyprus remains the most visible reminder.

Fifth, the recent crisis in the Gulf demonstrated how important cooperation between some of the frontline Third Mediterranean countries and the EU is for the strategic interests of the West. Further alienation of the nonmembers of the EU in the region might prove damaging to the long-term interests of the Union.

Sixth, the region continues to undergo an alarming accumulation of conventional weaponry and proliferation of nonconventional weaponry. The amounts of weaponry acquired in the southern and eastern regions and the growing importance of the armies in the area are particularly impressive, if compared with the figures for the countries to the north of the Mediterranean frontier.

What role will the Southern European states have to play during the current decade in this new contradictory context in which, since the disappearance of the

Soviet Union, divisions as well as opportunities for cooperation have emerged in North-South relations in the Mediterranean basin? This chapter will consider whether the Mediterranean member states of the EU have common and/or conflicting interests with the nonmembers in the Mediterranean basin, focusing on three issue-areas: military-security, political- diplomatic, and economic-developmental.

The Military-Security Issue-Area

As Vasconcelos points out, from the point of view of security there is a fundamental difference between the north and the south of the Mediterranean. In the north there are institutional frameworks for conflict management and the preservation of peace such as NATO, WEU, and the CSCE as well as the prospect for a common European security policy, whereas in the south there is a total lack of common security structures.[5]

The question now is whether, after a long period of confrontation, there can be a long period of cooperation and partnership. There simply is no chance of a peaceful and prosperous future for Southern Europe and the Third Mediterranean countries without a framework of solidarity and joint development, nor can there be security if countries regard one another as potential threats.

It has been argued that two trends seem to have emerged in the relations between the northern and southern shores of the Mediterranean. On the one hand, the transformation of the superpowers' international role has removed the global threat that conditioned the nature of relations across the Mediterranean. Thus, the first trend seems to be a new impetus for trans-Mediterranean relations, possibly in the direction of broader and more effective cooperation. "No splits are insuperable and there is no reason for the Mediterranean countries to be doomed to confrontation rather than laying the foundations for cooperation that would be fruitful for all."[6]

On the other hand, the demise of the Soviet threat came at the end of a decade of clashes, albeit very low-intensity, and difficult relations between Western and Arab-Islamic countries. Thus, the second possible trend is that, in the area to the south of Europe, new threats in the North-South context will alternate with old threats from the East-West one.[7] As Aliboni emphasizes, "The Mediterranean is not a 'centre,' naturally destined to breed solidarity, but rather a 'frontier' separating worlds that are culturally, economically and politically very far apart." This means, Aliboni adds, "that cooperation and security across the 'frontier' are not precluded but cannot be taken for granted."[8]

Common Interests: Creating a Security Community

The establishment of a security community in the Mediterranean area could be accomplished by first launching a Conference on Security and Cooperation in the Mediterranean (CSCM) and by achieving a successful outcome of the Middle East peace process.

Conference on Security and Cooperation in the Mediterranean (CSCM). If the Mediterranean member states of the EU do not take the necessary steps to lay new foundations for peace and security throughout the Mediterranean area, a new period of instability and tension is likely to ensue.

Security and stability in the southern periphery will also depend on the West's ability to promote, and possibly maintain, a new and flexible balance of power acceptable to all or most of the southern-periphery nations.[9] This is particularly true of southern EU states, which are more sensitive to requests for security coming from the countries on the southern shores of the Mediterranean. Accordingly, Italy and Spain have prepared a proposal for a conference on security and cooperation in the Mediterranean and the Middle East, which France and Portugal endorsed for submission at the Palma meeting held in September 1990 in the framework of the CSCE.

The CSCM is a product of the changed situation in Europe, which encourages regional initiatives by smaller and medium powers. "Notably, these initiatives, while reflecting a new interest in regionalism, emphasize the acceptance of existing frontiers as the 'price of entry."[10] The prospective CSCM should, according to the proposal, be an independent entity based on the principles set forth in the United Nations Charter and drawing on the experience of the CSCE, while taking into account that the problems that will have to be solved in this context will often be quite different from those encountered by the CSCE. However, the immediate objectives that the CSCM would pursue would include preventing new imbalances from emerging in the region; controlling the acquisition of arms and arresting the reemergence of an arms race; and creating a system of security for the region, which would not be dependent on the presence of troops from outside.[11]

Differences of opinion, however, soon emerged between France, Italy, and Spain over priorities in their Mediterranean initiatives. At the Rome ministerial meeting of October 10, 1990, at which the Group 5 + 5 (the western Mediterranean cooperation scheme) was launched, Paris was reluctant to go ahead with CSCM, as it considered this forum premature, and preferred to concentrate on the Group 5 + 5. Italy and Spain, however, opted to deal with both initiatives simultaneously. In September 1990 Greece had expressed support for the idea of CSCM;[12] Turkey also expressed its approval. Egypt, Jordan, and Syria welcomed a move toward closer links with the EU (thus increasing the pressure on Israel), as did the Arab

Maghreb Union (AMU), which nonetheless inclined toward the French view, concerned at how existing ties might become weakened. Israel, Iran, and Libya, however, remained circumspect.[13]

Undoubtedly a full CSCM, in the sense of a round table established to regulate relations around both the northern and southern rims, is not a realistic proposition at present because of the enormous complexity and multiplicity of problems to be resolved—the Arab-Israeli peace process, the situation in former Yugoslavia, the Cyprus question to mention but a few. Both the Italian and Spanish foreign ministers have admitted that there was an "element of utopia" in their CSCM scheme. Apparently, political initiatives alone such as the CSCM "stand little chance of success as long as those countries which promote them lack the economic and military tools to set them in motion."[14] CSCM will only be successful if Southern European countries manage to find support for it in the multilateral organizations to which they belong, especially the EU. To be effective, these initiatives must be Community policies.

Furthermore, the trauma undergone by many Arab countries as a result of the Gulf crisis and its aftermath will not make it easy for those countries to embark on preparations for such a conference. They will have their national interests, and particularly the Palestinian question, in mind.[15] On the other hand, the postponement of a full-scale CSCM should not be equated with inactivity. An obvious example is the foreign policy of France, which, while pointedly ignoring the "grand design," has been pursuing active links in North Africa, where it tries to monopolize relations except perhaps with Libya.[16]

However, if and when substantial progress will be achieved in the Arab-Israeli conflict, a CSCM "might be an ideal instrument for promoting and managing cooperation, as was the CSCE, at the time of the East-West divide."[17]

The role of the Middle East peace conference. The global nature of this conference demonstrates that the southern periphery is no longer merely a peripheral region of NATO but a major, political and strategic, southern center. The EU and its Mediterranean member states cannot simply stand by and observe how the conference unfolds, especially since the September 1993 signing of the Israel-PLO Declaration of Principles. There is indeed much at stake for the EU and particularly its Mediterranean member states, as they must demonstrate the necessary strength of will. The role that the EU can play in promoting peace and stability in the eastern Mediterranean will be determined primarily by developments in the political process at hand. The Mediterranean member states as well as the Commission could take the initiative toward adoption by the EU of a policy aimed at establishment of a security community in the entire Mediterranean area. A first step would be to turn EU development efforts in the West Bank and Gaza into instruments for enhancing intercommunal and regional cooperation. The social and economic development of the West Bank and Gaza will be vital for ensuring the stability of the region, and could become a focus of cooperation between Israel, neighboring (and some other) Arab states, and the Palestinian population.[18] Issues of environmental cooperation, the sharing of the Jordan River waters, labor exchange, the protection of human rights, arms control, expansion of trade, energy cooperation, and so on could then be introduced within this framework.

Conflicting Interests

The Gulf War left a strong impact on relations between countries north and south of the Mediterranean. Circumstances as perceived in the West did not necessarily coincide with what was actually experienced, particularly in the Arab countries. The majority of the Arab people (not necessarily the governments) had little feeling about the infringement of international law and the annexation of one country by another. Instead, they saw the crisis as a brutal action by rich and powerful northern countries to prevent an attempt at unifying the Arab world. Although it may certainly be hoped that the Gulf War will eventually prove propitious in facilitating the finding of solutions to problems such as the Israeli-Arab conflict as well as the Kurdish, Cypriot, Lebanese, and Algerian questions, the EU, for its part, must work out an organized response to problems of this sort that are common in the Mediterranean.

The new threats stemming from the regional conflicts drive the Southern European countries to act individually, bilaterally, and under the framework of NATO. Thus, though not officially rejected, the theoretical designs of Europe as a "civilian" power were progressively abandoned and the use of military instruments in addition to economic and diplomatic tools gained partial de facto legitimacy.

All the Mediterranean member states, which have traditionally paid particular attention to Arab concerns, tried systematically to individualize their positions and minimize the negative effects of the West's involvement in the Gulf War. "The inability of EPC stimulated in the Mediterranean group the search for alternatives and all of them developed a parallel unilateral diplomatic activity."[19]

As a result of their colonial involvement in the region, it is the Latin countries of southwestern Europe that are displaying the greatest unease at the threats coming from the South. In particular, Spain and Italy have deep-rooted historical sensitivities toward North Africa, producing a nervousness that has been reflected in military preparedness. The Spanish Legion of full-time professionals has as its primary role the safeguarding of Spain's remaining African territories of Ceuta and Mellila; Italy's territory came under Libyan attack in April 1986, when the island of Lampedusa was targeted in reprisal for the American air attack on Tripoli.[20] France, for its part, pursued a unilateral line through its peace plans; Greece pursued closer links with Egypt and Syria.

A greater confidence by Europe in its ability to use its military forces for the purpose of peacekeeping and peace-enforcing has also been manifested by increased cooperation in the Mediterranean involving Italy, France, and Spain. Joint exercises, as well as technical coordination involving the shared use of major tools such as control and communication systems, have laid the foundations for the operational compatibility of the forces of these countries in the Mediterranean.[21] In 1987-1988 France, Spain, and Italy signed three distinct bilateral defense agreements that, taken together, form the basis of the "Mediterranean Triangle."[22]

Finally, many European Mediterranean countries have also, particularly since the Gulf War, shown willingness to formulate security policies with a strong emphasis on the modernization and reorganization of forces to facilitate their participation in multinational, out-of-area operations of NATO. However, American decisions to intervene militarily in the Third World for reasons of national security and global responsibility often have undesired repercussions on European countries, especially on the interests and security of the countries of the southern flank, "as the impact, feasibility and probability of military actions must be considered limited, and the military threats they imply are not likely to be sufficiently serious to necessitate a full military response."[23]

The possibility of an expansion of NATO's area of responsibility would certainly not be perceived in the same way in the southern rim of the Mediterranean as it is in Central Europe: it would be widely perceived as exacerbating rather than alleviating insecurity, at least by major political sectors in all countries.[24] Consequently, Southern European countries risk being alienated from the southern Mediterranean, especially Arab, countries if their close relationship with the United States and NATO would lead them to support, even reluctantly, out-of-area operations. Thus, a distinction should be made between the European approach to the Mediterranean and the regional American policy in terms of "overall stability zones," with the former giving greater emphasis to political, the latter to military, means. "For Southern NATO members this distinction meant a need to separate political and military security policy, addressing their different demands to different partners within the same alliance."[25] Greece, France, and Italy, for example, have not been enthusiastic about the prospective extension of NATO competences to the South. For these countries, NATO has been and remains a military alliance and is therefore unable to deal with the nonmilitary aspects of Mediterranean security. Some maintain that the Atlantic Alliance should not deal even with military aspects, such as in former Yugoslavia.

The Political-Diplomatic Issue-Area

Common Interests

The main common interest in the political-diplomatic sphere is a desire to strengthen regional cooperation.

A distinctive aspect of the EU's approach to the Mediterranean countries in the past has been its interest in promoting regional cooperation and integration. So far, however, rather little has been done in practice in this direction. Nevertheless, despite obstacles, there are opportunities for the southern member states to promote this important aim, as we shall now see.

The advancement of the Forum of Ten. France, Italy, and Spain have opted for a subregional initiative originally known as the Group of Nine, dealing with the Western Mediterranean, on the assumption that this area has fewer security problems than its eastern counterpart, although the recent turmoil in Algeria might weaken that assumption. The initiative was launched by President Mitterrand in 1983, and has involved a process of political cooperation among France, Italy, Spain, Portugal, and the five members of the AMU; later, Malta joined as well.[26]

It is hoped that the Group of Ten will later be extended to the north (Europe) and to the east (the rest of the Mediterranean), thereby creating a bridge between the regions. Despite a strong desire to do so Greece has not yet taken an active part in this process, as some of the western Mediterranean countries, particularly Italy, have expressed reservations about its involvement. The main reason is that Greece, notwithstanding its being a full member state of the EU, is expected to bring the complex problems of the Greek-Turkish dispute into the Forum.

The European partners also have divergent views on the initiative itself. Although France has agreed to go ahead with the CSCM, it considers this forum "premature" and prefers to concentrate on the Forum of Ten. Italy and Spain, however, prefer to deal with both initiatives at the same time. As a result, the first formal meeting of the 5 + 4—involving the UMA as well as France, Italy, Portugal, and Malta as an observer only—took place in October 1990, at which time the Rome declaration was issued. The second meeting, set for June 1991 in Benghazi, was abruptly canceled because of internal UMA political problems connected to the Islamist tensions in Algeria. The meeting eventually took place in late October 1991, and Malta was accepted as a full negotiating partner.

Today the Forum of Ten is facing difficulties, stemming mainly from the conflict between London and Paris on the one hand and Tripoli on the other, as well as from Algeria's domestic situation.

EU support (particularly of its Mediterranean members) for the economic and political integration of the Maghreb (UMA). The July 1990 summit of the UMA

(Algeria, Libya, Mauritania, Morocco, and Tunisia) propounded a customs union as an intermediate objective. This achievement was, however, jeopardized not only by the unresolved political tensions among the member countries but also by the serious disequilibriums in the productive structures of the Maghreb countries.[27]

If the UMA is to succeed in its political as well as economic objectives, it will need considerable external aid, particularly from the EU and especially the EU's southern members. Spain, France, and Italy could draw other EU countries' attention to the need to anchor the Maghreb to the EU, somewhat as Germany does with respect to the new, still fragile East European democracies.[28] Given the EU's preponderant role in the Maghreb's foreign trade and financial flows, economic reforms in individual Maghreb countries and these countries' evolution toward common economic objectives are highly dependent on the financial support of the Community and the improvement of its trade regime for Maghreb products.[29] Such European support could also take the form of a stabilization fund for Maghreb currencies during a process toward achievement and maintenance of external convertibility and of official support for European industrial cooperation with the region.[30] Thus, economic cooperation can be used as an important, complementary diplomatic tool in the region. In this context, Spain proposed the acceleration and institutionalization of the EU-UMA cooperation.[31] The Commission also proposed a "new partnership policy" aiming at creation of a free trade area between the EU and the Maghreb countries.[32] The Commission's proposal was adopted by the European Council at the Lisbon meeting in June 1992.[33]

Encouragement of the Euro-Arab dialogue. The Euro-Arab dialogue has been plagued with difficulties since its inception in 1973. There have been three main problems: (a) fundamentally different perceptions of the nature and purpose of the dialogue, (b) institutional weaknesses and inability to deliver results, and (c) failure of both parties to insulate the relationship from the negative influence of external events and political interference. Consequently, progress in practical areas of cooperation has been held up by disagreements arising mainly on the political side of the dialogue. France's efforts to reactivate the dialogue succeeded modestly in securing agreement on new procedures and on the content of the dialogue's practical tasks, before events in the Gulf intervened. It is open to question whether the dialogue will live up to its name and become a real forum for the free exchange of political views between Europeans and Arabs.

Conflicting Interests

Regional conflicts. It should not be forgotten that growing conflicts in the Mediterranean region involve the Mediterranean member states of the EU. The

Arab-Israeli conflict, the question of the Western Sahara, the plight of the Kurdish population in southern Turkey, the struggle for political preeminence between Arab secularists and Islamic revivalists in the Maghreb, Egypt, and Jordan, are some of the difficult problems in the southern rim of the Mediterranean that need to be resolved. For example, any acute political, economic, or military crisis in the Maghreb would expose Spain, Italy, and France to multiple risks. A new crisis or war in the Middle East could have severe effects on all the Mediterranean member states of the EU, including possible terrorist acts.

New challenges from the South. Southern member states of the EU are concerned as to whether the developments in the Mediterranean, and particularly its southern shore, constitute a real threat. At present it is clear that there is no military threat to the Mediterranean EU member states from any of the states south of the Mediterranean. The military capabilities and the political intentions that would warrant even the perception of such a threat do not exist in any of these states. There are, however, risks and challenges that should be given due attention. The challenges are multifaceted and involve political and economic as well as military matters. From a Southern European point of view, these new security challenges such as mass migration, terrorism, and intercultural confrontation can be as disconcerting as the proliferation of conventional and unconventional arms in the region.

Migration, like terrorism and religious tensions, is a consequence of profound sociocultural unrest, and requires as much attention as do more conventional, military challenges. Especially for the Mediterranean member states, the immigration pressures are being further exacerbated by political instability, economic failure, and rapid growth of the population. There are only limited employment opportunities, and in general current economic circumstances, accompanied in some cases by an increase in immigration from East European countries (as the Albanians in the case of Greece and Italy), mean that foreign nationals, often ill-suited for the needs of modern industrial society, cannot be allowed to enter without appropriate preparation for their reception, settlement, and eventual repatriation. The countries of Southern Europe, like Italy, Spain and Greece, which had previously been countries of emigration, will be more exposed to immigration from the Mediterranean. "Thus, they will have to make particular efforts in order to implement EU restrictive policies and will have to deal with growing levels of intolerance and public disorder."[34] Southern EU members believe that ultimately only the development of the South can provide a solution to this problem by offering work and a standard of living acceptable to its people. In particular, EU countries could partially alleviate the migration problem from North Africa by making large-scale contracting arrangements with the North African countries, and by opening preparatory "schools" for prospective immigrants where they would be accorded vocational training as well as general social, cultural, and linguistic competences.

The Economic-Developmental Issue-Area

Common Interests

In the economic field, the formulation and implementation of the Renovated Community Policy indicate the convergence of interests between EU southern member states and the Third Mediterranean countries. The Community's Mediterranean policy involves a series of bilateral agreements for development assistance and trade cooperation with all littoral states facing its southern borders (except Libya) plus Jordan. The Community has also extended direct assistance to the Palestinian communities in the occupied territories and, since 1988-1989, trade concessions.

The most recent review of the EU's Mediterranean policy, agreed upon by the European Council in December 1990, has led to the improvement of relations, that is, to the Renovated Mediterranean Policy. Two important developments forced the EU officials to reevaluate Mediterranean policy: one was Project 1992, which it was thought might have a negative impact on the Third Mediterranean countries' trade relations with the EU; the other was the competition between the EU and its global rivals, namely, the United States and Japan, over investments in the Mediterranean basin.[35]

In the absence of progress in coordinating Western and Arab donors at the regional level, EU development assistance plays an important role. The new five-year EU Mediterranean policy constitutes a significant step forward in EU regional initiatives. Its innovative features include (1) dismantling of tariffs on all agricultural products, although tighter limits on sensitive products remain; (2) allocation of over 2 billion ECUs for horizontal financial cooperation to support regional projects; (3) allocation of 300 million ECUs for support of economic reforms in Mediterranean developing countries, under the new bilateral Financial Protocol; and (4) removal of exceptions to the free access of some textile products and improved regulations on the place of origin. The most important innovation, however, in the EU's Mediterranean policy is economic cooperation, which consists of measures to encourage relations between private companies. This enables European investors to obtain financial support for the creation of joint ventures in southern Mediterranean countries.

Nevertheless, the increase in EU financing that is part of the new Mediterranean policy still does not seem sufficient to attenuate the recessive effects of the initial stages of economic reform and, thus, to contain migratory pressure. Furthermore, member states are hesitant to assign increased importance and resources to a common policy of cooperation as opposed to separate, national ones. The EU should play a greater and more autonomous role in supporting programs aimed at increasing employment in the short and medium term. More important than that objective, however, are the restructuring and adjustment programs supported by IMF and the World Bank.[36] Moreover, improvements in the trade regime are too conservative, as is evidenced by the postponement of a more advanced phase of the Uruguay Round and by the proposal for free access to the Community of textile products from Egypt, Morocco, and Tunisia. In sum, EU development cooperation with the developing countries of the Mediterranean must be further intensified.

The Southern European countries' natural sensitivity to the problems and claims of the Third Mediterranean countries impels them to represent and support the latter within the EU. "The regional sense of community existing among the countries concerned and the definite importance on bilateral grounds of their multiple economic and political ties make this solidarity credible."[37] Of course, some of the southern EU members may look upon the "mandate" entrusted to them by the Mediterranean countries as a factor reinforcing their bargaining position within the EU policy framework. Nevertheless, the succession of proposals, including the Renovated Mediterranean Policy, by the southern EU countries clearly demonstrates "that there is concern for events in the region, though disorientation is evident about the best way to achieve concrete solutions."[38]

All the southern members of the EC have supported the Renovated Mediterranean Policy, especially Italy, and mainly on political grounds. Except, that is, for Greece: Athens threatened to block that policy if Turkey were to be included in the "horizontal" framework. Greece maintained that Turkey's participation would place in doubt the European Council's decision taken in Dublin (June 1990) to link any development of the EC-Turkey relationship with progress achieved on the Cyprus issue. In June 1992, however, Greece abandoned its objections because of the reactions expressed by many Third Mediterranean countries. The priority that Athens placed on the "Macedonian" question, together with a relaxation, albeit short-lived, of tensions between Greece and Turkey were perhaps other reasons for this shift in Greek policy.[39]

Conflicting Interests

The Southern European countries, given their agricultural interests, compete fiercely with the southern Mediterranean countries to preserve their preference in the EU market. In particular, Greece, Spain, and Portugal strongly defend the principle of the Union preference in agriculture, which can only mean protectionism against other Mediterranean products. Thus, in the field of trade, the most obvious limit of EU Mediterranean policy consisted of its protectionist measures (quotas, timetables) against the most competitive Mediterranean products (agricultural/food products, textiles, petrochemicals), which were introduced shortly after the agreements were drawn up. The enlargement of the then-EC to include Greece, Spain, and Portugal further infringed on the European-market share of Mediterranean products.[40]

In addition, the economic relationship between the two shores of the Mediterranean is based both on the trade of goods and services and on the exploitation (and conservation) of their common resource, the Mediterranean Sea. However, trade relations between southern EU countries and the Third Mediterranean countries are stagnating. Trade within the Mediterranean region is also very limited; what is remarkable is that the central role in Mediterranean trade relations is being played by two non-Mediterranean countries, West Germany and the United States.[41] There are many reasons for the lack of improvement in intra-Mediterranean trade, paramount among them being the adverse international economic conditions (i.e., recession in the West and a drop in oil revenues). Another reason is that, until recently, many of these states have pursued inward-looking policies; a whole gamut of protectionist measures have been used to insulate domestic industries against neighboring competition. For example, the economies of countries that adopted policies of industrialization geared toward export have fared better than those of countries, such as Algeria, that focused on the development of self-sufficiency.

Conclusions

It emerges, then, that the Mediterranean Sea unites as much as it divides its littoral countries, and that the Southern European states have both common and divergent interests with the Third Mediterranean states. We have also seen that the Mediterranean region is far from homogeneous. In addition to the political, social, and economic problems facing each country, there is a great disparity in economic performance. Growth rates vary from country to country, and in the southern rim of the Mediterranean poor performance is often compounded by rapid population growth. Creation of a security community in the Mediterranean would depend on many factors belonging to the security, political, and economic fields.

It is therefore clear that Southern Europe alone cannot generate the political and economic investment necessary for cooperation in the Mediterranean. "An overoptimistic assumption that cooperation under existing conditions is inevitably good, does not take into consideration that marginal levels of cooperation can aggravate problems and probably fail to resolve crucial questions such as that of Palestinian dispossession."[42]

If an alliance of the southern EU countries is to be established in order to cope with Mediterranean problems, this must be done with the aim of strengthening overall EU political and security integration processes rather than with only Southern European concerns in mind. Of course, the development of bilateral links between the Southern European states and Third Mediterranean countries, and the encouragement of regional cooperation—such as the Forum of Ten in the western Mediterranean, or the launching of another such forum in the eastern Mediterranean between, for example, Greece, Italy, and Egypt—could contribute much toward the gradual establishment of a security community in the Mediterranean region. The northern Mediterranean countries have taken pains to pursue neighborly policies, and France, Spain, Italy, and Greece have invested in energy ventures aimed at fostering goodwill and material development in the volatile south. Yet even though these states are in a position to formulate a grand strategy toward the southern rim, they have so far been unable to implement it.

Whether the southern EU member states will succeed in building a strong relationship with the Third Mediterranean countries depends on several factors. The first is the extent to which regional cooperation schemes such as the UMA, Forum of Ten, and CSCM will succeed—whether, in other words, the promotion of cooperation and integration is in fact a viable way of alleviating the existing rivalries and whether in both rims of the Mediterranean enough political will exists.

The second factor is the extent to which the growing economic gap between the north and south of the Mediterranean can be narrowed. The Renovated Mediterranean Policy is aimed directly at that objective.

The third is the extent to which NATO's objectives and policies toward the region will become complementary with those of the southern member states.

Last and not least is the extent to which some of the most serious disputes in the area, such as the Arab-Israeli one and the Greek-Turkish one, will move toward resolution.

Notes

1. A. Tovias, "The EC's Contribution to Peace and Prosperity in the Mediterranean and the Middle East: Some Proposals," *Jerusalem Journal of International Relations* 14, 2 (1992).

2. R. Aliboni, "Southern European Security Perceptions and Problems," in R. Aliboni, ed., *Southern Europe in the 1990s* (London: Pinter, 1992), p. 2.

3. A. de Vasconcelos, "The Shaping of a Subregional Identity," in Aliboni, *Southern Europe*, p. 18.

4. L. Guazzone, "The Mediterranean Basin," *International Spectator* 25, 4 (October-December 1990): 306.

5. A. de Vasconcelos, "Disintegration and Integration in the Mediterranean," *International Spectator* 28, 3 (July-September 1993): 71.

6. Assembly of Western European Union, Report submitted on behalf of the Political Committee, *Security in the Mediterranean*, rapporteur Mr. Roseta, Doc. 1371, 24 May 1993, p. 192.

7. Aliboni, "Southern European Security," p. 5.

8. R. Aliboni, *European Security Across the Mediterranean*, Chaillot Papers, no. 2, March 1991, pp. 1-2.

9. L. Caligaris, "Security Challenges in Alliance: The Southern Periphery," *International Spectator* 27, 4 (October-December 1992): 10-11.

10. I. Lesser, *Mediterranean Security: New Perspectives and Implications for U.S. Policy* (Santa Monica, Cal.: Rand Corporation, 1992), p. 18.

11. T. Niblock, "Towards a Conference on Security and Cooperation in the Mediterranean and the Middle East (CSCM)," in G. Nonneman, ed., *The Middle East and Europe* (London: Federal Trust for Education and Research, 1992), p. 247.

12. T. Veremis, "European Political Cooperation and the Pursuit of Security: Towards a Southern Position?" in Aliboni, *Southern Europe*, p. 31.

13. E. Foster, "'An interesting idea. . .': The Grand Mediterranean Design," *RUSI and Brassey's Defence Yearbook* (1992), p. 122.

14. Caligaris, "Security Challenges," p. 19.

15. Assembly of Western European Union, Report submitted on behalf of the Political Committee, *European Security and Threats Outside Europe: The Organisation of Peace and Security in the Mediterranean Region and the Middle East*, rapporteur Mr. Martinez, Doc. 1271, 13 May 1991, p. 1271.

16. Foster, "'An interesting idea . . .'," p. 126.

17. V-Y. Ghebali, "Toward a Mediterranean Helsinki-Type Process," *Mediterranean Quarterly* 4, 1 (Winter 1993): 101.

18. E. Murphy, "Economic and Social Development in the West Bank and Gaza Strip," in Nonneman, *Middle East*, pp. 127-133.

19. C. Closa, "The Gulf Crisis: A Case Study of National Constraints on Community Action," *Journal of European Integration* 15, 1 (Fall 1991): 47-67.

20. Foster, "'An interesting idea . . .'," pp. 116-117.

21. Guazzone, "Mediterranean Basin," p. 307.

22. M. Rant, "Cooperation in the Western Mediterranean: A New Role for NATO's Southern Flank Allies," *RUSI and Brassey's Defence Yearbook* (1990), p. 166.

23. Aliboni, *European Security Across the Mediterranean*, p. 28.

24. de Vasconcelos, "Disintegration and Integration," p. 73.

25. M. Kohler, "The Italian Search for Mediterranean Security in a Perspective of Transatlanic Security Relations," *Mediterranean Quarterly* 2, 4 (Fall 1991): 40.

26. J. F. Coustilliere, "Une politique de l'Europe latine en méditerranée occidentale," *Défense Nationale* 5 (1992): 103-119.

27. F. Zallio, "Economic Reforms and Community Aid in the Mediterranean Developing Countries," *International Spectator* 26, 2 (1991): 113-126.

28. Tovias, "The EC's Contribution," pp. 129-130.

29. A. Lorca and J. Nunez, "EC-Maghreb Relations: A Global Policy for Centre-Periphery Interdependence," *International Spectator* 28, 3 (July-September 1993): 57-63.

30. F. Zallio, "Regional Integration and Economic Prospects of the Developing Countries to the South of the Mediterranean," *International Spectator* 27, 2 (1992): 59.

31. *Agence Europe*, no. 56802, 3 March 1992.

32. Commission des Communautés Européennes, *Les relations CEE-Maghreb*, SEC (92)

401/4 Bruxelles, 25 April 1992.

33. In practice, however, the EU chose at the beginning to single out Morocco for its "new partnership policy." This choice was determined by the Islamic movement in Algeria and by the blockage of the 5 + 5 group by the Libyan problem. See Lorca and Nunez, "EC-Maghreb Relations," p. 56.

34. Aliboni, *European Security Across the Mediterranean*, p. 34.

35. B. Yesilada, "The EC's Mediterranean Policy," in L. Hurwitz and C. Lequesne, eds., *The State of the European Community* (London: Lynne Rienner/Longman, 1991), p. 359; R. Pomfret, "The European Community's Relations With the Mediterranean Countries," in J. Redmond, ed., *The External Relations of the European Community* (London: Macmillan, 1992), pp. 77-92.

36. Assembly of Western European Union, *Security in the Mediterranean*, p. 210.

37. R. Aliboni, "The Mediterranean Dimension," in W. Wallace, ed., *The Dynamics of European Integration* (London: Pinter/RIIA, 1990), p. 157.

38. Lorca and Nunez, "EC-Maghreb Relations," p. 58.

39. For an analysis of Greece's position, see C. Tsardanidis, *The Renovated Mediterranean Policy of the EC and Greece* (Athens: Hellenic Centre of European Studies, 1992). (Greek)

40. A. Tovias, *Foreign Economic Relations of the EC: The Impact of Spain and Portugal* (Boulder, Col.: Lynne Rienner), p. 108.

41. Aliboni, "Mediterranean Dimension," p. 166.

42. T. Niblock, "The Role of the European Community in the Middle East, in the Light of the Gulf War," paper presented at the conference on "The Middle East: Two Years After the Gulf War," Institute of International Relations, Panteios University, February 1993, p. 26.

PART II

THE ECONOMIC PERSPECTIVE

Chapter 3

The Effect of Europe 1992 on Outsider Firms: The Case of Israel

SEEV HIRSCH AND TAMAR ALMOR

Introduction

"Europe Ninety-Two" (EC92) is the term used to describe the measures the European Community has undertaken to complete the Community's internal market. To achieve this end, numerous measures at the Community and national levels are being adopted. These include abolition of border controls, amendment of technical regulations, opening of public procurement programs to all Community members, elimination of barriers to financial and business services, and numerous other steps to reduce intra-EC barriers to the movement of goods, services, capital, and people. In some cases national rules and regulations may be replaced by Community rules and regulations. In other cases integration will be achieved by "harmonization" or, alternatively, by "mutual recognition."

The Cecchini Report and other studies conducted by or on behalf of the Community suggest that the steps taken to complete the European internal market will enhance the economic welfare of the Community's residents, and increase the growth rate of the EC's economies.[1] The studies enumerate the positive effects that the adoption of these measures is expected to have on the economies of the member countries, distinguishing between different types of gains. These include gains from removal of barriers such as national borders affecting trade and overall production across countries; gains from exploiting additional economies of scale resulting from the removal of barriers; and gains from intensified competition, including the reduction of business inefficiencies, and loss of monopoly profits.

Clearly, not all economic actors stand to gain from the implementation of EC92. Community consumers will, on the whole, benefit, as consumers inevitably do when competition is intensified through economic integration. Community producers, too, will gain as a group, although some will inevitably fare better than others. This chapter focuses on the effects of EC92 on a third group—the outsiders, or more specifically, the producers who compete in the EC but are located in countries that do not belong to it.

The theoretical sections of this chapter examine two aspects of EC92: (1) its effect on the relative competitive position of outsider firms, and (2) response, by means of foreign direct investment (FDI), to EC92 by two groups of firms: producers of "Heckscher-Ohlin" goods, characterized by publicly available technologies, and producers of "Schumpeter" goods, characterized by firm-specific technologies. The theoretical models are tested on empirical data pertaining to FDI by Israeli firms in the period 1984-1991.

The Effects of EC92 on Outsider Firms: A Conceptual Framework

Trade theory teaches that international transactions are determined by relative rather than absolute costs. Costs have numerous components that include the outlays on gaining market access. When the access costs of one supplier decrease in relation to the access costs of his competitor, the competitive position of the latter deteriorates. This conclusion holds when other cost components such as costs of production remain unchanged, and even when the other cost components of both competitors change in a given proportion. It is thus conceivable that changes in relative access costs generated by EC92 could prevent the exportation of goods to the EC even when the absolute costs of outside suppliers remain unchanged or decline. This proposition is examined more formally below.

The EC92 process is an ongoing one. Many directives and other policy decisions pertaining to specific industries vary from case to case and, moreover, numerous directives have not yet been implemented or even approved. It is consequently difficult to speculate about the impact of EC92 on the competitive position of specific countries and industries. The following example illustrates, however, the effect of one EC92-related policy on outsiders, namely, the elimination of border controls between EC members.

Border controls symbolize, perhaps more than other barriers, the fact that the European Common Market has not yet been completed. The proliferation of border controls causes delays arising from the time spent on filling out forms, on clearing customs, and generally on activities associated with the obligation of complying with the rules and regulations governing the transfer of goods across national boundaries. Such activities add to the costs of doing business with foreign firms, thus protecting domestic firms against foreign competitors. It has been amply demonstrated in the Cecchini Report that the removal of border controls will increase the Community's Gross Domestic Product by as much as 0.4%, which amounts to about 8% of total estimated gains expected from the completion of the EC. Costs of outsiders will also be reduced, but by a smaller margin than the costs of insiders, since the Community's external border controls will not be dismantled.

To illustrate this point, consider two plywood suppliers to a Frankfurt-based customer, one located in Israel and the other in Spain. The Israeli plywood is shipped by sea from Haifa to Marseilles, and transported over land to Frankfurt. Following EC92 the border controls between France and Germany will presumably be eliminated, and the shipment from Israel will not be delayed beyond Marseilles. The Israeli plywood exporter will therefore gain in absolute terms from the removal of border controls. However, the Spanish plywood exporter benefits even more. Before EC92 his shipments to Germany have to bear the costs of border crossing at the Franco-Spanish and the Franco-German borders. After EC92 Spanish shipments to Germany encounter no border controls at all. In relative terms the Israeli exporter is consequently worse off in relation to the Spanish exporter. Worst off in our hypothetical example is the German domestic producer. Before EC92 he is protected against the Spanish and the Israeli suppliers by the existence of two border posts. After EC92 he loses all border-related protection against the Spanish exporter and his protection against the Israeli exporter is diminished by the elimination of the Franco-German border posts. The German supplier is, however, compensated in other EC markets where he competes mainly against other domestic firms and where, following EC92, the latter lose the protection provided by border controls.

A superficial analysis of other policies associated with EC92, such as public procurement,[2] technical regulation,[3] and trade in services, confirms the expectation that EC92 will benefit firms located in the EC more than firms located outside it. Since relative rather than absolute costs determine the competitive position of business firms, we must conclude that *ceteris paribus* the competitive position of outsiders is going to be adversely affected by EC92, even if the principle of Fortress Europe is rejected by the Community.

The adverse effects of EC92 on outsiders will, as noted above, vary by target market, source country, industry, and even by firm. The relative change in the competitive position of insiders and outsiders can nevertheless be assessed in advance as is shown in Figure 1. Consider four manufacturers located in four countries A, B, C, and R. The first three countries are EC members; therefore the A, B, and C firms are insiders, whereas the R firm is an outsider. All firms A, B, C, and R compete in the home markets of A, B, and C. EC92 affects access costs to the EC markets by eliminating entry barriers faced by the A, B, and C firms to each other's markets. The R firm, on the other hand, still encounters entry barriers as it has to enter the EC from the outside. Figure 1 illustrates the change in the competitive position of each of the four manufacturers in the three EC markets following EC92.

Figure 1
Change in the Relative Competitive Position of
Insiders and Outsiders Following the Implementation of EC92

		Target Market		
		A	B	C
A's Position Relative to:	B	-	+	O
	C	-	O	+
	R	(-)	+	+
R's Position Relative to:	A	(+)	-	-
	B	-	(+)	-
	C	-	-	(+)

The upper half of Figure 1 summarizes the changes in the competitive position of the A firm in relation to its three competitors: the B and C firms—the other insiders, and the R firm—the outsider. The lower half focuses on the change in the competitive position of the R firm in the three insiders' markets. The plus sign signifies an improvement, the minus sign deterioration, a zero no change in the competitive position of suppliers, and brackets a relatively small change in the competitive position of the firm.

The first row illustrates the changes in the A firm's competitive position vis-à-vis B's, in A's, B's and C's domestic markets. The second and third rows illustrate the changes in the competitive position of the A firm vis-à-vis the C and R firms in A's, B's, and C's domestic markets, respectively. The following changes in the competitive position of the different parties are indicated: the A firm's competitive position vis-à-vis B's, in A's home market, deteriorates. As barriers to entry facing insiders in A's market are eliminated, A's market is turned into a domestic market for B and C firms. Although the competitive position in its home market deteriorates, A's competitive position vis-à-vis B in B's home market and vis-à-vis C in

C's home market improves. A's competitive position vis-à-vis B's in C's domestic market, and vis-à-vis C's in B's market, remains unchanged.

Figure 1 omits the illustration of the effects of EC92 on the changes of the competitive position of B and C in their domestic and other EC markets. These effects are symmetrical to those experienced by A, which are examined at the top of figure. The figure shows that the insiders' competitive position in their home market vis-à-vis other insiders deteriorates significantly, and deteriorates marginally vis-à-vis the outsiders. Their competitive position in the home market of other insiders improves vis-à-vis domestic manufacturers, and vis-à-vis outsiders; it remains unchanged vis-à-vis other insiders.

The lower part of Figure 1 focuses on the changes of the competitive position of the R firm (the outsider) vis-à-vis the insiders, i.e., A, B, and C. The R firm's competitive position either deteriorates or improves moderately, depending on the source of competition. Its competitive position vis-à-vis domestic manufacturers improves marginally after unification, as R will have fewer borders to cross. Compared to other insiders, however, its position deteriorates.

Although the overall competitive position of outsiders will deteriorate as a result of EC92, it is clear that a firm's specific strategic response to EC92 is influenced by a host of additional factors. Daems, for instance, argues that response of insiders as well as outsiders is dependent on the industry to which the firm belongs.[4] In the same article it is further argued that product line, production facilities, and configuration of value activities shape the individual firm's response to the program as well. Heitger and Stehn argue that European protectionist measures, more than other factors, are shaping the response of Japanese companies.[5]

Buigues and Jacquemin as well as Franko view market position in the home and target markets as dominant factors shaping a firm's response.[6] In addition, it is suggested by various researchers that the objectives and existing strategies of the individual firm play a major role in determining its response to EC92.[7]

Thus, it seems that a firm's competitive strategy in the post-EC92 environment is shaped by various factors that may be either firm, industry, or source-country specific.

One response strategy that has gained popularity is foreign direct investment (FDI). The use of FDI can transform outsiders' status into that of insiders.[8] The wish to achieve insider status seems indeed to have been the main motivation behind many FDI decisions by outsider firms in recent years. For example, in its "Fourth Following Report," dealing with the effects of EC92 on the U.S., the United States International Trade Commission noted: "Another important factor in drawing direct investment to the EC has been the 1992 single-market program. Fear of being excluded from the EC market after the integration program is complete has apparently increased the willingness of US and Japanese companies to earmark funds for European projects."[9] Similar views about the motivation behind increased FDI in the EC by outsiders have been expressed by others.[10] Balasubramanyam and Greenaway found evidence that Japanese FDI has increased as a consequence of the 1992 program.[11] Dunning reports a marked increase in U.S. direct investment in all EC countries toward 1992.[12] He notes that investment in the EC in 1989 and 1990 accounted for nearly 50% of all U.S. foreign plant and equipment expenditure, as opposed to 38.8% in 1985.

As stated above, the propensity of outsiders to invest in the EC, as well as the scope and actual mode of investment are influenced not only by overall worsening of competitive position but by other, more specific, factors as well. Industry and firm characteristics as well as related product attributes are likely to figure prominently among these factors. The relationship between these attributes and the response to EC92 is discussed in the following section.

Firm Characteristics, Product Attributes, and the Response to EC92

Firms are engaged in three major sets of activities: (1) production of goods and services, (2) their marketing, and (3) knowledge creation, i.e., the acquisition and utilization of know-how.[13]

Production involves the transformation of primary inputs such as labor, capital, and purchased inputs such as materials, subassemblies, and energy into intermediate inputs or final products. Marketing consists of all activities that link the firm to its customers—sales, distribution, and servicing. Acquisition of knowledge pertains to applied technological knowledge including process (i.e., technical) knowledge, product knowledge, and managerial knowledge.

Some production factors used by firms are universal, others are firm-specific factors. Universal factors are available at the prevailing market price to all economic entities, regardless of whether they are owned by domestic or foreign firms. Examples include natural resources, unskilled and skilled labor, physical, financial, and human capital, infrastructure, and the services provided by public institutions. Firm-specific factors are represented by the technical and managerial know-how and experience embodied in a firm's managers, engineers, skilled workers, and other employees. This takes the form of codified and noncodified operating norms and policies, as well as past investments in process engineering and in product research and development. These factors contribute to the firm's "technological competence," which is a major determinant of its "ownership advantage."[14] An important attribute of firm-specific knowledge is that competitors can be effectively prevented from having access to it. Another attribute is that it is not obtainable in the marketplace. It must either be "produced" by the firm that uses it, or it can be obtained through licensing, or through contract research.

Both types of production factors are combined with purchased inputs to produce outputs that, in turn, can be divided into (1) universal or Heckscher-Ohlin goods and (2) firm-specific or Schumpeter goods.[15]

Schumpeter goods (S-goods) contain a significant element of proprietary knowledge—knowledge that imparts unique characteristics to the product and that, as noted above, can be effectively withheld from competitors. In contrast, the manufacture of Heckscher-Ohlin goods (H-goods) does not depend on the possession of proprietary knowledge by the producer. The technology is easily acquired and absorbed, and does not confer a competitive advantage on the firm that possesses it.

Competitive advantage in H-goods is determined by the relative cost and share of the universal production factors such as labor, capital, raw materials, and other inputs used in their manufacture. Competitive advantage in S-goods is, by contrast, determined essentially by the manufacturer's ability to differentiate his output from that of his competitors, and to convince potential customers of its uniqueness.

Goods cannot be marketed (either in the domestic market or internationally) unless they are accompanied by some services, transportation being an obvious example. Unlike goods, services are intangible. They cannot be inventoried and, most important, to render a service, the provider must interact with the user. These characteristics have an important impact on the transaction modes of the goods with which they are associated.[16]

Firms can produce goods, or services, or combinations of the two, i.e., goods with varying service intensities. In this chapter we are concerned with a special group of services—those that are associated with goods, i.e., services whose availability determines the usefulness of the goods to the buyer. In services as in goods we distinguish between universal and firm-specific. Universal services—finance, insurance, and transportation—can be acquired in the open markets. Firm-specific services—instruction, installation, repairs, etc.—depend on proprietary knowledge originating with the manufacturer of the goods. These product characteristics influence the operating modes employed in their manufacture and distribution both within a country's boundaries and internationally.

Considering H-goods first, recall that the knowledge required for their manufacture and servicing is in the public domain. Transactions in H-goods can therefore be unbundled in the sense that the goods and associated services can be provided by different, unrelated firms. Transactions in S-goods are likewise influenced by their characteristics. Since the process technology, product specifications, and the associated services all depend on firm-specific knowledge that is not publicly available, unbundling is difficult, if not impossible.

The relative advantage associated with unbundling the value chain of H- and S-goods is reflected in the operating modes of firms manufacturing the two types of goods. S-goods industries tend to be dominated by firms characterized by vertical integration where R&D, manufacturing, distribution, and servicing are undertaken by units owned or controlled by a single firm. The operating modes of H-goods firms are likely to be more varied, and unbundling to be more common. Thus, contract research, subcontracting of key components, distribution and servicing by independent agents, are more prevalent in the H-goods than in the S-goods industries.

Having specified the attributes of S-goods and S-goods industries, we are ready to examine the likely response to EC92 of outsider firms producing one of the two types of goods for EC markets. Consider non-EC producers of S-goods seeking to market their products in the EC. Before EC92, cross-border provision of associated services was severely limited. Hence, they were obliged to choose between using independent service providers and operating their own service facilities in all markets that they served. It is to be expected that only few, relatively large producers of S-goods opted to become forward market integrated in all EC markets. Most S-goods producers probably preferred to have the less important markets serviced by independent agents, thus forgoing both revenues and market power while minimizing investments. EC92 will change the economics of forward market integration, as shown in the following example.

Consider German and Israeli manufacturers of medical scanning equipment—a typical S-good, requiring intensive associated services such as instruction, installation, maintenance, and repairs (all S-type services). The firms operate manufacturing plants in their respective home countries from which they ship their output to customers located throughout the EC. Before EC92 these services could not be provided across national boundaries, and the firms' customers had to be serviced by local facilities in the target markets. Since the number of installations in each country was considered too small to justify the establishment of distribution and service subsidiaries, the servicing was provided by local independent distributors.

Comparing the position of the two firms before EC92, note that they compete on more or less equal terms in the different EC markets. The only exception is Germany, where the local firm can use its manufacturing base to service its local customer.

Following EC92, the relative competitive position of the two firms changes radically since EC-based firms are able to export their services across national boundaries. Thus the German firm can service all its EC customers from any location inside the Community. The firm is able to transfer its servicing operations to the home facility, which it owns and controls. The home facility shares overheads with production, R&D, and other functions. To compete with the

German firm on a similar basis in the EC markets, the Israeli firm must engage in FDI in at least one market. *Ceteris paribus* its competitive position has deteriorated following EC92.

The detailed example discussed above is, on the face of it, highly specific. It does, however, suggest a testable general hypothesis, namely: although EC92 enables insiders to consolidate their operations, outsiders are obliged to engage in FDI to counteract its negative effects. To test our model, we shall look at Israeli firms employing FDI.

Outsider Response to EC92: The Case of Israel

The discussion in the preceding sections suggests that FDI is likely to figure prominently among the instruments employed by outsiders to counteract the negative, and exploit the positive aspects of EC92. FDI is likely to be particularly important in economies that trade intensively with the EC. Israel is such an economy.

Israel is a small country with an open economy, highly dependent on international transactions for its economic well-being. Exports plus imports reached 83% of its GNP in 1990. The country's two largest trading partners are the EC and the United States; Israel has Free Trade Area agreements with both. The agreement with the EC was signed in 1975, allowing most Israeli manufacturers to sell their products on the EC market without tariff or quota restrictions since the late 1970s. Tariffs on imports from the EC have been eliminated since the beginning of 1990. The agreement with the U.S., which is more comprehensive in terms of coverage (it includes fresh produce), was signed in 1985 and will be implemented in full by 1995. Israel finds itself in a unique position as no other country has Free Trade Area agreements with both trading blocs.

Nevertheless, the agreements focus mainly on tariffs and quotas and are only marginally concerned with other types of nontariff barriers. Although the Free Trade Area agreements improve the country's position in the two trading blocs vis-à-vis other third countries, they do not offer equal terms to Israeli companies competing with EC- and U.S.-based firms in their home markets.

Israel's economic relations with the EC are close. Exports to the EC accounted in 1991 for 36% of total exports, and imports from the EC for 48% of total imports.

The analysis in the preceding sections indicates that the Free Trade Area Agreement between Israel and the EC notwithstanding, the competitive position of Israeli firms will be adversely affected by EC92. Therefore, we argue that Israeli firms will tend to engage in FDI in the Community to counteract these negative effects.

To test this hypothesis, we looked at Israeli FDI in the period 1984-1991. Data concerning FDI by Israeli firms were provided to us by the Foreign Exchange Department of the Bank of Israel, which supervises foreign investments. Permission to invest abroad is, as a rule, granted only to firms that can demonstrate that their investment will increase exports. Exceptions may of course occur, but it is probably safe to accept the view that FDI is intended to enhance exports as our working hypothesis. In fact, over 70% of foreign investments made by Israeli manufacturing firms over the years were in marketing and service facilities.[17] This means that FDI is used mostly to establish sales and distribution facilities, pre- and postsales servicing centers, or other market support operations. These may, and in some cases do, include integration and assembly operations. Additional investments may be related to the public procurement component of EC92. Foreign firms seeking to participate in public procurement programs must acquire EC-based manufacturing facilities to satisfy the condition that local (i.e., Community) contents must exceed 50%.

Two types of figures were made available to us: number of investments (or rather of approvals) and their value.[18] The decision of firms to engage in forward market integration is manifested by the number of foreign affiliates they control and not necessarily by the amount of money spent on their acquisition, which may vary between firms, industries, countries, and functions; thus both types of figures are presented.

Table 1
Israeli FDI total, in the EC and in the U.S.,*
1984-1991, in million USD (current prices)

Year	Total	EC	U.S.
Until 1984	450.0	74.7	262.9
1985	14.6	4.8	8.2
1986	44.1	21.0	22.4
1987	129.7	68.8	46.7
1988	36.2	15.6	12.8
1989	163.5	85.7	65.7
1990	351.5	94.6	119.6
1991	373.5	66.3	267.3
Total 1985-1991	1,113.1	356.8	542.7
Cumulative	1,563.1	431.5	805.6

Source: Bank of Israel.
* U.S. includes Canada.

The use of FDI among Israeli firms is a relatively new phenomenon. Figures presented in Table 1 show that the cumulative value of foreign investments represented less than half a billion dollars by the end of 1984, or about 10% of industrial exports in that year. By comparison, Japan, which started using FDI only during the 1970s, had, in 1984, a cumulative FDI of $71,431 million, representing about 30% of that year's exports.[19]

Cumulative FDI by Israeli companies tripled during the subsequent six years, reaching $1563 million by December 1991. In terms of the number as well as value of investments, growth in FDI has been very rapid since 1985. By comparison, growth in exports fluctuated around 10% except for 1987, when exports increased by 17%.

To test the theoretical arguments presented in the first part of this chapter, we looked at Israeli FDI in the EC in terms of number of investments as well as the amount invested, in 1985-1991. We also noted changes that took place after 1987, the year in which the Single European Act was approved by all members of the EC. Passage of the act enabled the Community to hasten the process of approving the directives and other pieces of legislation required to translate the ideas of EC92 into reality. We consequently expected Israeli FDI in the EC to gain momentum after 1987.

Data presenting the number of Israeli investments in the EC and in the United States are presented in Table 2.[20] The number of Israeli investments in the Com-

Table 2
Number of Israeli Investments, Total, in the EC and in the U.S.*

Year	Total	EC	U.S.
Until 1984	586	190	184
1985	63	16	32
1986	74	22	31
1987	98	36	44
1988	121	44	42
1989	263	102	85
1990	303	115	76
1991	348	126	96
Total 1985-1991	967	461	406
Cumulative	1,553	651	590

Source: Bank of Israel.

* U.S. includes Canada.

munity increased from 137 in 1985-1987 to 416 in 1988-1991, showing a definite increase toward 1992. The value of Israeli FDI in the EC increased from $95 million for the first period to $262 million for the second period.

In other words, FDI in the EC increased significantly toward 1992, supporting the argument that outsiders will engage in FDI to counteract worsening of competitive position. To further strengthen our results we also compared Israeli FDI in the EC and in the U.S. The data in Table 2 clearly show that, compared to the U.S., relatively more investments were made in the EC in 1988-1991. In the years 1985-1987, 74 investments were made in the EC, compared to 107 in the U.S. During the second time period, 387 investments were made in the EC compared to 299 in the U.S. In other words, compared to the U.S., 88 more investments were made in the EC in 1988-1991.

In dollar terms the picture is less clear as, on the average, investments in the U.S. are larger than in the EC. As stated previously, we believe the number of investments is more indicative of change in strategy than size of investment. Thus we conclude that Israeli firms use FDI in the EC to counteract worsening of competitive position.

Our second theoretical argument concerns the different propensity of Heckscher-Ohlin and Schumpeterian manufacturers to engage in FDI. The FDI data were divided into two categories: Schumpeter and Heckscher-Ohlin industries. The division was based on the share of skilled employees in the labor force and on relative employment costs in each group. Data obtained from the Israel Central Bureau of Statistics cover employment costs and the percentage of technical personnel, i.e., technicians, engineers, and scientists, in the labor force of the different industrial branches. Industries with a ratio of technical to total employees of under 15%, and where monthly employment costs per employee are under $1500, are classified as H-goods manufacturers. Industries where the ratio of technical personnel is 15% and above, and the monthly employment costs exceed $1500, are classified as S-goods producers. Thus, chemicals, electrical and electronic products are classified as S-goods industries whereas foods and beverages, textiles and clothing, plastics and rubber, and the metals industries are classified as H-goods industries.

Table 3 presents figures concerning FDI by manufacturers of S-goods and H-goods in the EC. The data clearly show that S-goods manufacturers employ FDI more frequently than H-goods manufacturers. S-goods manufacturers made 110 investments in 1988-1991, compared to 46 investments made by H-goods manufacturers. Figures also show that both groups have increased their investments in the EC toward 1992; however, S-goods manufacturers increased their investments by $212 million during 1988-1991, whereas H-goods manufacturers increased theirs by only $26 million in the same period. Thus, the data presented in Table

3 support the second theoretical argument, namely, that S-goods manufacturers will be more inclined to employ FDI toward 1992 than H-goods manufacturers.

Table 3
Israeli FDI by S- and H- Industries in the EC

	1984-1987	1988-1991	Total
S-Goods $M	77	212	289
Cases	36	110	146
H-Goods $M	3	26	29
Cases	11	46	57

Concluding Remarks

By establishing affiliates in the EC, outsider firms can acquire the status of insiders that, in theory at least, have the same rights and obligations as firms owned by EC nationals. Admittedly, the experience of Japanese automotive and computer firms indicates that the right of non-EC firms to insider status is not automatically guaranteed; it may be challenged from time to time. It is nevertheless likely that the principle of "national treatment" will, on the whole, be observed in the Community, provided non-Europeans, on their part, demonstrate their adherence to the idea of "reciprocity." The findings reported in the last section are consistent with the view that FDI is indeed frequently adopted by outsider firms to counteract the negative and exploit the positive effects of EC92. The findings are also consistent with the assertion that Schumpeter goods manufacturers are more likely to engage in FDI than manufacturers of Heckscher-Ohlin goods. It should, however, be remembered that the FDI patterns exhibited by Israeli firms may well be influenced by the restrictions imposed on capital exports. It is possible that, in countries where capital exports are less restricted, patterns of behavior will be different.

Bearing these caveats in mind, it is probably safe to generalize from our findings concerning the response of different outsider groups to EC92. These findings, underpinned by the theoretical analysis, are:

1. Firms prefer to establish affiliates in large nonfragmented markets. Outsider firms have been anticipating the completion of the Single Market, and are increasing their FDI in Europe at a higher rate than previously.

2. The propensity of Schumpeter goods manufacturers to engage in FDI has been higher than that of Heckscher-Ohlin products manufacturers. Moreover, FDI

in the EC by Schumpeterian firms compared to Heckscher-Ohlin firms has been increasing at a higher rate in recent years in apparent response to EC92.

These findings support the view propounded in this chapter that the competitive position of outsiders deteriorates in the EC market and that outsiders react by becoming insiders. Moreover, in the case of S-goods manufacturers, the change in competitive position seems to be larger than for H-goods manufacturers. Thus, S-goods manufacturers are more prone to engage in FDI in the EC as the unification of the single market approaches.

Notes

1. R. Baldwin, "The Growth Effects of 1992," *Economic Policy* (October 1992): 248-281; P. Cecchini, M. Catinat, and A. Jacquemin, *1992 The European Challenge: The Benefits of a Single Market* (London: Wildwood House, 1988); Commission of the EC, "The Economics of 1992: An Assessment of the Potential Economic Effects of Completing the Internal Market of the EC" (1988).

2. A. Tovias, "The Impact of Liberalizing Government Procurement Policies of Individual EC Countries on Trade With Non-Members," *Weltwirtschafliches Archiv* 126 (1990): 723-736.

3. S. Hirsch, "Nineteen Ninety Two: How Will Outsiders Be Affected?," Working Paper 66/90, Israel Institute of Business Research, Tel Aviv University, 1990.

4. H. Daems, "The Strategic Implications of Europe 1992," *Long Range Planning* 23 (1990): 41-48.

5. B. Heitger and Z. Stehn, "Japanese Direct Investment in the EC: Response to the Internal Market 1993?," *Journal of Common Market Studies* 29 (1990): 1-15.

6. P. Buigues and A. Jacquemin, "Strategies of Firms and Structural Environments in the Large Internal Market," *Journal of Common Market Studies* 28 (1989): 53-67; L. G. Franko, "Europe 1992: The Impact on Global Corporate Competition and Multinational Corporate Strategy," *European Business Journal* 1 (1989): 23-32.

7. Buigues and Jacquemin, "Strategies of Firms"; Daems, "Strategic Implications"; T.R.M. Line, "The Acquisition Route to a European Presence," *European Management Journal* 6 (1988): 359-366; L. Ohlsson, "EC-EFTA Relations: The Case of Sweden," Working Paper 10/89, Israel Institute of Business Research, Tel Aviv University, 1989.

8. T. Almor-Ellemers and S. Hirsch, "Patterns of Foreign Direct Investment: Israel, a Small Country Situated in Between Trading Blocs," Business and Economic Studies on European Integration, Working Paper 9-91, Institute of International Economics and Management, Copenhagen, 1991.

9. U.S. International Trade Commission, "The Effects of Greater Economic Integration Within the European Community on the United States: Fourth Following Report," Washington, June 1992.

10. T. Ozawa, "Cross-Investment Between Japan and the EC: Income Similarity, Technological Congruity, and Economies of Scope," in J. Cantwell, ed., *Multinational Investment in Modern Europe: Strategic Interaction in the Integrated Community* (Cheltenham, U.K.: Edward Elgar, 1992); G. Yannopoulous, "Foreign Direct Investment and European Integration: Evidence From

the Formative Years of the European Community," *Journal of Common Market Studies* 28 (1990): 235-259; A. M. Rugman and S. A. Verbeke, "Competitive Strategies for Non-European Firms," in B. Burgenmeier and J. L. Mucchielli, eds., *Multinationals and Europe* 1992 (London: Routledge, 1991).

11. U. N. Balasubramanyam and D. Greenaway, "Economic Integration and Foreign Direct Investment: Japanese Investment in the EC," *Journal of Common Market Studies* 30 (1992): 175-193.

12. J. H. Dunning, "European Integration and Transatlantic Foreign Direct Investment: The Record Assessed," Business and Economic Studies on European Integration, Working Paper 3/91, Institute of International Economics and Management, Copenhagen.

13. M. Casson, "Internationalization and Beyond," Discussion Papers in International Investment and Business Studies 148 (mimeo), Department of Economics, University of Reading, 1990; S. Hirsch and A. Meshulach, "Towards a Unified Theory of Internationalization," Business and Economic Studies on European Integration, Working Paper 1/92, Institute of International Economics and Management, Copenhagen, 1992.

14. J. Cantwell, "The Technological Competence Theory of International Production and Its Implications," Discussion Papers in International Investment and Business Studies 149 (mimeo), Department of Economics, University of Reading; J. H. Dunning, "The Eclectic Paradigm of International Production: A Restatement and Some Possible Extensions," *Journal of International Business Studies* 19 (1988): 1-31; Dunning, "European Integration."

15. Hirsch and Meshulach, "Towards a Unified Theory."

16. S. Hirsch, "Services and Service Intensity in International Trade," *Weltwirtschafliches Archiv* 125 (1989): 45-60.

17. Almor-Ellemers and Hirsch, "Patterns of Foreign Direct Investment."

18. The FDI data obtained pertain to all approvals granted by the Bank of Israel, aggregated by country of destination and by industry. Obviously, approvals of FDI do not necessarily correspond to FDI actually taking place in a given year. Some investments are inevitably delayed and others are canceled. We believe, however, that the figures provided by the Bank of Israel represent a reasonable proxy for FDI undertaken by Israeli firms in the period under consideration.

19. K. Kojima, "Japanese Direct Investment Abroad," International Christian University, Tokyo, 1990.

20. The Bank of Israel would not provide us with data for FDI in the U.S. only, and supplied data on North America (U.S. and Canada) instead. Since Canada accounts for less than 3% of Israel's exports, we assume that FDI in Canada is marginal as well.

Chapter 4

*Trade Liberalization Under GATT and By the EC: Implications for Israel**

JACOB KOL

Introduction

Nondiscrimination is the main principle underlying the present system of world trade under GATT. From its inception in 1947, however, the GATT did not cover world trade in its entirety. Several sectors were kept outside GATT: agriculture, textiles, clothing, as well as services, together accounting for one-third of total world trade in merchandise and services. The recent conclusion of the Uruguay Round on December 15, 1993, may be regarded as a major breakthrough, already on the ground alone that the four sectors just mentioned have been brought into the GATT system. That is, upon ratification of the agreement by the members of GATT, virtually all of their international trade will take place under the aegis of GATT.

Furthermore, several tendencies are at odds with the principle of nondiscrimination. A sensitivity toward unfair trade, the tendencies toward bilateralism and aggressive unilateralism, and inward-looking regional trading blocs are important examples.

In this perspective, this chapter looks at some recent developments in the world economy. It discusses the nature of the EC's 1992 program, and reviews present EC trade policies and the formation of the European Economic Area. It then considers the possible emergence of regional trading blocs and the implications for nondiscrimination in world trade. The first part of the chapter concludes with a

---

* The author gratefully acknowledges the comments of Professor Alfred Tovias as well as the statistical assistance of Mr. B. Kuijpers of the Erasmus Centre for Economic Integration Studies at Erasmus University.

review of trade liberalization under GATT and the consequences for world economic welfare.

The second part of the chapter focuses on the position of Israel in international trade, in particular Israel's revealed comparative advantage on the EC market. The final section summarizes the conclusions of the chapter and notes some implications for Israel.

The EC's 1992 Program and Mercantilism

In the mid-1970s the process of economic integration in the European Community stagnated. Because of declining economic growth and rising unemployment, EC member states were less prepared for adaptations in their national economies that were necessitated by further economic integration.[1] European companies, however, stressed the importance of continued economic integration and pressed for the creation of an Internal Market in particular.

The EC Commission responded with the White Paper of 1985, which included 304 concrete measures to arrive at an Internal Market by the end of 1992. This program came to be called the 1992 program of the EC and was meant to remove the barriers that still interfered with the free movement of products (goods and services) and production factors (labor and capital) in the EC. These barriers were grouped under three headings:

1. *Physical barriers*. These mainly included customs formalities and delays at the intra-EC borders, which are abolished under the 1992 program.

2. *Technical barriers*. The many barriers under this heading include technical specifications of products, of procedures for testing new products, and of regulations regarding safety and health. The aim is that the differences in these specifications and regulations among member states be harmonized or mutually recognized among EC member states. The latter procedure has turned out to be much less cumbersome, of course, than the former.

3. *Fiscal barriers*. Differences in tax rates, especially of VAT rates and excises, also are barriers to intra-EC trade and are diminished under the 1992 program.

The 1992 program of the EC has been complemented by a program for monetary integration, the European Monetary Union.

In the seventeenth century, mercantilism dominated economic policies in Western Europe. The mercantilist doctrine is well known for its application to trade policy. Maximizing exports while minimizing imports would bring the maximum of foreign gold to the domestic economy. International trade was regarded as profitable to the exporting country but unprofitable to the importing partner to an equal extent: international trade as a zero-sum game.

Less well known is that mercantilism also advocated a program for economic integration within the nation-state. At the time, nation-states such as France, England, or Germany did not constitute an economic unity: counties, duchies, and kingdoms within these nations still maintained their own economic and legal authorities. The mercantilist program for economic integration had four main elements: (1) abolition of the toll system; (2) unification of measures and weights; (3) unification of the tax system; and (4) unification of the coinage system. This seventeenth-century program shows a striking resemblance to the three elements of the 1992 program and the program for monetary integration within the EC.

The abolition of the toll system within the European nation-states under mercantilism corresponds directly, of course, to the abolition of physical barriers to trade in the 1992 program of the EC. The present harmonization of technical specifications of products and procedures in the EC can be seen as a necessary follow-up, with technological advancement, to the successful unification of weights and measures on the continent from the mercantilist period till around Napoleonic times. Likewise, the harmonization of taxes and monetary unification are further elements of correspondence between the programs at the two different periods.

We shall turn now to the question of whether the parallel with mercantilism also exists with respect to present EC external policies regarding international trade.

Trade Policies of the EC

The effects of the 1992 program on non-EC members have been studied widely.[2] In itself the 1992 program is designed to generate additional economic growth in the EC, some 5%-7% of GDP as a static effect and an estimated dynamic effect of about 0.5% of GDP per annum.[3] How far this extra growth translates itself into trade creation involving more exports from outside the EC and to what extent trade diversion will occur depend, to a considerable extent, on the future shape of EC trade policies.

At present, trade policies of the EC are characterized by many preferential agreements. With the EFTA countries a free trade area has existed since 1966. Many countries in the Mediterranean region have a special agreement on trade with the EC: Cyprus, Israel, the Maghreb countries (Algeria, Morocco, and Tunisia), Malta, the Mashreq countries (Egypt, Jordan, Lebanon, and Syria). The General System of Preferences (GSP) extends preferential access for a range of products to developing countries in general. The Lomé conventions do so for a group of former colonies in Africa, the Caribbean, and the Pacific, the ACP countries. With individual countries of the former Comecon, separate trade agreements have been concluded. The impression is that the EC, far more than the United States or Japan, has surrounded itself with layers of preferential trade agreements, together forming a pyramid of preferences or, in the words of Wolf, "the EC is embedded in concentric circles of discrimination."[4]

Measures of protection presently in use by the EC—as well as by other bodies—include quotas on imports, voluntary restraints on exports, and antidumping procedures. Import quota and voluntary export restraints apply to specific trade partners of the EC and are therefore discriminatory in nature. Moreover, these measures limit the extent of the market by fragmenting it. Antidumping procedures are targeted even more precisely, namely, to individual firms allegedly dumping their products on the EC market.

In conclusion, it appears that discrimination is an important element of present-day EC trade policies.

The European Economic Area

The agreement on the European Economic Area (EEA) substitutes for previous agreements between the EC and EFTA. To the already existing free EC-EFTA trade in manufactures, the EEA adds free trade in services, free movement of labor and capital, and the adoption by EFTA countries of EC competition policies and company laws.

With respect to manufactured goods the EC and EFTA already constitute a free trade area, but it is only through the EEA that the EC-EFTA area can be treated by firms as a unified market. The elements of the 1992 program of the EC incorporated in the EEA agreement would increase EFTA GDP by some 0.5%.[5] Moreover, EC-EFTA trade in manufactures for Austria, Sweden, and Switzerland is to a large extent of the intra-industry type. This suggests that the firms involved would also to a large extent operate under conditions of imperfect competition. This in turn would imply benefits from the EEA in terms of increased competition. The costs for EFTA of not joining the EEA would also involve a loss in competitiveness of EFTA-based firms relative to EC-based firms, calculated to amount again to 0.5% of EFTA GDP.[6]

Services have a higher average share in GDP in EFTA (60% in 1990) than in the EC (53%). Services usually are designed for national markets, with national regulation fencing off international competition. The EC1992 program and the EEA imply national deregulation and hence increased competition in the service industries. Regarding financial services the benefits of the EEA would be about 1% of GDP both in the EC and EFTA, with Austria and Switzerland benefiting more than the Nordic EFTA countries.[7]

Agriculture is a highly protected sector in the EC and even more so in EFTA. This sensitive sector has been excluded from the earlier free trade arrangements and has been largely left out of the EEA agreement as well.[8]

In addition to the static effects discussed above, the dynamic effects of the EEA are of specific importance. The EC share in direct foreign investment (DFI) going into EFTA has already fallen from 47% in 1986 to 36% in 1990; on the other hand, the EC share in DFI going out from EFTA increased from 30% to 63% in the same period.[9] There is no doubt that the technical harmonization in the EC under the 1992 program and the setting of EC standards lead EFTA firms to desire a presence within the EC. Outside the EEA the EFTA countries would experience a reduced rate of investment,[10] lower returns to capital and to skilled labor, as well as increased flows of investment and skilled labor to the EC, all reducing the growth rate in EFTA.

Under the EEA agreement, the EFTA countries are only informally consulted regarding new EC legislation. The economic consequence is that EFTA countries and firms do not partake in the process of shaping EC policies and formulating EC technical standards. This position as outsiders will almost automatically lead to applications by EFTA countries for EC membership.[11] CEPR concludes for that reason that the present EEA agreement is only a transitory arrangement.[12]

Regional Blocs in World Trade

Bhagwati discusses four threats to the world trading system, whose main underlying principle, under GATT, is nondiscrimination.[13] The four are:

1. *The sensitivity toward unfair trade.* This sensitivity has led, among other things, to the use of countervailing duties against foreign subsidization of exports and of antidumping measures to counteract dumping.

2. *The flight into managed trade.* This involves the fear that high-technology industries will be lost to countries such as Japan, which has been more successful in supporting such industries than other countries. This fear leads to the application of measures such as voluntary export restraints.

3. *Aggressive unilateralism.* This relates to the use of section 301 and so-called super-301 provisions of U.S. trade legislation, which allows the U.S. to demand negotiations with specific countries on trade practices that it finds unacceptable and to seek their abolition on a tight time schedule that it sets, resorting to tariff retaliation if necessary.

4. *Regionalism in world trade.* The impression has spread that the regional Free Trade Areas and Customs Unions are fragmenting the world economy into three internally coherent trading blocs that are hostile to the outside world.

Bhagwati comments that the first three elements are undoubtedly undermining nondiscrimination in world trade. With respect to the fourth element, regionalism, the matter is more complicated. Anderson, Lloyd, and Schott[14] have investigated the question of whether regional trading blocs are emerging in world trade, using as the criterion the development over time of intra-area trade relative to total imports of the area. Intra-EC trade in total EC imports rose from 40% in 1960 to 60% in 1989.[15] Intra-area trade rose only slightly to 40% of total imports of North America in 1989, and remained fairly constant at one-third in East Asia.[16] The conclusion, then, is that in terms of the criterion chosen the EC is clearly emerging as a trading bloc, East Asia is not, and North America is in an intermediate position.

These figures already indicate that the East Asian countries have an ongoing interest in open trade relations with the outside world and thus have an interest in an open multilateral system of world trade, that is, without discrimination.[17] The figures cited equally indicate the lesser interest of the EC in open trade relations with the outside world. Again, the United States or NAFTA take an intermediate position.[18] A relatively inward-looking attitude by the EC is made the more likely by the tendency toward discrimination in present-day EC trade policy practice.

Of course, any Free Trade Area or Customs Union by definition discriminates against its nonmembers. Yet article 24 of the GATT allows the formation of such areas provided they are complete, that is, not selective in terms of commodity coverage. Viner explains that the same principle applied in economic diplomacy in the nineteenth century when international disputes concerned the incompatibility of preferential trade agreements with the most-favored-nation principle, i.e., the principle of nondiscrimination in world trade.[19]

On various grounds the complete Free Trade Area was seen as a reasonable compromise between discriminatory economic integration and the principle of nondiscrimination in trade worldwide.[20] The most important reason, however, was that a Free Trade Area can be considered as an experiment with relatively low risk on a relatively small scale of what eventually may become liberalized worldwide trade.

In conclusion, Free Trade Areas as trading blocs in world trade by definition discriminate against nonmembers. Whether such trading blocs pose a threat to the nondiscriminatory multilateral trade system is, however, uncertain. This depends on the extent of openness that the trading bloc develops toward the outside world.

Trade Liberalization Under GATT

We have noted various developments in world trade relations. Several of these contravene the continuation and improvement of an open, multilateral, nondiscriminatory trade system. Among these developments are the discrimination inherent in main present-day trade policies of the EC, the aggressive unilateralism of U.S. trade policies, and the possible formation of inward-looking regional trading blocs.

The recently concluded Uruguay Round of GATT negotiations was primarily meant to keep these tendencies in check and ensure that the world trade system would remain based as far as possible on the main principle underlying GATT, namely, nondiscrimination. Thus, the program of the Uruguay Round sought to bring under GATT a range of trade flows and trade measures, and its conclusion in December 1993 has been largely successful in doing so. The relevant topics include:[21]

1. *Agriculture*, protection of which has been outside GATT
2. *Textiles and clothing*, protection of which has been under the Multi-Fibre Arrangement
3. *Services*, trade in which was outside GATT
4. *Trade-related intellectual property rights* (TRIPs)
5. *Trade-related investment measures* (TRIMs)
6. *Safeguard clauses*
7. *Dispute settlements*

It is difficult if not impossible to prove that an open multilateral system of world trade without discrimination is always preferable to any alternative. Yet there is important circumstantial evidence, involving both empirical experience and theoretical insight. Convincing empirical experience is provided by the growth rates of world output and world trade in various periods. These figures are represented in Table 1. It appears that over the years 1953-1990 world trade grew faster than world output. This, of course, indicates that specialization in production and trade is increasing in the world economy and that, as a consequence, countries get more interdependent. With respect to periods, in the years 1963-1973 the growth rates for output and trade are high and their difference is large relative to the period 1973-1983. In the latter period the use of NTBs increased considerably. Also, the figures for 1930-1938 are illustrative. These are the years of the Great Depression, increasing protectionism, and the implementation of bilateral trade agreements.[22] In that period world output (in manufactures) still increased by 3% per annum, but world trade declined by 0.5%; both figures combined reveal a tendency toward autarky.[23]

Table 1
World Output and World Trade 1930-1990
(annual growth rates in percentages)

	1930-1938	1953-1962	1963-1972	1973-1982	1983-1990
World output	3[1]	4	5	2.5	4
World trade	-0.5[1]	6	9	3	6

Sources: UNCTAD, *Handbook of International Trade and Development Statistics* (1972); G. Hufbauer and J. Schott, *Trading for Growth* (Washington, D.C.: Institute for International Economics, 1985); GATT, *International Trade 90-91* (1992).
[1]Manufactures only.

The interpretation of the figures in Table 1 also supports an insight from theory. Trade liberalization under GATT favors international specialization and economic growth. On the other hand, protectionism and bilateralism imply a tendency toward autarky and depression. This brings to memory the insight of Adam Smith that growth of welfare is based in no small measure on the division of labor, which in turn is limited by the extent of the market. In this perspective, liberalization of trade without discrimination extends the world market and therefore stimulates the international division of labor. Protection[24] and bilateralism, on the other hand, limit the extent of the market and hence block the process of further international specialization.

Israel in the World Trade System

Israel's Profile in International Trade

Israel's merchandise exports increased from U.S. $2 billion in 1975 to well over U.S. $11 billion in 1991 (Table 2). This sixfold increase implies a rise in Israel's share in world exports from 0.22 in 1975 to 0.34 in 1991. Throughout this period the EC was the main market of destination, absorbing around 40% of Israel's exports.[25] The United States doubled its share in Israel's exports to reach 31% in 1991, at the expense of the rest of the world, with Japan having a share of around 5%.

Table 2
Profile of International Trade, 1975-1991

Exports of Israel	in $US million				
Destination	1975	1980	1985	1989	1991
EC-12	807	2415	2218	3847	4484
Japan	89	227	215	758	737
USA	314	971	2200	3325	3571
Rest of world	731	1930	1655	3164	2806
Total	1941	5543	6288	11094	11598

Exports of Israel	in percentages of total exports				
Destination	1975	1980	1985	1989	1991
EC-12	42	44	35	35	39
Japan	5	4	3	7	6
USA	16	18	35	30	31
Rest of world	38	35	26	29	24
Total	100	100	100	100	100

Share in world exports	in percentages				
	1975	1980	1985	1989	1991
	0.22	0.28	0.33	0.37	0.34

Imports of Israel	in $US million				
Origin	1975	1980	1985	1989	1991
EC-12	1624	2372	2992	5589	7229
Japan	73	109	170	318	738
USA	1508	1942	1808	2697	3554
Rest of world	2794	5262	5040	5546	5298
Total	5999	9685	10010	14150	16819

(Cont'd.)

(Table 2 cont'd.)

Imports of Israel		in percentages of total imports			
Origin	1975	1980	1985	1989	1991
EC-12	27	24	30	39	43
Japan	1	1	2	2	4
USA	25	20	18	19	21
Rest of world	47	54	50	39	32
Total	100	100	100	100	100

Share in world imports			in percentages		
	1975	1980	1985	1989	1991
0.66	0.47	0.50	0.45	0.56	

Sources: UN trade data, UN Statistical Office, Geneva; IMF, *Direction of Trade Statistics Yearbook* (Washington, D.C.).

Israel's merchandise imports increased much less than its exports, from U.S. $6 billion in 1975 to U.S. $17 billion in 1991, representing a declining share in world imports from 0.7% to 0.6% in the same period. On the import side, the EC increased its importance in Israel's trade relations from 27% to 43% between 1975 and 1991. The United States continued to have a share in Israel's imports of around 20%. Japan's share recently rose to 4%.

Taken together, these developments in exports and imports imply a trade deficit for Israel in the entire period, although declining between 1975 and 1991 from 51% to 18% of Israel's total merchandise trade.

Appendixes A1-A4 display the product composition of Israel's exports and imports, distinguishing as trade partners the EC-12, Japan, and the United States. At the 1-digit level of the SITC, the product composition of Israel's exports to the EC shows that the share of food and live animals in total exports dropped from 35% in 1975 to 15% in 1991. The remainder of exports was largely concentrated in manufactures (SITC 5-8), with raw material based manufactures as the largest group (SITC 6) at 27% of total exports. The same group (SITC 6) is dominant in exports to Japan and the U.S., with much higher shares in total exports than for the EC with 73% and 40% in 1991, respectively.[26] For the remainder—again unlike exports to the EC—exports to Japan and the U.S. are unimportant outside manufactures (SITC 5-8).

Imports of Israel from the EC, Japan, and the United States are all concentrated on manufactures. Within that, however, there is a marked difference in the product composition of imports from the EC on the one hand and from Japan and the U.S. on the other. Imports from Japan and the U.S. are predominantly found in SITC section 7, that is, machinery and transport equipment. Not less than 79% of total imports from Japan were classified under that heading in 1991, a remarkable increase from 22% in 1975. In contrast, imports from the EC consist for the major part of around 40% of raw material based manufactures (SITC section 6).

At the 5-digit level of the SITC, Appendix A4 lists the 25 most important products of Israel's exports and imports with the EC. Within exports the 10 most important products are all primary products, apart from diamonds, which are the most important export products in 1991. The positions 11-25 comprise 12 manufactured products, among which are two bulk chemicals and three clothing products but also three modern types of instruments.

Imports from the EC in 1991 at the 5-digit level show diamonds as the most important product, just as at the export side. The other important import products include a variety of motor vehicles, communication equipment, and chemicals. Only one primary product is among the 25 most important import products: sugar.

Israel's Revealed Comparative Advantages on the EC Market

We turn to an analysis of the revealed comparative advantage (RCA) of Israel's exports on the EC market. Balassa's RCA index (B_i) will be used to measure the position of Israel's exports on the EC market:

$$B_i = (X_{ij} / X_j) \; / \; (X_i / X)$$

In which:

X_{ij} = exports of product(group) i from country j to the EC;
X_j = exports of all products from country j to the EC;
X_i = exports of product(group) i from the world to the EC;
X = exports of all products from the world to the EC.

When the value of the Balassa index B_i is greater than one, the share of the product i in total exports from country j to the EC is greater than the share of product i in total exports from all countries to the EC. This implies that country j has a revealed comparative advantage (compared to the rest of the world) in exporting product i to the EC. Similarly, a value of Bi smaller than one indicates that country j has a revealed comparative disadvantage in exporting product i to the EC.

The concept of revealed comparative advantage is closely related to that of comparative advantage (CA), but the two concepts are clearly distinguished.

Comparative advantage relates to the *advantage* that a certain country has in the production of certain goods *comparative* to other countries. Such advantages relate to the price of the product, which in turn is based on the costs of production. Such production costs differ among countries due to differences in climate, mineral deposits, and the costs of production factors: land, labor, and capital. Countries are different in these respects and hence will produce in autarky the various goods at different costs and prices. From a welfare point of view it is profitable that such differences in production costs among countries are exploited; each country specializes in those products in which it has a comparative advantage and exchanges these products in international trade for products for which its trading partners have a comparative advantage. David Ricardo (1772-1823) illustrated the principle of comparative advantage in his *Principles of Political Economy* (1817).[27] Later on, Heckscher and Ohlin[28] attributed differences in production costs among countries to differences in relative availability of the factors of production capital and labor.

In practice, however, it turned out not to be easy to measure a country's comparative advantage; in particular, the availability of production factors turned out to be difficult to assess and the relation between costs of production factors and product prices is not straightforward.[29]

Aware of these difficulties, Balassa introduced the concept of revealed comparative advantage.[30] His reasoning was that whereas a country's comparative advantage was difficult to observe, it would "reveal" itself in the emerging product pattern of trade. The product composition of a country's exports would be an indicator of the country's comparative advantage, with the merit of being an observable one. Of course, Balassa realized that trade patterns between countries are influenced not only by comparative advantage, but also by tariffs and nontariff barriers, trade agreements, and preferential access. Such factors obscure to some extent the direct relationship between revealed comparative advantage and comparative advantage and should be borne in mind when interpreting the Balassa RCA index.

Israel's comparative advantage on the EC market has been assessed by calculating the Balassa-index (B) for revealed comparative advantage. Data have been used at the 2-digit level of the SITC for EC imports from Israel relative to total EC imports in 1989. The seven product groups with the most pronounced RCA of Israel on the EC market are represented in Table 3. The product groups include food products and bulk chemicals, corresponding to the observations on the product pattern of EC imports from Israel given above.

Similar calculations on RCA on the EC market have been made for other exporting countries and country groups. Hence Table 3 shows, for each of the import products with a high RCA on the EC, Israel's main competitors.

Table 3
Israel's Revealed Comparative Advantages on the EC Market, 1989
(Balassa-index, 2-digit SITC)

SITC	Product	B[1]	Main competitors	B[1]
56	Chemical fertilizers	11.8	Mediterr. agr. countr.[2]	5.6
66	Nonmetallic mineral manuf.	8.0	India	6.8
09	Misc. edible products	7.8	China	2.8
29	Crude animal/vegetable mat.	7.3	China	4.8
05	Vegetables and fruit	6.8	New NICs[3]	4.1
52	Inorganic chemicals	5.9	China	2.4
27	Crude fertilizers and minerals	4.7	Mediterr. agr. countr.[2]	3.9

Source: UN trade data.
[1] B = Balassa index for revealed comparative advantage.
[2] Mediterranean Agreement countries: Algeria, Cyprus, Egypt, Malta, Morocco, Tunisia, Turkey.
[3] New NICs: Chile, Indonesia, Jordan, Macau, Malaysia, Peru, the Philippines, Sri Lanka, Thailand.

Conclusions and Implications for Israel

From the review of recent developments and tendencies in the world trade system in the preceding sections, the following main observations emerge:

- The 1992 program of the EC shows a striking resemblance to the program of economic unification within the nation-state under the system of mercantilism.
- Present trade policies of the EC show a tendency toward discrimination in trade relations.
- The formation of the European Economic Area probably is a transitory arrangement only; the EFTA countries in general will opt for EC membership because the EEA gives them only little say in shaping EC policies.
- Insofar as regional trading blocs are emerging, the East Asian bloc can be shown to have a continued interest in an open multilateral world trade system. Such

a system is less likely to be supported by the EC given the nature of its 1992 program and its trade policies. North America has an intermediate position.

- The conclusion of the Uruguay Round will keep in check the tendencies away from nondiscrimination in the world trade system by bringing more sectors under GATT, such as agriculture and services, and by improving the functioning of GATT.

The EC and the United States are the main markets for exports from Israel, each receiving more than 30%; the share of the EC has been stable around 40% of total exports from Israel in the period 1975-1991 but has doubled for the U.S. in that time, reaching 31% in 1991. Both markets receive mainly basic and resource-based manufactures with the EC also importing substantial amounts of vegetables and fruit, though with a declining share in EC imports from Israel.

Israel has concluded a free trade arrangement with the United States. This provides a good basis for developing this trade relationship further, in the direction of more diversified exports from Israel, also in view of the North American Free Trade Agreement (NAFTA) recently concluded by Canada, Mexico, and the United States and of other free trade arrangements possibly to be expected on the American continent.

A similar reasoning applies to trade agreements between Israel and the EC, with the latter concluding trade agreements with other European countries. This applies in particular to the EFTA countries, with which Israel recently concluded a free trade arrangement. With EC membership of EFTA countries to be expected, in this way Israel comes very close to EC membership itself (Appendix B) without giving up its position in order to be able to conclude trade agreements independent of the EC trade policy framework.

The declining share of vegetables and fruit in Israel's exports to the EC may testify to a diversification of Israel's export package. On the other hand, the fact that the Uruguay Round has brought agriculture under GATT might provide new opportunities for Israel's export of such products.

It seems advisable for Israel to expand trade relations with East Asia—if possible—in view of East Asia's high growth rates and continued interest in an open multilateral world trade system.

Notes

1. J. Pelkmans and A. Winters, *Europe's Domestic Market*, Chatham House Papers 43, Royal Institute of International Affairs (London: Routledge, 1989).

2. See, e.g., R. Portes, "The EC and Eastern Europe After 1992," *Essays in International Finace*, no. 182, pp. 31-43 (Princeton University, 1991); K. Shigehara, "The External Dimension

of Europe 1992: Its Effects on Relations Between Europe, the United States and Japan," *Essays in International Finance*, no. 182 (Princeton University, 1991), pp. 17-30; and the overview in J. Kol, "The ACP Countries and the 1992-Programme of the EC," Report to the Commission of the EC, Erasmus University, 1992, also published in *The Courier*, no. 120, 1990.

3. R. Baldwin, "The Growth Effects of 1992," *Economic Policy*, 1989, pp. 248-281.

4. M. Wolf, "An Unholy Alliance: The EC and Developing Countries in the International Trading System," in L.B.M. Mennes and J. Kol, eds., *European Trade Policies and the Developing World* (London: Croom Helm, 1988).

5. CEPR, "Is Bigger Better?: The Economics of EC Enlargement," *Monitoring European Integration* 3, CEPR Annual Report (London, 1992).

6. Ibid.

7. E.P.M. Gardener and J. L. Teppett, "The Impact of '1992' on the Financial Services Sectors of EFTA Countries," EFTA Occasional Paper 33 (Geneva, 1992).

8. Including the agricultural sectors and policies of EFTA in the EC Common Agricultural Policy would have important consequences for prices and trade of agricultural products in EFTA countries upon their EC membership.

9. CEPR, "Is Bigger Better?"

10. Induced capital formation through the EEA increases EFTA gains with 1%-2% of GDP (ibid.).

11. For instance, as an EC member Finland would have a say in shaping EC forestry policies, Norway in policies on fishing and petroleum, Sweden on automobiles and capital goods policies, and Switzerland regarding policies on banking and pharmaceuticals (ibid.).

12. Ibid.

13. J. Bhagwati, "The Threats to the World Trade System," *World Economy* 15 (1992): 443-456.

14. K. Anderson, "Is an Asian-Pacific Trade Bloc Next?," *Journal of World Trade* 25 (1991): 27-40; P. J. Lloyd, "Regionalisation and World Trade," *OECD Economic Studies* 18 (1992): 7-43; J. J. Schott, "Trading Blocs and the World Trading System," *The World Economy* 14 (1991): 1-17.

15. Figures for 1960 relate to the present 12 EC members for reasons of comparison.

16. North America comprises Canada, Mexico, and the United States; East Asia includes Australia, Hong Kong, Indonesia, Japan, Korea, Malaysia, New Zealand, the Philippines, Singapore, Taiwan, and Thailand.

17. An array of additional supporting arguments may be found in Anderson, "Asian-Pacific Trade Bloc."

18. Schott, "Trading Blocs."

19. J. Viner, *The Customs Union Issue* (London: Stevens & Sons, 1950).

20. Bhagwati, "Threats."

21. An overview is given in Bhagwati, "Threats."

22. Tovias makes an interesting comparison of geographical discrimination in world trade in the 1930s and 1980s and concludes: "moving from unconditional most-favoured-nation treatment to something else, as is witnessed today, is like opening a Pandora's box" (A. Tovias, "Trade Discrimination in the Thirties and Eighties," *The World Economy*, 11, 1988, pp. 501-514).

23. Five hundred years ago China was by far the richest country in the world. Gradually China tended toward autarky and the government stopped international trade. The outcome over time was not rewarding (M. Wolf, "European Community 1992: The Lure of the Chasse Gardée," *The World*

Economy, 12, 1989, pp. 373-376).

24. In this regard, Wolf ("Unholy Alliance") explains that tariffs still allow prices to play the role as indicators of relative scarcity and thus are a market-conforming instrument of protection. Quota and other NTBs, however, stop the functioning of the market by fragmenting it.

25. For reasons of comparison, the EC-12 country group has been taken to represent the EC throughout the period of investigation.

26. SITC group 6 contains diamonds, the major export product of Israel (see also Appendix A-4).

27. Ricardo's well-known example is that of England and Portugal each specializing in a specific product—textiles and wine, respectively—and exchanging these in foreign trade to their mutual advantage. Ricardo also pointed out that differences between countries in production costs need not be absolute, but can be relative for international trade to be of mutual benefit.

28. E. F. Heckscher, "The Effects of Foreign Trade on the Distribution of Income," *Economisk Tidskrift* 21 (1919): 497-512 (in Swedish), reprinted in abridged and translated form in H. S. Ellis and L. A. Metzler, eds., *Readings in the Theory of International Trade* (Blakiston, Phila., for the American Economic Association, 1949), pp. 272-300; B. Ohlin, *Interregional and International Trade* (Cambridge: Harvard University Press, 1933).

29. A. V. Deardorff, "Testing Trade Theories and Predicting Trade Flows," in R. W. Jones and P. B. Kenen, eds., *Handbook of International Economics* (Amsterdam: North-Holland, 1984).

30. B. Balassa, "Trade Liberalisation and 'Revealed' Comparative Advantage," *Manchester School of Economic and Social Studies* 33, 2 (1965): 99-123.

Appendix A1
Product Composition of Trade of Israel With EC-12, 1975-1991

Exports of Israel to EC-12	in $US million				
SITC section	1975	1980	1985	1989	1991
0 Food and live animals	279	521	528	596	660
1 Beverages and tobacco	1	2	1	9	5
2 Crude materials	86	332	292	330	373
3 Mineral fuels	48	118	57	23	87
4 Oils and fats	8	1	1	0	1
5 Chemicals	89	279	348	691	780
6 Raw material based manufactures	175	650	446	1057	1211
7 Machinery and transport equipment	38	112	183	476	637
8 Miscellaneous manufactures	79	337	284	520	691
9 Commodities n.e.s.	4	62	79	145	39
Total	807	2415	2218	3847	4484

Appendix A1 (cont'd.)

Exports of Israel to EC-12 — in percentages of total exports

SITC section	1975	1980	1985	1989	1991
0 Food and live animals	35	22	24	15	15
1 Beverages and tobacco	0	0	0	0	0
2 Crude materials	11	14	13	9	8
3 Mineral fuels	6	5	3	1	2
4 Oils and fats	1	0	0	0	0
5 Chemicals	11	12	16	18	17
6 Raw material based manufactures	22	27	20	27	27
7 Machinery and transport equipment	5	5	8	12	14
8 Miscellaneous manufactures	10	14	13	14	15
9 Commodities n.e.s.	0	3	4	4	1
Total	100	100	100	100	100

Imports of Israel from EC-12 — in $US million

SITC section	1975	1980	1985	1989	1991
0 Food and live animals	55	129	125	259	314
1 Beverages and tobacco	7	9	10	21	23
2 Crude materials	28	38	48	82	81
3 Mineral fuels	4	9	14	30	71
4 Oils and fats	9	9	17	12	18
5 Chemicals	145	276	381	710	855
6 Raw material based manufactures	651	926	1154	2527	2958
7 Machinery and transport equipment	604	726	981	1435	2270
8 Miscellaneous manufactures	85	132	220	462	557
9 Commodities n.e.s.	37	118	43	49	83
Total	1624	2372	2992	5589	7230

Appendix A1 (cont'd.)

Imports of Israel from EC-12	in percentages of total imports				
SITC section	1975	1980	1985	1989	1991
0 Food and live animals	3	5	4	5	4
1 Beverages and tobacco	0	0	0	0	0
2 Crude materials	2	2	2	1	1
3 Mineral fuels	0	0	0	1	1
4 Oils and fats	1	0	1	0	0
5 Chemicals	9	12	13	13	12
6 Raw material based manufactures	40	39	39	45	41
7 Machinery and transport equipment	37	31	33	26	31
8 Miscellaneous manufactures	5	6	7	8	8
9 Commodities n.e.s.	2	5	1	1	1
Total	100	100	100	100	100

Source: UN trade data, UN Statistical Office, Geneva.

Appendix A2

Product Composition of Trade of Israel With Japan, 1975-1991

Exports of Israel to Japan	in $US million				
SITC section	1975	1980	1985	1989	1991
0 Food and live animals	6	7	15	19	25
1 Beverages and tobacco	0	0	0	1	7
2 Crude materials	3	2	2	12	12
3 Mineral fuels	0	0	0	0	0
4 Oils and fats	0	0	0	0	0
5 Chemicals	11	28	29	54	63
6 Raw material based manufactures	68	183	151	597	536
7 Machinery and transport equipment	1	5	9	47	66
8 Miscellaneous manufactures	1	3	8	27	27
9 Commodities n.e.s.	0	0	1	0	1
Total	89	227	215	758	737

Appendix A2 (cont'd.)

Exports of Israel to Japan	in percentages of total exports				
SITC section	1975	1980	1985	1989	1991
0 Food and live animals	6	3	7	2	3
1 Beverages and tobacco	0	0	0	0	1
2 Crude materials	4	1	1	2	2
3 Mineral fuels	0	0	0	0	0
4 Oils and fats	0	0	0	0	0
5 Chemicals	12	12	14	7	9
6 Raw material based manufactures	76	80	70	79	73
7 Machinery and transport equipment	1	2	4	6	9
8 Miscellaneous manufactures	1	1	4	4	4
9 Commodities n.e.s.	0	0	0	0	0
Total	100	100	100	100	100

Imports of Israel from Japan	in $US million				
SITC section	1975	1980	1985	1989	1991
0 Food and live animals	1	2	1	1	0
1 Beverages and tobacco	0	0	0	0	0
2 Crude materials	5	5	4	3	2
3 Mineral fuels	0	0	0	0	0
4 Oils and fats	0	0	0	0	0
5 Chemicals	7	13	9	17	27
6 Raw material based manufactures	32	19	18	19	20
7 Machinery and transport equipment	16	52	100	223	579
8 Miscellaneous manufactures	11	14	31	34	47
9 Commodities n.e.s.	1	4	6	21	62
Total	73	109	171	318	737

Appendix A2 (cont'd.)

Imports of Israel from Japan — in percentages of total imports

SITC section	1975	1980	1985	1989	1991
0 Food and live animals	1	1	0	0	0
1 Beverages and tobacco	0	0	0	0	0
2 Crude materials	7	5	2	1	0
3 Mineral fuels	0	0	0	0	0
4 Oils and fats	0	0	0	0	0
5 Chemicals	10	12	5	5	4
6 Raw material based manufactures	44	17	11	6	3
7 Machinery and transport equipment	22	48	59	70	79
8 Miscellaneous manufactures	15	13	18	11	6
9 Commodities n.e.s.	1	4	4	7	8
Total	100	100	100	100	100

Source: UN trade data, UN Statistical Office, Geneva.

Appendix A3
Product Composition of Trade of Israel With USA, 1975-1991

Exports of Israel to USA — in $US million

SITC section	1975	1980	1985	1989	1991
0 Food and live animals	7	18	63	70	72
1 Beverages and tobacco	2	3	4	3	2
2 Crude materials	11	23	33	17	24
3 Mineral fuels	0	0	23	15	32
4 Oils and fats	0	0	0	0	1
5 Chemicals	17	62	160	242	280
6 Raw material based manufactures	182	543	984	1512	1416
7 Machinery and transport equipment	35	180	547	844	1035
8 Miscellaneous manufactures	49	114	302	549	616
9 Commodities n.e.s.	12	29	85	72	93
Total	314	971	2200	3325	3571

Appendix A3 (cont'd.)

Exports of Israel to USA	in percentages of total exports				
SITC section	1975	1980	1985	1989	1991
0 Food and live animals	2	2	3	2	2
1 Beverages and tobacco	1	0	0	0	0
2 Crude materials	3	2	2	1	1
3 Mineral fuels	0	0	1	0	1
4 Oils and fats	0	0	0	0	0
5 Chemicals	5	6	7	7	8
6 Raw material based manufactures	58	56	45	45	40
7 Machinery and transport equipment	11	19	25	25	29
8 Miscellaneous manufactures	16	12	14	17	17
9 Commodities n.e.s.	4	3	4	2	3
Total	100	100	100	100	100

Imports of Israel from USA	in $US million				
SITC section	1975	1980	1985	1989	1991
0 Food and live animals	207	213	163	205	187
1 Beverages and tobacco	4	8	11	40	41
2 Crude materials	112	94	124	122	151
3 Mineral fuels	2	2	21	50	65
4 Oils and fats	3	5	3	1	4
5 Chemicals	38	76	66	133	194
6 Raw material based manufactures	118	173	209	399	284
7 Machinery and transport equipment	444	712	1020	1299	1984
8 Miscellaneous manufactures	35	90	143	347	490
9 Commodities n.e.s.	17	19	48	101	153
Total	979	1393	1808	2697	3553

Appendix A3 (cont'd.)

Imports of Israel from USA in percentages of total imports

SITC section	1975	1980	1985	1989	1991
0 Food and live animals	21	15	9	8	5
1 Beverages and tobacco	0	1	1	1	1
2 Crude materials	11	7	7	5	4
3 Mineral fuels	0	0	1	2	2
4 Oils and fats	0	0	0	0	0
5 Chemicals	4	5	4	5	5
6 Raw material based manufactures	12	12	12	15	8
7 Machinery and transport equipment	45	51	56	48	56
8 Miscellaneous manufactures	4	6	8	13	14
9 Commodities n.e.s.	2	1	3	4	4
Total	100	100	100	100	100

Source: UN trade data, UN Statistical Office, Geneva.

Appendix A4
Main Products in Trade Between Israel and the EC-12, 1991

Main export products of Israel to EC-12, 1991

	SITC	Basic Heading	in $US million	in %
1	66729	Diamonds, worked, not mounted or set	514	11.5
2	66722	Diamonds, sorted, unworked	213	4.8
3	0591	Orange juice	136	3.0
4	29271	Cut flowers and flower buds	118	2.6
5	56231	Potassium chloride	83	1.9
6	05722	Grapefruit, fresh or dried	68	1.5
7	27231	Natural calcium phosphates, unground	63	1.4
8	52352	Potassium nitrate	60	1.3
9	05797	Avocados, guavas and mangoes, fresh or dried	55	1.2
10	2631	Cotton, not carded or combed	53	1.2
11	69562	Plates and the like for tools, of metal	53	1.2
12	56222	Superphosphates	52	1.2

Appendix A4 (cont'd.)

13	52234	Diphosphorus pentoxide	51	1.1
14	75997	Parts of automatic data processing machines	46	1.0
15	05711	Oranges, fresh or dried	46	1.0
16	0592	Grapefruit juice	45	1.0
17	33419	Light petroleum oils, not crude	44	1.0
18	84629	Other hosiery, knitted or crocheted	42	0.9
19	89731	Articles of jewellery, of precious metals	42	0.9
20	59225	Peptones and derivatives	36	0.8
21	84381	Underpants and briefs, for men	34	0.8
22	84482	Briefs and panties, for women	34	0.8
23	9310	Special commodities not classified	34	0.8
24	76417	Apparatus for carrier-current line systems	32	0.7
25	87229	Other instruments for medical purposes	31	0.7
		Total	1985	44.3

Main import products of Israel from EC-12, 1991

SITC		Basic Heading	in $US million	in %
1	66722	Diamonds, sorted, unworked	1232	17.0
2	7812	Motor vehicles for the transport of persons	270	3.7
3	66729	Diamonds, worked, not mounted or set	260	3.6
4	79327	Other vessels for the transport of goods	143	2.0
5	78219	Motor vehicles for the transport of goods, n.e.s.	114	1.6
6	9310	Special commodities not classified	74	1.0
7	78439	Other parts and accessories of motor vehicles	68	0.9
8	06129	Other beet or cane sugar, flavoured	56	0.8
9	7841	Chassis fitted with engines of motor vehicles	55	0.8
10	68241	Copper wire of refined copper	48	0.7
11	54293	Medicaments, n.e.s., in measured doses	44	0.6
12	7523	Digital processing units	43	0.6
13	89731	Articles of jewellery, of precious metals	41	0.6
14	75997	Parts of automatic data processing machines	39	0.5
15	76491	Parts of telephone and telegraph equipment	38	0.5
16	72651	Reel fed offset printing machinery	31	0.4
17	66245	Glazed ceramic flags and paving	28	0.4
18	65133	Cotton yarn, > 85% weight of cotton	27	0.4
19	67421	Flat-rolled iron products, plated, > 0.6m	27	0.4

Appendix A4 (cont'd.)

20	77511	Household washing machines, capacity < 10 kg	27	0.4
21	72842	Machinery for working rubber or plastics	27	0.4
22	74412	Self-propelled trucks, not electric	27	0.4
23	7478	Taps, cocks and valves, n.e.s.	26	0.4
24	89399	Other articles of plastics, n.e.s.	26	0.4
25	72321	Front-end shovel loaders	25	0.3
		Total	2796	38.7

Source: UN trade data, UN Statistical Office, Geneva.

Appendix B
EEC Treaty Provisions

Article 237

Any European State may apply to become a member of the Community. It shall address its application to the Council, which shall act unanimously after consulting the Commission and after receiving the assent of the European Parliament which shall act by an absolute majority of its component members.

Lisbon Report of the European Commission (June 1992)

The "three basic conditions" of EC membership:

- European identity
- Democratic status
- Respect of fundamental human rights

The limits of Europe:

The term "European" has not been officially defined. It combines geographical, historical and cultural elements which all contribute to the European identity. The shared experience of proximity, ideas, values, and historical interaction cannot be condensed into a simple formula, and is subject to review by each succeeding generation. The Commission believes that it is neither possible nor opportune to establish now the frontiers of the European Union, whose contours will be shaped over many years.

Chapter 5

The European Economic Area: Implications for Nonmembers in General and Mediterranean Countries in Particular

VICTORIA CURZON PRICE

Introduction

The efficiency implications of growing regionalism in the global economy are the subject of much recent debate. The "multilateralists," perhaps best represented by Bhagwati,[1] deplore the trend and see it as a long-term threat to the multilateral system as embodied in GATT. The "regionalists," perhaps best represented by Krugman,[2] argue that regional integration between countries that anyway trade a lot with each other is likely to be beneficial *and* that it will become easier to proceed to multilateral free trade in due course, since it seems intuitively obvious that negotiations between a handful of trading blocs should progress faster than the current system of attempting to reach consensus between the 105 members of GATT.[3]

But irrespective of the efficiency implications, the *fact* of the matter is that the crisis of GATT and the patent reluctance to do something about it in the context of the Uruguay Round are forcing countries that might otherwise prefer a multilateral approach to seek an insurance policy in the form of regional trade arrangements with their main trading partners.[4]

Nowhere is this trend more apparent than in Europe, where not only have the EFTA countries (minus Switzerland) signed a far-reaching integration treaty with the European Community (the EEA agreement) but some are preparing (despite major reservations among their respective electorates) to join the EC as full members. Malta, Cyprus, and Turkey also form part of the growing queue of applicants. The Central European countries have all expressed the wish to join as soon as possible and in the meantime have negotiated the standard EC-type preferential "free trade area" agreement reserved for the EC's less developed neighbors.[5] They are also in the process of negotiating similar agreements with the EFTA countries.[6] Other Mediterranean countries, with the exception of Libya, are anxious to enhance their existing preferential trade agreements with the EC. Where will this enormous snowball come to rest? (As some may remember from their childhood, snowballs grow until they get too heavy to push. . . .)

Can we look forward to a situation, somewhere in the distant future, where the whole of Europe (however defined), the Middle East, and North Africa become a single integrated trade zone? The "regionalists" would thereby be vindicated, for such a vast area would represent free trade on a scale unimaginable in the GATT context. But there are several snags, at least in the short run.

The "free trade area" agreements on offer from the EC to its neighbors to the east and south are not really free trade area agreements at all. They are not reciprocal, they contain many restraints and safeguards on both sides, they exclude agricultural products, they do not always provide for free trade between the nonmembers themselves, and limitations on the "cumulation" of origin reduce the value of the free trade regime on offer. They tend to be short on free trade and long on aid, technical assistance, and social and cultural matters (generally a bad sign).

The fact that most of the countries seeking preferential access to the EC market are sheltering behind long transitional periods in order to protect their emerging market economies is predictable but still to be deplored. To the extent that this is justified with reference to the infant-industry argument, the practical difficulties of implementing such an industrial policy successfully should not be overlooked. To the extent that the justification for asymmetrical trade regimes is in terms of the idea that competition with the "strong" economies of Western Europe would harm the "weak" economies of Central and Eastern Europe, it is simply wrong economics, denying the principle of comparative advantage. Although competition, by definition, rewards efficient and penalizes poorly run firms, the same cannot be said of countries as a whole. Quite to the contrary, competition will reveal which firms are better, and which worse, within the national context.

It is worrying that the Central and East European countries seem bent on repeating the mistakes made by developing countries from 1964 onward, in asking for nonreciprocal trade arrangements with their more developed neighbors and in remaining uninterested in developing free trade arrangements among themselves. It suggests that their leaders consider international trade to be a dangerous, zero-sum or even negative-sum game. The Visegrad group (Hungary, Poland, and the Czech and Slovak republics) have indeed established a free trade area among themselves, but significantly enough, only at the insistence of the EC and against their better judgment. The EC wields an incentive to form such free trade areas in that it accepts the cumulation of origin for products originating in more than one associated country, provided it forms part of a regional free trade arrangement. But one does not see countries rushing to form free trade agreements among themselves in order to benefit from this unusually enlightened policy.

We must, however, view the present untidy and fragmentary situation as being simply a stage in an evolving diplomatic and political process that is being impelled by hard economic realities: modern methods of production, hugely efficient in a technical sense but very expensive in terms of up-front investment, need large, secure markets, often well beyond the "size" of most emerging industrial economies. If GATT cannot deliver these, regional arrangements are the next best solution. The generally small, emerging countries that surround the EC have little alternative for the time being than to seek such secure access bilaterally with the EC. Not only is the GATT route highly imperfect and uncertain, but the EC presents outsiders with an irresistible diplomatic simplification: a preexisting concentration of some 12 to 18 national markets, large enough to justify investments designed to capture most known minimum-efficient-scale economies.

And what is the interest of the EC in all this? Long ago, the original EEC chose to favor the preferential and discriminatory trade route over the multilateral one in its dealings with its immediate neighbors and former colonies. The reasons were "strategic" in the true sense of the word. In the battle for influence during the Cold War, trade preferences in favor of Mediterranean countries, in particular, seemed the best way to bind them to the West. Even the United States saw the point and made no more than a symbolic effort to uphold GATT as the EC's preferential system developed.

However, the "pyramid of preference" that resulted now constitutes one of the most glaring denials of multilateralism in existence, an anomaly that not only cannot be reversed but is now being extended to the whole of Central and Eastern Europe. The challenge for the future will be to convert this hodgepodge of preferential, bilateral trade ties into a *single, multilateral, pan-European-Mediterranean free trade area* for industrial products.[7]

The Community has every motive to pursue this objective. By offering only selective, conditional, and restricted access to the goods of its Mediterranean and Central European neighbors it would condemn them to economic stagnation, and by the same token would condemn itself to an ever larger and unstoppable flow of economic immigrants, as the gap in living standards would remain dramatic and demographic pressures continue unabated. By championing multilateral regional free trade among all countries in this vast area, it would not only offer them the best road to rapid economic development but would also permit its own firms and citizens to participate in what would surely become the economic miracle of the next century.

The vehicle for realizing this vision already exists: the EEA Agreement. This agreement suffers from none of the drawbacks mentioned earlier with respect to the existing hodgepodge of preferential arrangements. Countries joining the EEA obtain virtual *economic* membership in the EC, without political ties. They are subject to the same rights (and duties) as full EC members with respect to market access. The essential difference between the EEA and all other previous arrangements on offer by the EC is that the EC extends the *acquis communautaire* to signatories, who in turn accept it (in both its present and future shape). This means that the EC defines a minimum "level playing field" in terms of state aids, public procurement, mutual recognition of norms and regulations, tests and certification procedures, rules of competition, environmental regulation, and so on. In exchange for accepting this package, EEA signatories enjoy full, reciprocal access to the EC market for goods, services, and factors of production. They are automatically placed in an equally free trade relationship with each other. The cumulation of origin within the area is guaranteed.[8] The only difference between an EC and an EEA member is that the latter retains its border controls, since it maintains its own customs tariffs, and its own agricultural policy, since basic foodstuffs are excluded.

Far from being a transitory arrangement while EFTA countries negotiate their full accession to the EC, the EEA agreement might well become a permanent feature of the European trade system. First, some EFTA governments may not be able to persuade their electorates that full membership in the EC is an improvement on the EEA. Second, after absorbing Austria, Finland, and perhaps Sweden, the EC itself may wish to exclude new members for a long time to come while it sorts out its institutional future. Third, the EEA offers a convenient substitute for membership that might prove attractive to applicants in Central and Eastern Europe who become impatient with the EC's foot-dragging. And finally, a number of near-applicants might view membership in the EEA as a permanent solution to their relationship with the EC.

However, as we are still a very long way from opening up the EEA arrangement in this manner, the question arises in the meantime of its immediate implications for nonmembers. This chapter will first discuss the implications of the EEA agreement for nonmembers in general terms; it will then address implications for Mediterranean countries in particular. After that it will take a longer-term perspective and return to the idea that the EEA arrangement might form the basis for a coherent EC policy toward its immediate neighbors to the south and east.

The EEA Arrangement: Broad Implications for Nonmembers

The EFTA countries (minus Switzerland) are, as of January 1, 1994,[9] linked to the EC in an entirely novel form of economic integration, namely, the 17-nation EEA.

What are the efficiency and trade implications of the EEA agreement for nonmembers in general?

The EEA agreement has merged five countries with the 12-nation Single European Market.[10] They collectively "add" some $630 billion GNP to an EC GNP of $8841 billion—the equivalent of two-thirds of the United Kingdom, or two Netherlands. However, with respect to industrial trade, these countries (including Switzerland) were already linked to the EC in a series of bilateral free trade areas, and much of the trade diversion that was inherent in these older agreements is already in operation.[11] The damage, so to speak, is already done. What the EEA agreement does is to eliminate nontariff barriers to these trade flows, without altering the fact that it is still no more than a free trade area, and that rules of origin still have to be complied with (a significant nontariff barrier in their own right).

The EEA and Nontariff Barriers

The principal nontariff barriers that fall as a result of the EEA are (1) technical barriers due to differing norms and regulations, and (2) discriminatory public procurement.

The EEA states are fully integrated into the EC's system of "mutual recognition" of differing national norms, specifications, and regulations, and the development by industrial associations and private standards-setting bodies of harmonized Euro-norms.

To what extent does this system put a nonmember exporter at a disadvantage? Once Euro-norms are established they become available to outsiders and insiders alike, and the Community cannot, in principle, refuse "national treatment" to nonmember products that meet its specifications.

However, the whole point of the EC's "new approach" to standardization is to rely more on *mutual recognition* of different norms and regulations than on their *harmonization* at the political level. This "soft" approach is harder for third countries to live with, since they have no clear Euro-standard to meet. It works well for products whose production or sale constitutes no major threat to consumers, workers, or the environment, or where these interests can be protected by means of Directives that establish "minimum essential requirements." In these cases, the Community farms out the task of drawing up the detailed specifications to private standards-setting bodies, such as CEN and CENELEC.

The vast majority of traded goods fall within the ambit of this new system and the EC is quite clear in its policy with respect to third parties: mutual recognition (of standards themselves, and of tests and certifications) is reserved "for members only."[12] But it is willing to discuss extending the privilege on a reciprocal basis, and has indeed done so in the context of the "Europe agreements" (i.e., with the Visegrad countries).

When products are potentially dangerous for users, consumers, or the environment, the EC uses a modified version of the "new approach." The Council of Ministers issues minimum essential requirements, in the same way as for medium-risk products, but instead of handing the task of drawing up the actual standards to private bodies it delegates this task to the Commission, which draws up the compulsory detailed standards that have to be translated into each national legal system by the member states. As mentioned above, third countries should find this "hard" system of Euro-standards-setting easier to live with than the "soft" system of mutual recognition, since in principle GATT's article III (national treatment) should apply. By contrast, the principle of mutual recognition cannot be "multilateralized" automatically along GATT lines, since it implies a high degree of mutual trust.

The fact that the EEA agreement adds only a small number of small countries to the Single EC Market implies that third parties will scarcely feel the difference in terms of extra trade diversion. However, this cannot obscure the fact that *if* the question of technical barriers to trade is important,[13] and the system of mutual recognition works, then third parties have every incentive to negotiate EEA-type accreditation agreements with the EC.

As far as public procurement is concerned, the EC has adopted far-reaching measures to open up a "market" of some 600 billion ECUs, from paper clips to locomotives and telecommunications equipment, until now entirely subject to the noncommercial whims of government purchasing agents. In 1990 the unbelievable occurred: the Council of Ministers agreed to include the "excluded" sectors (water, energy, transport, and telecommunications) in the general rules of open and non-discriminatory tendering procedures.[14] These had been excluded for the good reason that behind these public monopolies lay highly protected "national champions" supplying expensive items of capital equipment in a cosy monopoly-monopsony relationship.[15]

This Directive opens up many new opportunities for profitable enterprise for Community firms; but where does it leave outsiders?

Article 29 of the 1990 Directive creates a Community preference in the following way: (1) if a tender contains more than 50% by value of non-Community products it "may" be rejected; (2) if two or more tenders are "equivalent" (i.e., if the price difference does not exceed 3%) then a Community preference "shall" be given to the tender that meets the 50% rule.

At first sight the 3% preference threshold seems modest, but one must remember that most public purchasing authorities do not need such guidelines at all; they quite spontaneously give huge preferences to local suppliers. If such "loyalty" is transferred to Community suppliers, and they "may" reject non-Community tenders, one may be forgiven for thinking that they might do exactly that.

For the moment it is impossible to predict how this rule will work, especially since the whole subject is under negotiation both in the Uruguay Round and in the context of the "Europe agreements." As with norms, regulations, and standards, the EC is prepared to offer access on the basis of reciprocity, but negotiations take time. In any event, "outsiders" should have a far more transparent system to deal with. How this combination of transparency and protection balances out in practice for nonmembers depends on the circumstances.

For instance, exporting to the Italian or British public sectors should become easier, since the current levels of import penetration amount to only 1% and 4%, respectively,[16] suggesting virtually automatic preference to local suppliers at any cost. According to the new rules, open tender procedures should force public purchasing agents to consider all bids, including non-EEA ones, and (in the most generous interpretation of article 29 of the 1990 Directive) offer EEA suppliers only a 3% margin of preference. This presumably constitutes an improvement over the previous level of access.

However, the same need not be true of smaller countries, which cannot afford to nurture large "national champions." They tend to purchase much more from foreign suppliers than large countries, especially in the fields of heavy transport, energy, and communications equipment, and until the recent extension of EC open tender rules to these sectors, were free to purchase from the lowest-cost world supplier without (in theory at least) discriminating in favor of EC suppliers. In the case of small countries, and in particular the EFTA states, the application of the EC's procurement directives therefore suggests a potential for trade diversion, especially in the so-called excluded sectors.

Agriculture

As far as agriculture is concerned, the EEA agreement continues to exclude basic foodstuffs, although processed food products are generally included, subject to adjustments to compensate for negative effective protection due to the EFTA countries' generally higher levels of domestic price support for agriculture. In other words, value-added in the agro-industrial sector is granted area preference.

However, in the course of the EEA negotiations, the EC asked for, and obtained, two concessions of particular interest to the southern EC members: a significant contribution by EFTA countries to the EC's "financial mechanism" in favor of poorer regions,[17] and the extension of free trade to specifically "Mediterranean" agricultural products such as flowers, vegetables, fruit, and olive oil. If one were to pinpoint a particular sector where trade diversion to the detriment of Mediterranean nonmembers is likely to occur as a result of the EEA agreement, this would be it.[18]

Services, People, Capital

For the remainder of the EEA agreement, covering free provision of services as well as free movement of people and capital, the scope for "trade diversion" in the traditional sense is low, as the EFTA countries were either very protectionist anyway (regarding immigration, provision of nontraded services, or acquisition of assets by foreigners) or very liberal (few or no exchange controls on financial transfers). However, from the point of view of the EFTA countries themselves, one of the most important parts of the EEA agreement lies in the first of these areas. Thanks to the free movement of people and the free provision of services, the whole "sheltered" (nontraded) service sector becomes subject to competition. This is potentially an important source of efficiency gains for their economies, since lack of competition in areas such as construction, retail distribution, and the professions has led in some cases to extraordinarily high domestic price levels for nontraded and semitraded services,[19] and generally high wage levels (paid for by an increasingly "squeezed" export sector).[20] Needless to say, the same types of gains are also potentially available within the EC, and were estimated in the Cecchini Report to amount to 13-58 billion ECU annually (equivalent to 0.4%-1.8% of EC GDP).[21] If the dynamic effect of competition in these sheltered sectors fulfills its promise, nonmember countries should feel the beneficial impact of the higher real incomes in the form of higher exports to the EEA.

Foreign Direct Investment Flows

Economic integration does not only take the form of trade flows. Direct investment is also an important part of the process as firms rationalize, relocate, and search for the optimal combination of costs of production and closeness to markets. For the EFTA countries, one of the greatest incentives for pursuing ever-closer integration with the EC was the fear that the magnetic attraction of the great Single Market would drain their small economies of new investments for years to come. During the 1980s there was some evidence that this was in fact happening. During the 1960s EFTA's outward and inward flows were more or less balanced, amounting to, respectively, 0.5% and 0.4% of GNP. During the 1980s the relative importance of inward flows had risen slightly to 0.6% of GNP; outward flows had expanded to 2% of GNP. Of this, over half went to the EC.[22] It is worth noting that this "investment diversion" *accelerated* in 1989-90, despite the fact that a comprehensive EEA agreement was being negotiated.[23]

In point of fact, the EFTA countries have on the whole ceased to be attractive locations for industrial investment because of the high price and wage levels mentioned earlier. By the same token, however, inward foreign (EC) investment in the sheltered sectors, accompanied by free movement of labor and provision of services, should in due course iron out the differences. Until this happens, however, the EFTA countries are likely to remain large net exporters of capital. Where is it likely to go in the future? European investment resources in general, and EFTA investment resources in particular, are likely to be pulled toward Central Europe as preferential trade agreements with these countries create the beginnings of a propitious legal framework for expanded trade.

Agreements With Central Europe

It must not be overlooked that concurrently with the introduction of the EEA agreement, both the EC and EFTA have negotiated (or are negotiating) so-called free trade agreements with the Central and East European Countries (see Introduction).

The current state of Central Europe does not permit one to make more than the wildest guesses as to the trade-diverting implications of these agreements. In the absence of supply-side constraints, the difference in cost for labor-intensive products between Western and Central Europe is so great that one can predict with certainty that safeguards will be introduced whenever "necessary" (as they already have been for steel). Access for agricultural goods is carefully controlled through tariff quotas, as we have seen. If we assume (1) that the EEA's capacity for importing labor-intensive and agricultural goods is limited and (2) that it is politically necessary to expand trade from Central and Eastern Europe, it seems inevitable that this will occur at somebody's expense. The question is: whose? In particular, do the Mediterranean nonmember (MNM) countries risk trade diversion from this source? The answer is yes, unless they upgrade their trade agreements with both the EC and the EFTA countries, thus making themselves part of the emerging free trade system.

Implications of the EEA for Mediterranean Nonmembers

The share of MNMs[24] in EFTA imports is minuscule (less than 1% even if oil imports from Algeria and Libya are included; see Table 1). Similarly, EFTA does not figure largely in MNM exports (see Table 8). If one looks at growth of trade flows from 1984 to 1990 (Table 5), one sees only stagnation or decline (especially by comparison with Spain and Portugal). One gets the impression that the EFTA-MNM trade flows have been "crowded out" (with the exception of Swiss-Israeli trade; see Tables 2, 4, and 8). This is attributable not only to the lack of particular historical or cultural ties, or geographic distance, but doubtless also to "double" trade diversion, resultant to the fact that *both* parties have had preferential arrangements with the EC but not with each other. This is gradually being corrected. In 1991 the EFTA countries concluded a free trade agreement with Turkey (entry into force April 1992), and in the following year with Israel (entry into force January 1993).

The remaining EFTA-MNM trade relations are governed by GATT and, within GATT, by the GSP and the Multifibre Arrangement, when applicable. The EEA agreement cannot add noticeably to the trade diversion that has already taken place, with the exception of horticultural products, as already mentioned, because there is almost no trade to be diverted. On the other hand, change will occur when some EFTA countries become full members of the EC (in about five years) and begin to apply EC preferences to MNM trade. In anticipation, the MNMs could do worse than to follow the Israeli and Turkish example and negotiate free trade areas with the EFTA countries. Although small in absolute terms, these trade flows have enormous potential for growth in relative terms; welfare effects are more ambiguous.

If we consider that EFTA markets amount to about 10% of those of the EC, then (all other things equal) EFTA should account for about 10% of the MNMs' exports to the EC. In the first two columns of Table 8, we see that this is far from being the case. For instance, the EC accounts for 77.2% of Tunisia's exports, whereas EFTA accounts for only 0.8%. Some rebalancing of trade is clearly in order, even if we agree that geographical factors explain part of the difference.

The same type of distortion appears if one looks at the shares of MNMs in EFTA and EC imports. If we compare the top part of Table 1 with Table 7, we see that whereas MNMs account for only 0.6% of Swedish imports, they amount to 5% of Dutch imports, or 7% of Belgian imports. This striking difference must have something to do with the EC's preferential arrangements and perhaps with the absence of preferential arrangements between EFTA and the MNMs.

The size of this gap gives one an idea of the potential for the reversal of existing trade diversion. Even though such a redirection of trade would not be wholly efficient (since some trade would be diverted from other third countries, such as Chile or South Africa), it would reduce the artificial intensity of existing MNM-EC and EFTA-EC trade flows, and reverse the artificial boost to EFTA-EC trade

Table 1
Shares of Mediterranean Nonmembers* in Total EFTA Imports
(in pctg.)

	1970	1980	1991
Switzerland	1.1	1.02	0.82
Austria	1.16	1.29	1.45
Sweden	0.69	0.51	0.61
Norway	0.58	0.77	0.6
Finland	0.69	1.74	0.51
EFTA	0.85	0.94	0.86
	(without Algeria and Libya)		
Switzerland	0.81	0.91	0.8
Austria	1.16	0.7	0.75
Sweden	0.65	0.48	0.5
Norway	0.53	0.75	0.6
Finland	0.68	1.59	0.5
EFTA	0.75	0.75	0.7

Source: IMF, direction of trade statistics.
* Western Mediterranean: Morocco, Algeria, Tunisia, Libya, Malta. Eastern Mediterranean: Egypt, Israel, Lebanon, Cyprus, Turkey.

Table 2
Share of Israel in EFTA Imports (per mil)

	1970	1980	1991
Switzerland	2.93	3.44	3.8
Austria	2.65	2.41	1.4
Sweden	2.15	1.91	1.6
Norway	1.22	3.1	1.9
Finland	3.33	7.65	1.8
EFTA	2.43	2.91	2.23

Source: IMF, direction of trade statistics.

Table 3

Share of Mediterranean Nonmembers in Total EFTA Exports (in pctg.)

	1970	1980	1991
Switzerland	2.28	3.7	2.88
Austria	1.45	1.7	1.9
Sweden	1.2	1.4	1.4
Norway	0.8	0.8	1.23
Finland	1.18	1.5	1.6
EFTA	1.46	2.0	1.78

Source: IMF, direction of trade statistics.

Table 4

Share of Israel in EFTA Exports (per mil)

	1970	1980	1991
Switzerland	7.2	17.6	18.6
Austria	3.3	1.6	1.4
Sweden	3.5	1.9	3.3
Norway	1.8	0.8	3.7
Finland	5.4	3.0	3.0
EFTA	4.4	6.0	5.4

Source: IMF, direction of trade statistics.

Table 5

Share of EFTA Imports From Selected Mediterranean Countries
(Poland and Hungary included for comparison)
(as pctg. of total EFTA imports)

	1984	1985	1986	1987	1988	1989	1990	Trend
Morocco	0.07	0.07	0.06	0.08	0.08	0.08	0.06	No change
Algeria	0.44	0.33	0.16	0.13	0.12	0.14	0.18	Down: tot
Tunisia	0.09	0.03	0.03	0.02	0.03	0.02	0.03	Down/no change
Egypt	0.09	0.13	0.05	0.04	0.03	0.05	0.06	Down
Israel	0.24	0.23	0.22	0.21	0.20	0.23	0.23	No change/ down
Spain	0.96	1.09	1.12	1.12	1.12	1.05	1.13	Up
Portugal	0.56	0.6	0.68	0.74	0.73	0.77	0.85	Up
Poland	0.74	0.69	0.59	0.58	0.55	0.54	0.56	Down (supply
Hungary	0.67	0.63	0.54	0.50	0.49	0.51	0.53	Down -side constraints)

Source: OECD, *Foreign Trade by Commodities*, vol. 2 (1991).

Table 6

Product Composition of EFTA Imports From Selected Mediterranean Countries (in pctg., 1980:1988)

		Israel		Turkey		Greece	
		1980	1988	1980	1988	1980	1988
SITC							
0	Food	37.8	34.3	49.8	29.8	19.2	8.8
(0.5)	Fruit & veg.	(33.0)	(29.2)	(44.8)	(26.9)	(17.2)	(7.8)
2	Raw materials	28.7	12.1	30.9	12.2	6.4	1.9
3+4	Fuel/oils	2.1	0.8	6.7	2.5	25.6	3.1
5	Chemicals	3.4	7.0	0.4	1.4	4.4	1.2
6.1	Leather goods	0.26	—	—	0.7	6.4	1.4
6.5	Textiles	1.86	1.4	7.2	10.3	5.9	4.6
6.6	Nonmetalic mf	13.8	13.7	—	1.8	0.9	1.0
6.7	Iron & steel mf	0.53	0.05	0.9	1.65	7.9	3.7
6.8	Nonfer met mf	0.53	0.4	—	0.26	0.5	1.6
6.9	met mf nes	1.06	1.8	—	1.07	—	0.4
7	mach & transp	2.9	12.3	0.4	2.3	2.0	31.8
8	misc mf	6.91	16.1	3.6	35.9	20.7	40.2
	Aggregation into broad categories						
SITC							
0-2	Food + rm	66.5	46.4	80.7	42.0	25.6	10.7
3-4	Fuel/oils	2.1	0.8	6.7	2.5	25.6	3.1
5-6	Intermediates	21.5	24.3	8.5	17.2	26.1	14.1
7-8	Mf goods	9.8	28.5	4.0	38.2	22.6	72.0

Source: OECD, *Foreign Trade by Commodities*, vol. 2 (1991).

Table 7
Shares of Mediterranean Nonmembers in Total (Extra) EC Imports
(in pctg., 1960; 1990)

	1960	1990
Belgium	3.6	6.9
Denmark	2.9	2.0
Germany	4.8	8.5
Greece	8.0	15.2
Spain	5.7	10.6
France	20.6	10.8
Ireland	3.3	2.0
Italy	7.6	18.8
Netherlands	7.5	5.1
Portugal	2.8	9.8
UK	2.7	3.1
EEC	6.7	8.8

Source: *Trends in EC Trade*, 1992, Table 6, p. 84.

Table 8
Shares of EC and EFTA in Exports of Principal Nonoil,
Non-EC Member Mediterranean Basin Countries
(in pctg., 1990)

	EC	EFTA	EC + EFTA
Western Mediterranean			
Morocco	64.5	4.8	69.3
Tunisia	77.2	0.8	78.0
Malta	77.4	2.2	79.6
Eastern Mediterranean			
Egypt	42.4	2.1	44.5
Israel	36.2	4.2	40.4
Lebanon	22.8	1.5	24.3
Turkey	52.2	4.6	56.8
Cyprus	47.6	3.4	51.0

Source: IMF, direction of trade statistics.

flows in garden products about to be given by the EEA. There is also a good chance that the EFTA countries' highly protected agricultural markets in general, and fruit and vegetable markets in particular, would be opened up to competition, giving rise to classical trade creation.

The other area of concern—heavy industrial equipment purchased by governments—is unlikely to affect MNM exports, with the possible exception of Israel (which is a competitive producer of specialized capital goods). For other manufactured goods, as argued above, the EEA agreement, in conjunction with the Single Market and the "Europe agreements," makes it urgent for MNM countries either to upgrade their old trade agreements, to include the *acquis communautaire* on a reciprocal basis, or to join the EEA.

Finally, it should be reiterated that the EFTA-EC links take the form of free trade areas. This means that each EFTA country retains its own commercial policy, applies its own GSP system, does not follow the EC's "contingent" protection (antidumping duties, VERs, etc.), and (as far as industrial goods are concerned) practices very low levels of tariff protection (the Nordic countries especially). So insignificant are most tariffs that the GSP take-up rate is notoriously low; it is just not worth the trouble for a 2%-3% margin of preference. As far as the MNMs are concerned, the open nature of EFTA markets is a double-edged sword: access is easier for labor-intensive products than to the EC market, but it takes place on a multilateral basis. This means that the scope for conventional trade diversion from the EEA arrangement is low and that any positive dynamic effects will flow easily toward members and nonmembers alike. This situation will reverse itself if and when some EFTA countries become full members of the EC.

The EEA: A Vehicle for the Next Generation of Agreements With the EC?

As mentioned in the Introduction, the EEA agreement is revolutionary in that it extends to a select group of non-EC members almost all the elements of full membership in economic terms, without the costs and benefits of full membership in political terms. European countries that are presently outside the EC are in the process of weighing up these alternatives. Some (such as the Visegrad countries) have clearly stated their preference for joining. Others (such as Norway or Sweden) find it harder to make up their minds. Switzerland has taken the decision not to join even the EEA, largely because the electorate feared this would be an intermediate stage to joining the EC outright.

But there is another interested party in this game: the EC itself. Although it could possibly absorb a few small EFTA countries without a basic change in its constitution, the same cannot be said for an EC of 20, 25, or 30 members. In the ongoing debate between "deepening" and "widening," one sees great pressure in favor of "deepening" (the Maastricht treaty), which in itself makes "widening" more and more problematic. This is no accident.

In the 1960s and 1970s the EC was at pains to offer the EFTA countries as little as was decently possible, to encourage new applicants and to avoid creating a parallel system comfortable enough to offer a close substitute for membership itself. This strategy was successful in that Britain, Denmark, and Portugal (which had initially preferred the EFTA track) finally did join the EC. By 1989, however, the 12-member EC was already beginning to consider strategies to ward off new applicants, at least until the "deepening" process was complete. The EEA was thus initially conceived as a permanent or at least long-term alternative to membership for the EFTA countries, some of them precluded from joining because of their neutral status. In terms of past EC policy toward the EFTA countries, the EEA agreement was almost inconceivably generous: while far from perfect, it was a good substitute for joining. Then came the fall of the Berlin Wall and the collapse of the USSR. Suddenly, neutral countries could join the EC as full members—and their governments all expressed an interest in doing so. The EEA became a mere staging post on the road to full membership.

Simultaneously, the whole of Central and Eastern Europe, freed from Soviet-imposed communism, presented the prospect of large numbers of democratic market economies all wanting to join the EC as soon as possible. However, it is not clear at all that the original 12 members of the EC view this sudden popularity of their organization with enthusiasm, and it is quite possible that they will diplomatically "close the door" to new members once a few EFTA countries are "in."

On the other hand, the pressure from the outside will not abate unless something almost as good as membership is offered. That is why, in my assessment, the EEA agreement (or modified versions thereof) will in due course be offered by the EC to a large number of applicants and near-applicants as an intermediate stage. Afterward, as the French say, "il n'y a que le provisoire qui dure." The concept (virtual economic membership in the EC without political ties) has the great virtue of having already been worked out in detail in the EEA agreement; it already exists. Furthermore, despite the "E" in its title, there is no reason why the concept itself should be geographically bound (since "political" aspects of EC membership are excluded). In short, the EEA concept is the natural vehicle for creating a single, multilateral free trade area between the EC and its many neighbors to the east and south, and it is one that the EC itself might well prefer to a radical enlargement of its own membership.

Conclusion

The old "pyramid of preference" was conceived in the midst of the Cold War. Many of its beneficiaries were running frankly Marxist economies. Few of them were therefore able to benefit from what on paper, at least, looked like an incredibly good deal: free access to the EC market for industrial products.

The Cold War is at an end—so much so that the EFTA neutrals see no external constraint on joining the EC. The Marxist model of economic development is also at an end. Although the transition to capitalism is tortuous, it is gradually occurring both to the east and the south of the EC. Slowly, the supply-side constraints, which made it costless for the EC to offer free access for industrial products to its markets, will diminish. Will the enlarged EC15-16 of the end of the century be adequate to the task of accommodating vastly increased trade with its immediate neighbors?

The EC can either rise to the occasion, offering opportunities for trade and wealth-creation to its own citizens and those of its neighbors, or it can retreat into a fear-ridden, autistic cocoon.

If the former, the level of trade diversion suffered by "outsiders" will be low, and genuine market access (whether via GATT, an extension of the EEA, or expansion of EC membership) will be assured. If the latter, the emerging capitalist countries in Central and Eastern Europe and the Mediterranean would have to begin searching for alternatives: multilateral links with the CIS, Southeast Asia, Latin America, Japan, the United States via GATT, and/or preferential trade among themselves. Unfortunately, there is a third possibility: economic disintegration, nationalism, and attempts at autarky on the scale of the tiny economies that are now emerging at the end of the Cold War. This happened once before at the end of World War I and would have happened again after World War II, but for enlightened leadership by a strong and prosperous United States. If we are now to avoid this tragic possibility and instead participate in a new economic miracle, the EC must rise to the occasion, not with aid but with open trade policies.

Notes

1. Jagdish Bhagwati, "Multilateralism at Risk: The GATT Is Dead, Long Live GATT," *The World Economy*, June 1990, pp. 149-169.

2. "Is Bilateralism Bad?," in E. Helpman and A. Razin, eds., *International Trade and Trade Policy* (Cambridge: MIT Press, 1991).

3. For a dissenting view on the seeming ease with which genuine free trade is achieved within regional trade systems, see Bernard Hoekman and Michael Leidy, "Holes and Loopholes in Regional Trade Arrangements and the Multilateral Trading System," paper presented at the Workshop on Regionalism and the Global Trading System, GATT Secretariat, Geneva, September 1992.

4. Jaime de Melo and Arvind Panagariya, *The New Regionalism in Trade Policy* (World Bank and Centre for Economic Policy Research, 1992).

5. The first "Europe Agreements," signed in December 1991, covered Poland, Hungary, and the Czech and Slovak republics. Identical agreements were negotiated in 1992 with Bulgaria and Romania; similar agreements are in preparation with Albania and the Baltic states.

6. Bulgaria, the Czech Republic, Hungary, Poland, Romania, and Slovakia have all negotiated free trade agreements (covering industrial products, processed agricultural goods, and some fisheries products) with the EFTA countries. Agreements with Slovenia and the Baltic states are expected shortly.

7. Free trade in agricultural products is something that will doubtless have to wait: the best should not be the enemy of the good.

8. Article 2, Title II, of the EEA Agreement states: "A product shall be considered to be originating in the EEA within the meaning of this Agreement if it has been either wholly obtained or sufficiently worked or processed in the EEA . . . the territories of the Contracting Parties . . . shall be considered as a single territory." This is a major revolution in comparison with the 1972 free trade agreements between the EFTA countries and the EC, which were strictly bilateral and permitted only very limited cumulation.

9. The initial date for entry into force was January 1, 1993, but Switzerland's refusal of the agreement meant that many points had to be renegotiated, setting back the process by a year.

10. Sweden, Austria, Finland, Norway, and Iceland. Although Liechtenstein (FL) has accepted the EEA in a referendum, it is not clear that it can in fact accede to it (so long as Switzerland refuses it) unless it denounces, or at least alters, the customs union treaty of 1922 that links it to Switzerland. Products entering FL from the EC under the terms of the "minimum essential requirements" directives would somehow have to be stopped from going further into Switzerland (unless Switzerland were prepared to grant EC goods nonreciprocal rights of recognition). Conversely, goods exported from FL to the EC would have to carry newly designed origin certificates, and might involve FL in considerable trade diversion (unless the EC were prepared to accept "cumulation" of origin between Switzerland and FL). The free movement of people and provision of services between FL and the EC, but not between the EC and Switzerland, might also affect these very freedoms between FL and Switzerland, unless Switzerland is prepared to let FL become a kind of back-door access to its market for EC nationals. Economic integration poses unanticipated complexities!

11. I have argued earlier ("The European Free Trade Association," in El-Agraa, ed., *International Economic Integration*, Macmillan, 1988, pp. 96-127) that strict origin rules in the EFTA-EC free trade areas provoked a measurable degree of trade diversion in semiprocessed products, especially in chemicals and textiles.

12. Odile Keller, *L'élimination des entraves techniques dans la Communauté européenne* (Bern: Peter Lang SA, 1992), p. 154.

13. How much is a lot? The EC calculated the loss due to multiple certification procedures to amount to 160-260 million ECU in 1985, or 0.5%-0.8% of industrial costs. See "The Economics of 1992" in *European Economy*, no. 35, March 1988, p. 53. However, this calculation does not capture the dynamic gains from more rational production and distribution, economies of scale, and enhanced competition, which are deemed to be much greater. For an assessment of the effects of "1992" on third countries, see L. Alan Winters, "European Trade and Welfare after '1992,'" CEPR Discussion Paper no. 678, June 1992.

14. Directive 90/531/EEC of September 17, 1990, on "the procurement procedures of entities operating in the water, energy, transport and telecommunications sectors."

15. According to the Management Consultants W. S. Atkins, engaged by the EC Commission to study "The Cost of Non-Europe in Public Sector Procurement," 30% of public contracts in the EC used to be arranged with a single supplier. See "The Economics of 1992" in *European Economy*, No. 35, March 1988, p. 56.

16. GATT, *Trade Policy Review: European Communities*, vol. 1 (Report by the GATT Secretariat, Geneva, 1991), p. 130.

17. This "entry fee" is quite steep. It involves the provision of 1,500 million ECUs in soft loans and 500 million ECUs in outright grants per annum. Switzerland's refusal to ratify the EEA agreement has meant that the other EFTA countries must now shoulder most of this financial package themselves. The EC has agreed to make the soft loans a little less soft (the interest subsidy will be cut from 3% to 2%), but the absolute amounts remain, apparently, untouched. The interest subsidy is estimated to be worth some 50 mn. ECUs per point.

18. The actual product coverage was a matter of bilateral negotiation with each EFTA country (notwithstanding the theoretically "multilateral" approach imposed by the EC). The EC-Sweden Agreement, for instance, opens zero-duty tariff quotas for (inter alia): fresh asparagus (100 tons), frozen beans (700 tons), frozen spinach (500 tons), frozen carrots, onions, and shallots (1000 tons), and "other" frozen vegetables (2000 tons), and eliminates tariffs on a preferential basis for: fresh carnations, other cut flowers, onions, lettuce (from November 1 to February 29), cherries (from June 16 to July 31), strawberries (from September 1 to June 7), olive oil, and so on. One can only marvel at the loving detail with which farming interests are protected and promoted.

19. See, e.g., *OECD Economic Survey: Switzerland* (Paris: OECD, 1992). According to this survey, the overall domestic price level in Switzerland is 35% higher than the average for the EC, with peaks of well over 50% for restaurants, hotels, food, medical services, beverages, and rent and water charges. Only in fuel, personal transport equipment, tobacco, furniture, and textiles (i.e., sectors open to trade) are prices in line with the EC average. The *OECD Economic Survey: Austria* (Paris: OECD, 1990) also notes that VAT-adjusted price levels in Austria are 20% to 30% higher than in Germany. The *Gatt Trade Policy Review: Austria* (1992) attributes this to "a comparatively low intensity of competition, resulting from market barriers, State intervention in economic life and the corporatist nature of Austrian society" (p. 110).

20. K. W. Clements and L.A. Sjaastad, *How Protection Taxes Exporters*, Thames Essay no. 39 (London: Trade Policy Research Centre, 1984). Although EFTA tariffs are generally low, sheltered distribution systems and cartels keep domestic price levels high. On the other hand, their export sectors are exposed to international price levels. Following the Clements/Sjaastad argument, they are thus "squeezed" since they have to compete with the sheltered sector for domestic resources.

21. "The Economics of 1992," *European Economy*, no. 35, March 1988, p. 123.

22. Jukka Leskelä, "EFTA Countries' Foreign Direct Investment," in *EFTA Trade* (Geneva: EFTA, Economic Affairs Department, 1990).

23. Ibid.

24. Morocco, Algeria, Tunisia, Libya, Malta (Western Mediterranean); Egypt, Israel, Lebanon, Cyprus, Turkey (Eastern Mediterranean).

Chapter 6

*The Shape of the EC's Pyramid of Privilege in The Year 2000: What Is in Store for Israel?**

ALFRED TOVIAS

Introduction

The main economic objectives of the European Community at present are to prepare the ground for monetary union toward the end of this decade and to enlarge to include Sweden, Austria, Finland, and Norway by 1996. In spite of the EC's desire not to be distracted by other agendas, several other governments have also asked for accession negotiations (Turkey, Malta, Cyprus). Even the government of Switzerland asked to initiate negotiations for accession into the EC, although this seems in question now that the cantons, as of December 1992, have rejected entry into the European Economic Area (EEA), a much more modest step than actual membership. Hungary, Poland, the Czech Republic, and Slovakia have also expressed, both officially and unofficially, their interest in future membership. According to a poll, in 1991 76% of Hungarians wanted to join the EC within five years.[1]

The purpose of this chapter is to explore the wider economic implications of further EC enlargements[2] for Israel (see the next section). Of course, the terms of the enlargement agreements to be negotiated are not yet known. Therefore, to give a foretaste, the main focus of the chapter is on a particular case study, namely, the progressive economic and political integration of Turkey and Cyprus into the EC (see the third section). The reason for this particular choice is that such a move by the Community may have more implications for the Middle East and Israel in

* I wish to thank Eyal Inbar and Noam Givoli for their assistance in the collection and computation of data.

particular than would membership of northern, Central, and even East European countries. Turkey's GNP and population are, indeed, the largest of the Mediterranean nonmember countries.

The final section will offer some concluding remarks.

EC Enlargement From an Israeli Perspective

Viewed from an Israeli perspective, the accession of third countries to the EC entailed until January 1993 several different but, in each case, significant steps, deriving from the adoption by new members of the *acquis communautaire*: (1) the establishment of a customs union between the Community and the new members (relating to trade in goods), (2) the application by one more country of the Common Agricultural Policy, and (3) the adoption by the new member of the contractual relationship that the EC has with Israel. Since the ratification of the Single European Act in 1987, whose main outcome was the completion of the Single Market by January 1, 1993, Israel must also be aware of the possible implications for itself of (4) the establishment of a free trade area in services between the EC and the new member.[3] Israel must also consider (5) what new membership means in terms of the EC's new economic and political size, and (6) how the center of gravity of the Community changes with the incorporation of new members.

Some of the steps specified above may be of little practical consequence depending on the existing relationship between the new member and Israel. For example, if at the time of membership the acceding country already conducts industrial free trade with Israel, as is likely to be the case with Austria, Sweden, Finland, and Norway,[4] then the adoption by the latter countries of the 1975 Israel-EC FTA will not make much of a difference.[5] Or, as we shall see later, Turkey's formal entry into the EC, say by 2010, would not add much as far as Israel's industry is concerned to the completion of the customs union between Turkey and the EC scheduled to take place already by January 1, 1996.

The Israeli government has in the past been concerned by and large with the implications of steps (1) and (2)—for example, as a result of the United Kingdom's or of Spain's accessions into the EC. The reason seems obvious: (a) if the new member must align itself on a more protectionist policy than the one applied by itself until entry, this will impair previous trade relations between Israel and the new member country; (b) if the new member was competing with Israel in the EC market before the latter's entry, there is a danger of trade diversion; and (c) if the new member and/or the EC are important actors in world trade for a product exported by Israel to the EC (e.g., citrus fruit), the trade diversion caused by the enlargement may lead in turn to a deterioration of Israel's terms of trade. A typical example of (a) was the UK's adoption upon entry of both the CAP and the EC's Common Customs Tariff. Typical examples of (b) and (c) were, respectively, Spain's new preferences acquired in EC fruit and vegetable markets and the negative impact of the enlargement to Spain on world market prices of citrus fruit.

Until now the best means political economists have had for assessing the importance of the potential for trade diversion as a result of enlargement is to look at the degree of similarity in the range of products supplied by the new member on the one hand and the outsider on the other (e.g., Israel). A number of export-similarity indexes are mentioned in the economic literature, among which the best known is the Finger-Kreinin index of similarity of export patterns. For two countries (a and b) exporting to a third market (c), the formula is as follows:

$$S = \sum_i \min (Si_{ac} , Si_{bc}) \times 100$$

where Si_{ac} and Si_{bc} represent the export shares of commodity i in the exports to c of a and b, respectively. For each commodity the lower of the two is selected. An index of 100 indicates perfect overlap; 0 represents no overlap whatsoever.

I have used this index to assess the degree of overlap of Israel's (a) agricultural, (b) industrial, and (c) overall export patterns (to the EC) in 1990 with a number of candidates to EC membership.

Data were taken from the UN Commodity Trade Statistics, disaggregated at the SITC three-digit level, i.e., a relatively high level of disaggregation.[6] Agricultural and raw material exports are taken as those included under categories SITC 0, 1, 2, and 4; industrial exports are represented by the remaining SITC categories. Results are indicated in Table 1.

Table 1
Similarity of Export Patterns to the EC
Between Israel and Selected Countries

	Agric. exp.	Ind. exp.	Total exp.
Israel-Poland	21.32	25.78	23.31
Israel-Switzerland	15.68	42.59	37.04
Israel-Austria	11.06	34.91	0.41
Israel-Sweden	6.46	33.75	28.38
Israel-Turkey	48.35	24.95	30.64
Israel-Cyprus	37.38	14.74	21.44

Source: UN Commodity Trade Statistics, 1990.

From the table several important conclusions emerge:

1. Overall, Israel's export patterns to the EC appear to be no more similar to those of EFTA-candidate countries than to those of Poland, Cyprus, and even Turkey. This rather interesting conclusion can only be drawn, it seems to me, by doing the kind of analysis presented here.

2. If we focus on primary products, as Pomfret and others did in the early 1980s for all Mediterranean countries, it is obvious that Israel's export patterns are much more similar to those of Turkey or Cyprus than to those of all the other countries under analysis. In fact, Israel's agricultural exports to the EC have almost nothing to do with those rather few sold by Austria, Sweden, and Switzerland (e.g., dairy products). It is also interesting to note that similarity of export patterns is higher between Turkey and Israel than between Cyprus and Israel (basically because in the former case there is overlap in cotton, preserved fruit and vegetables, and flowers).

3. The pattern of Israel's industrial exports to the EC is totally dissimilar to that of Cyprus and rather dissimilar to those of Poland and Turkey. This is much less the case when comparing to EFTA countries' export patterns to the EC, especially Switzerland's.[7]

4. A comparison of similarity indexes at different points of time (1980, 1987, and 1990) has been done for the case of Turkey in relation to Israel (see the next section) with the main result being that, although decreasing, the level of similarity of exports of primary products to the EC remains very high.

Therefore, in terms of potential trade diversion against Israeli agricultural products, it seems a priori that only the entry of Turkey and Cyprus into the EC should be of some concern. As explained later (see section 3), however, there are many considerations that considerably reduce this potential. The case of Hungary is also pertinent in this context. Although data for Hungary could not be obtained, it is well known that Israel and Hungary are competing in EC markets of goose liver and some fruits. On the other hand, Sweden and Switzerland are known to be even more protectionist in agriculture than the EC. Thus, a priori, the adoption by the former two of the EC's CCT and also of the CAP, which by the mid-1990s will have been somewhat liberalized, should be a bonus rather than a minus for Israeli agricultural exports to these countries (of fruit, flowers, or wine for example). As for Eastern Europe, by the end of the century exports from Israel will have reached fairly significant levels, particularly in regard to Hungary with its relatively low levels of barriers on agricultural imports. Entry into the EC may, however, impair those exports.

Turning now to industrial exports to the EC, both Israel and EFTA countries have had tariff- and quota-free access to the EC for over a decade. Membership of EFTA countries in the EC or in the EEA would not change anything in this respect.

However, as is well known the problem for Israel in penetrating or maintaining market shares in the EC is the existence of NTBs, such as government procurement or technical barriers. It is from this standpoint that the creation of the Single Market has brought about a high level of anxiety and, since 1988, a willingness by successive Israeli governments to negotiate with the EC. *This anxiety is compounded by the prospect of the enlargement of the Single Market to include EFTA countries (i.e., the EEA).* My research supports the view of the different Israeli governments: industrial export patterns to the EC are fairly similar to those of Switzerland and even Austria or Sweden. If, for example, mutual recognition of laboratories, certificates, standards and so on is applied in Switzerland-EC trade but not in Israeli-EC trade, some trade will be diverted away from Israel (e.g., in measure and control instruments, tools, pharmaceutical products). Although it may sound cynical, the rejection by the Swiss of EEA membership is good news for Israel. Not for nothing did past and present Israeli governments seek a status similar to those EFTA countries joining the EEA. Barring this, the aim has been to review the 1975 EC-Israel agreement so as to eliminate some of the NTBs on mutual trade. In fact, in industrial exports it is membership of Austria, Sweden, and other EFTA countries in the EEA that is the critical step for Israel, not future membership, which may come several years later.

The extension of free trade in commercial services to EFTA countries does not seem to pose new sorts of problems for Israel, but it aggravates those deriving from the creation of the Single Market, for example, in the field of air transport services. For El Al it is not the same thing if Swissair is an insider or an outsider in relation to the Single Market. If Swissair can compete in the winter season with Iberia and Finnair together with British Airways and KLM over the line Santa Cruz-de Tenerife-Helsinki, this works to the detriment of El Al services from Helsinki to Eilat!

East European countries will only progressively be given tariff- and quota-free access to EC markets in the context of the new association agreements signed in 1991. Insofar as there is some overlap between Israeli and East European exports to the EC (e.g., in textiles or clothing), some trade diversion against Israel will be inevitable as a result of preference erosion, and this will take place in the mid-1990s *even without accession of East European countries into the EEA or the EC*. There is nothing Israel can do about it.

A Case Study: Impact of the Completion of Turkey's and Cyprus's Customs Unions With the EC on Israeli Exports

EC Relations With Turkey and With Cyprus

This is not the place to review the history of these two countries' *economic* relations with the EC. Note simply that Turkey is not part of the Single Market created in January 1, 1993, nor of the EEA to enter into force soon. However, in February 1990, and as a result of some improvement in EC-Turkey relations since the mid-1980s, the European Council adopted a recommendation by the Commission to *establish the Customs Union by the end of 1995.*

As for Cyprus, the Association Agreement of December 1972 provided for the creation of a customs union in two stages, the first of which was only completed by 1988. In October 1987, Cyprus and the EC signed a protocol laying down the conditions and procedures for the implementation of the second stage, which was divided into two phases. The first will last 10 years until 1997. During this period, Cyprus will entirely abolish all customs duties for industrial products originating in the EC and will adopt the EC's CCT.[8] Thus *by 1997 a customs union will be in place between Cyprus and the EC*. The two parties will also have to eliminate by that date all tariffs on a number of key agricultural products in Cyprus's export basket including new potatoes, citrus fruit, and wine; QRs imposed by the EC on Cyprus will be progressively enlarged. The second stage will last four or five years, during which both parties will take the necessary steps to complete free trade in agricultural products. Notwithstanding all this, Cyprus submitted a formal application for accession to the EC on July 4, 1990.

In spite of other precedents, I have assumed for the purposes of this chapter that the schedule for the creation of the two customs unions will be respected.

Export Similarity

Pomfret and Donges et al.[9] have used this index in the past for analysis of similarity among Mediterranean countries' agricultural exports to the EC. The first, using 1977 EC import data at the SITC three-digit level, arrived at the following results with respect to Israel:

Spain	Greece	Portugal	All three
51.6	43.8	8.0	45.6

In order to maintain some parallelism, I have calculated the same index (i.e., only for SITC categories 0,1,2,4) using the UN Commodity Trade Statistics. Below are the results obtained for 1980, 1987, and 1990 (the last year for which I found homogeneous data at the three-digit level):

Turkey 1980	Turkey 1987	Turkey 1990
55.3	47.0	48.4

Several interesting conclusions follow:

1. Similarity between Israel and Turkey regarding agricultural exports to the EC diminished substantially during the 1980s.

2. In the early 1980s the overlap was at least as large as the one between Israel and Spain, rated to be on collision course in the EC market at the time of Spain's entry into the EC.

3. The overlap remains high even now, particularly if we compare with results obtained for Greece (not to speak of Portugal) in 1977.

Given the fact that most Turkish and Israeli exports to the EC are industrial, I have also calculated the overall index as well as the degree of overlap in industrial exports for 1980, 1987, and 1990.

	Turkey 1980	Turkey 1987	Turkey 1990
Industrial exports	28.71	36.77	24.95
Total exports	33.18	40.68	30.64

Again, several interesting conclusions may be drawn:

1. Similarity of industrial exports to the EC is smaller than in agricultural products.

2. In the mid-1980s there was a tendency for both countries' patterns of industrial exports to become more similar, but in recent years this trend was reversed.

3. With respect to total exports, the similarity of Israeli exports with those of Turkey increased rapidly from 1980 to 1987 but after that the trend was reversed. At present, export patterns of Israel and Turkey to the EC appear to be more dissimilar than at the beginning of the decade. This result is akin to my own findings in a previous study regarding Spain and Israel in the 1970s,[10] where it was shown that Spanish and Israeli exports to the EC were also increasingly dissimilar. The most plausible explanation is that Spain then and Turkey now have been shifting away from labor-intensive industries (such as clothing) and toward standardized capital-intensive products (such as petrochemicals or simple machines), whereas Israel has continued to concentrate on sales of labor-intensive products to the

Community, *both industrial and agricultural*, but has also begun to export high-tech products to the EC.[11]

Revealed Comparative Advantage in Trade With the EC

Here I shall take an alternative approach to the issue of Israel's competitiveness in EC markets in relation to that of Turkey. I assess the evolution of Israel's comparative advantage in EC markets in the 1980s and compare the trend with that of Turkey. Moreover, I try to discover whether the sectoral composition of Israel's comparative advantage coincides with that of Turkey and whether there was a change over time in this respect.

First, I calculated indexes of "revealed comparative advantage" (RCA) by sector (at the SITC two-digit level) for the two countries, using 1988 data published by the OECD.[12] Second, I calculated rank correlation indexes between Israel's sectoral RCAs and the corresponding RCAs of Turkey. Third, I repeated the same procedure for Israel and Turkey for the year 1983.

There are different indexes of comparative advantage. I used the "relative trade-balance" index[13]—a relative export-to-import ratio of each sector, used originally by the late B. Balassa to identify RCAs of a given country. A positive trade balance in a given sector is said to represent a comparative advantage of that sector; a negative trade balance reveals a disadvantage. The balance is then related to total trade, which acts as normalizer. Nevertheless, the RCA index is only a rough approximation of the "true" comparative advantage. Ideally, the index should be based on trade figures resulting from a free trade setting and not on "real world" figures, which are obviously the only ones available. The index is also very sensitive to the level of disaggregation used and to product heterogeneity. Furthermore, the index implicitly assumes that balance of payments and the exchange rate are in equilibrium. Finally, since it is a ratio, it does not distinguish between large and small absolute values of trade.

Bearing all these shortcomings in mind, on the basis of a quick analysis of Appendix A1 I arrive at the following conclusions:

1. Israel displays high RCA indexes (larger than 0.4) in trade with the EC for the following categories in 1988, presented in decreasing order of RCA:

SITC	Name	Index
56	Fertilizers (excl. group 272)	0.94
05	Vegetable and fruit	0.88
29	Crude animal and vegetable materials (incl. flowers)	0.88

28	Metalliferous ores and metal scrap	0.83
72	Specialized machinery	0.76
84	Articles of apparel and clothing	0.73
27	Crude fertilizers (excl. category 56)	0.69
01	Meat and meat preparations	0.69
52	Inorganic chemicals	0.60
26	Textile fibers and wastes	0.54
22	Oil seeds	0.51
71	Power-generating machinery and equipment	0.49

Source: Appendix A1.

These indexes can be compared with those I calculated for 1983 (see below) as well as with those in Tovias (1988) (see note 10) relating to 1979. What is worth noting is that in 1979 Israel displayed RCA in petroleum and petroleum products and cork and wood manufactures but not in any kind of machinery or chemicals as it did a decade later.

2. The corresponding list for Turkey is:

SITC	Name	Index
05	Vegetable and fruit	0.99
84	Articles of apparel and clothing	0.98
72	Specialized machinery	0.96
33	Petroleum and petroleum products	0.92
41	Animal oils and fats	0.90
83	Travel goods	0.90
27	Crude fertilizers (excl. category 56)	0.87
12	Tobacco and tobacco manufactures	0.84
22	Oil seeds	0.82
03	Fish, crustaceans, and preparations	0.76
51	Organic chemicals	0.72
06	Sugar, sugar preparations, and honey	0.72
65	Textile yarn and fabrics	0.69
34	Natural gas and manufactures thereof	0.51

Source: Appendix A1.

The following categories overlap with those of Israel: vegetable and fruit, articles of apparel and clothing, specialized machinery, crude fertilizers, and oil seeds.

I calculated the Spearman rank correlation index of RCA index series of Turkey and Israel for 1988. Perfect correlation means an index of 1, no correlation an index of 0.

Spearman rank correlation index for 1988 = 0.459

For purposes of comparison, it is worth noting that this index is lower than the one I found using 1979 data for the pairs Israel-Spain (0.687) and Israel-Greece (0.559), but higher than the one for the pair Israel-Portugal (0.352).[14]

Turning now to 1983 (see Appendix A2), the following goods were not among the 1988 categories on the Israeli list, reflecting new Israeli comparative advantage developed during the 1970s: specialized machinery, meat and meat preparations, oil seeds, power-generating machinery and equipment. On the other hand, the list did include the following categories that did not appear subsequently in 1988: miscellaneous edible goods and preparations, petroleum products. Clearly, Israel has been shifting comparative advantage in the direction of machinery and equipment, including high-tech products.

The following products are not included in the 1983 list for Turkey: specialized machinery, animal oils and fats, organic chemicals. On the other hand, there are many categories that appeared in the 1983 RCA list for Turkey but did not reappear in the 1988 list: meat and meat preparations; coffee, tea, and spices; feedstuff for animals (excluding unmilled cereals); miscellaneous edible preparations; textile fibers and wastes; cork and wood; crude animal and vegetable materials; cereals and cereals preparations. Note that these are all agricultural products and raw materials.

All this points to the important fact that Turkey's performance in EC markets in the 1980s increased for industrial products, such as machinery and chemicals, but decreased for agricultural products. In the case of Israel, the performance increased for machinery and meat preparations, and was roughly maintained in agriculture. Note that there is new overlap of comparative advantage between Israel and Turkey in specialized machinery, but diminished overlap in miscellaneous edible products, meat and meat preparations, textile fibers, and crude animal and vegetable materials. Although I do not have empirical evidence to support this, it is almost certain that specialized machinery exports by Turkey and Israel are not competing, since they tend to embody very different levels of technology and are for very different end uses.

The 1983 Spearman rank correlation index of RCA between Israel and Turkey reached 0.338, which is much lower than the one obtained for 1988. Accordingly, it appears that over the 1980s the level of similarity between Turkey's and Israel's comparative advantages in EC markets increased. This seems to contradict somewhat the results obtained for export similarity to the EC. The problem may lie in the differing levels of disaggregation used in the two tests, in which case it is better to rely on the results for export similarity, where the level of disaggregation used was higher (very important, e.g., for machinery exports).

I have confirmed as well with the inquiry into RCAs that overlap in agricultural exports is diminishing progressively, not so much because the two countries have diversified their exports but because Turkey seems to have lost competitiveness in this area.

Preference Erosion

All that has been said on export similarity and RCA indexes can be instrumental for making predictions about the potential of trade diversion in EC-12 markets in favor of Turkey and against Israel once the customs union between the EC and Turkey is concluded at the end of 1995, leading to erosion in the preference margins that Israel now has in the EC. Apparently, the fear that trade diversion will take place for some agricultural products is unwarranted. To begin with, by and large Turkey and Israel do not export the same vegetables and fruits to the EC. Turkey is very strong in dry fruit (e.g., nuts, figs, grapes), legumes, and tobacco, Israel in citrus fruit. There is some overlap for grapes, tomatoes, and other fresh vegetables and of course for cotton.[15] But by the time Turkey would benefit from the protection and support of the CAP (i.e., no sooner than in a decade), those products would be even less important than they are now in the Israeli export basket to the EC. As far as industrial products are concerned, both countries, generally speaking, already have duty- and quota-free access to the EC. Even assuming that Turkey becomes a member of the Single Market (and benefits from, e.g., Community preference in government procurement) and Israel remains outside, it would not change this assessment, since by and large both countries specialize in heterogeneous products incorporating different levels of technology (e.g., specialized machinery). Much more problematic would be the case of clothing, given the fact that, whereas Israeli exports to the EC enter unhampered by any restrictions, this is certainly not the case for Turkey. The creation of customs unions would, however, change the situation. Up to the completion of the two customs unions later in this decade, rivalry between Turkey and Israel could even increase. After all Turkey is, like Israel, close to the European fashion centers, an advantage that distinguishes both countries as compared to Southeast Asia or Latin America.

Preferential Access to the Markets of Turkey and Cyprus[16]

Upon completion of their customs unions with the EC, Turkey and Cyprus will have to apply the EC-Israel FTA to imports originating from Israel.[17] Israel's exports to Turkey and Cyprus in 1990 were $88.4 million and $33.3 million, respectively.

For Israel, Turkey's customs union with the EC involves the addition of a market (until now very closed) with a GNP not much under that of Portugal and Greece together (about 5% of the EC-12 GNP), to which Israel will be able to export at privileged prices (because of the Israel-EC FTA). Turkey (Cyprus) is much closer than Greece, Portugal, or Spain, with all three of which Turkey (Cyprus) can be compared in many ways. Distance is a factor facilitating servicing and replacement of spare parts and, potentially even more important, intra-industry trade (e.g., trade in components). Bulk products can also enter international trade more easily (e.g., cement, building materials) as well as highly perishable goods (such as live animals). There is much room for optimism about industrial exports that would attain duty- and quota-free access to the Turkish (Cypriot) market; but not so for agricultural products since the CAP would apply (e.g., reference prices), although for most products Turkey's (Cyprus's) imports would also be duty-free because of application by the EC of new rules on agricultural trade contained in the additional EC-Israel protocol that was signed upon Spain's and Portugal's accession into the Community. Although Turkey's GDP per capita is less than a third that of any OECD country (excepting Portugal), the picture changes somewhat if GDP per capita is calculated on a PPP basis, in which case it appears that real income per capita is more than half what it is in Greece and Portugal.[18] Moreover, in the 1980s Turkey's GDP growth was the highest in the OECD (and Cyprus's GDP growth was even larger than Turkey's), and this trend could well continue.

A prospect of further integration in the EC could itself stimulate growth in Turkey (Cyprus) as it did for Spain and Portugal. Turkey's population is much larger than that of either of these countries, and almost equal to that of Spain, Portugal, and Greece together.[19] Demographic data are particularly relevant for the Israeli exporter of mass consumption products (including food). In Table 2 it is clear that Israel's exports to Turkey are currently abnormally small, not because of Turkey's low GNP per capita but because tariffs and NTBs on Israeli exports are high whereas they are fairly nonexistent on Israeli exports to Greece, which is farther from Israel than Turkey and has a GNP two-thirds the size of Turkey's.[20] Using Greece as a yardstick, we could expect annual exports to Turkey, upon completion of the customs union in 1995, to be at least twice as large as they were in 1990 in constant terms.[21] For instance, Spain and Portugal entered the EC only in 1986, and tariffs on Israeli exports to both newcomers were scaled down to zero progressively up to January 1993. Using 1990 data we already find a tremendous expansion of Israeli exports to Spain and Portugal compared to 1987.[22] Roughly speaking, exports to Turkey could expand by $80-$100 million in real terms compared to 1990 if free trade were applied by Turkey. New export potential to Cyprus seems to be smaller, given the high levels already achieved.

Although it is true that Israel would be competing *in the Turkish and Cypriot markets* on a par with all 18 members of the European Economic Area as far as tariffs and most NTBs are concerned, it would have clear location and language advantages in relation to most West European competitors.

Table 2

Israel's Exports to Six Mediterranean Countries
Ranked According to Their GNP, 1990

Destination	Israeli exports (million $)	GNP of country Per capita	Overall	Population (millions)
Italy	502,839	16,850	970,619	57,588
Spain	169,639	10,920	429,404	39,326
Turkey	88,438	1,630	91,742	56,277
Greece	105,118	6,000	60,245	10,048
Portugal	39,436	4,890	50,692	10,372
Cyprus	33,324	8,040	5,633	701

Source: World Bank Atlas, UN Commodity Trade Statistics.

Israeli exports would expand greatly, for two reasons. First, the MFN tariff applied by Turkey (Cyprus) on Israeli imports is at present rather high, particularly compared to the zero-rates that Israel's main trade partners, namely, the United States, the EC, and EFTA, all apply on Israeli exports. Other OECD countries apply very low tariffs. In some cases Israel benefits from GSP treatment (e.g., in Japan). In other words, Israeli exporters now look elsewhere than Turkey or Cyprus. Second, currently Israel suffers from trade diversion in the two countries' markets against itself and in favor of EC countries (and now of EFTA as well).[23] Since many of Israel's industrial and agricultural exports overlap with those of one or the other EC or EFTA member country, particularly those close to Turkey or Cyprus (such as Greece, Austria, Italy, or Germany), at present this is particularly damaging.

Industrial products that Israel exports would be favored almost across the board, given the relative high income and price elasticities in destination countries for these products. The list includes machinery, transport equipment, instruments, pharmaceuticals, electronic and telecommunication equipment. At present many of these products are not exported at all to Turkey (Cyprus), for the reasons mentioned above. Israel would have an advantage over some European countries in that many of these products require servicing and follow-up (e.g., scanners), something that could be done cheaply from Israel compared to, say, Britain, Germany, or Sweden. Israel would also tend to displace, in the two Eastern Mediterranean markets, some advanced NICs whose exports to the latter would be subject to the CCT and EC NTBs (such as antidumping duties). It is unlikely that Turkey (Cyprus) would be obliged by the EC to apply GSP rates to Third World countries' exports at least in the foreseeable future.

One can also envisage semimanufactured products and components being shifted back and forth between Turkey (Cyprus) and Israel for further processing, with the intention of ultimately exporting the product to the EC or the U.S. market. This is a matter, in other words, of intra-industry trade with a view to selling the end product worldwide. Some parts of the production process would be completed in Turkey (Cyprus), others in Israel. As a general rule it seems more appropriate that the final processing stage be done in Israel, particularly because the final product could then be sold in the United States as an Israeli product and thus benefit from the U.S.-Israel FTA, provided of course that the product conforms with the agreement's rules of origin. In other words, the potential for Turkish-Israeli or Cypriot-Israeli intra-industry trade seems enormous, as, for related reasons, does that for trade in industry-related services (transport, telecommunications, banking, business and professional services, software, technology transfer, etc.).

Concluding Remarks

This chapter shows that the adoption of the EC agreements with Israel by non-EC European countries would have a very positive effect on Israel's trade with those that do not have preferential relations with Israel whatsoever, such as the Visegrad countries, Turkey, and Cyprus. As explained in the preceding section, the two latter countries will eliminate tariffs and QRs on imports originating in Israel upon completion of the customs union with the EC in the mid-1990s. If, as shown, tariff-free trade in industrial products between Turkey and Israel will be a real boon for Israel, the same applies regarding Eastern Europe. In fact, in less than a decade the 1991 association agreements will cause trade diversion against Israel and in favor of EC countries in East European markets, which are becoming important for the

Israeli exporter. This can only be avoided if Israel on the one hand and the Visegrad countries on the other conclude agreements of the sort both sides have with the EC and EFTA. If, however, the Visegrad countries enter the EC's customs union as Turkey is supposed to do by 1996, this would be unnecessary. Although Israel is geographically closer to Turkey than to Eastern Europe, it is culturally closer to the latter, so that relations with all those countries should attract the highest attention of Israel's authorities. In a sense, it is more important for Israel to have Turkey and Hungary apply the EC's trade policy to Israel than to have Norway in the EC!

This is true also from another perspective: the entry of the Visegrad countries, Cyprus, and Turkey into the EC would shift the EC's center of gravity toward Israel. If today there is a lobby within the EC advocating, for strategic reasons, the raising of EC-Maghreb relations to a higher level (composed of Spain, Italy, France, and Portugal), one would expect Turkey to push for the same in the Eastern Mediterranean once it is in the EC.

Thus, for Israel full memberships of Turkey and the Visegrad countries in the EC seem to bring more benefits than their hypothetical membership in the EEA. In the latter case their influence on the EC's decisionmaking would be nil, and trade discrimination against Israeli high-tech exports to these new growing markets would become the rule as is much the case in the EC at present. In this respect, it is worth noting that at the moment East European countries (and Hungary in particular)[24] place Israeli suppliers of goods and services in the same category as EC and EFTA suppliers as far as NTBs are concerned.

Finally, with respect to the increasing economic size of the EC two contradictory forces are at play. On the one hand, it seems obvious that the EC's leverage over Israel increases with its size. On the other, if enlargement means less rather than more cohesion the net result could be more opportunities for the outsider to advance its interests in Brussels.

Notes

1. See "Eurobarometer," *Foreign Affairs*, February-March 1991, p. 68.

2. By enlargement, I mean either full membership or at least membership in the EEA.

3. Free labor movements in the EC or the EEA are of no present concern to Israel because up to now there has been no significant migration of Israelis to Western Europe. This may change, however, in the future.

4. Israel concluded an FTA with EFTA in 1992. Seventy percent of Israel's exports to EFTA enter there duty-free.

5. It may, however, lead to a totally new definition of the area of origin of the goods exported by Israel or the new member.

6. Data for 1990 are not available for all the potential member countries at this level of disaggregatoin (e.g., Hungary).

7. The rather high export overlap between Israel and Switzerland is due to their parallel sales to the EC of chemicals, textile yarn, polished stones, aluminium, tools, heating and cooling equipment, measure and control instruments, articles of plastic, and jewelry.

8. The EC long ago abolished tariffs on Cyprus's industrial exports.

9. R. Pomfret, "The Impact of EEC Enlargement on Non-Member Mediterranean Countries' Exports to the EC," *Economic Journal* 91 (September 1981): 726-729; J. Donges et al., *The Second Enlargement of the European Community* (Tubingen: Mohr/Paul Siebeck, 1982).

10. See A. Tovias, "The Impact of the Second Enlargement of the EC Upon Israel's Balance of Payments," in I. Greilsammer and J. Weiler, eds., *Europe and Israel: Troubled Neighbours*, for the European University Institute, Series C: Political and Social Sciences 9 (Berlin: Walter de Gruyter, 1988), pp. 173-194.

11. Much of what is said here about Turkey applies to Cyprus as well, particularly regarding agricultural products such as fruit and vegetables.

12. OECD, *Foreign Trade by Commodities*, vol. 5, 1988.

13. The methodology is explained in, e.g., H. Giersch, ed., *The Economic Integration of Israel in the EEC* (Tubingen: Mohr/Paul Siebeck, 1980), pp. 132-143.

14. Tovias, "Impact of the Second Enlargement."

15. It is worth noting in this context that competition between Cyprus and Israel in EC markets of citrus fruit and potatoes is much stronger than between Israel and Turkey.

16. In what follows, I have mentioned the case of Cyprus after the Turkish case whenever the expected effect on Israel is qualitatively the same as with the entry of Turkey into the EC. Of course the quantitative impact is always much smaller, but this must be qualified by two elements: first, the GNP/head of Cyprus is about five times as large as Turkey's; second, Cyprus is much closer to Israel than Turkey and access to its economic center Nicosia is easier than comparable access to Izmir, Istanbul, or Ankara.

17. Of course the reverse applies as well, benefiting Israeli consumers of products from Turkey and Cyprus. We ignore in this chapter consumer interests, however, and focus on the interests of exporters, which are what the Israeli government has in mind when assessing the impact of any new move by the EC.

18. See *OECD Economic Surveys: Turkey 1990-1991* (Paris: OECD, 1991), where the Turkish GDP per capita on a PPP basis is $4348 for 1988, and those for Portugal and Greece are $6737 and $6786, respectively. Even more striking is the fact that Turkey's GDP calculated on a PPP basis is two-thirds that of Spain and almost four times that of Greece.

19. Note as well that the three countries' populations tend to stagnate, which is not the case for Turkey. By 2000 Turkey's population will reach 72,000,000.

20. Trade between Israel and Turkey may also be low because both countries give tariff preferences to the EC that they do not apply to their mutual trade. At present this affects Turkey much more than Israel, since Israel has been giving duty-free access to EC exports since 1989. Moreover, Israel is progressively dismantling its tariff vis-à-vis the United States and the EFTA countries.

21. Note that 1990 seems to have been an exceptionally good year for Israeli exports to Turkey. In 1991 they dropped back to $43.1 million; in 1987 they were $34.2 million.

22. For instance, in 1987 exports were, respectively, $99 mo. and $19 mo.

23. For instance, by 1989 Cyprus was already offering the EC a 60% preference on the latter's exports. By now the preference is much larger.

24. For instance, the Hungarian Postal Authority has bought large amounts of software from Israel. The Hungarian Ministry of Building, Industry and Trade has invited Israeli building contractors to present projects for the Budapest-hosted Expo 96 and to cooperate in building projects in other East European countries and the CIS. See *Israel Business Today*, July 24, 1992, October 30, 1992.

Other Works Consulted

Books and articles

Aktan, O. (1985). "The Second Enlargement of the European Communities: Probable Effects on the Members and the New Entrants." *European Economic Review*, no. 28, pp. 279-308.

Baysan, T. (1984). "Some Economic Aspects of Turkey's Accession to the EC: Resource Shifts, Comparative Advantage, and Static Gains." *Journal of Common Market Studies* 23, 1 (September): 15-34.

Gruen, G. E. (1985). "Turkey's Relations With Israel and Its Arab Neighbours: The Impact of Basic Interests and Changing Circumstances." *Middle East Review* 17, 3: 33-43.

Kramer, H. (1988). *Westeuropa und die Turkei: auf dem Weg zum 13.Mitglied der EG?* Ebenhausen: Stiftung Wissenschaft und Politik.

Palankai, T. (1991). *The European Community and Central European Integration: The Hungarian Case*. Occasional Paper Series, No. 21. New York: Institute for East-West Security Studies.

Redmond, J. "The Next Mediterranean Enlargement: Turkey, Cyprus and Malta." Paper presented at the ECSA Conference, George Mason University, Fairfax, Virginia, May 22-24, 1991.

Sinkovics, A. and Angresano, J. "Hungary and the European Community: Problems and Prospects." Paper presented at the ECSA Conference, George Mason University, Fairfax, Virginia, May 22-24, 1991.

Tovias, A. (1992). "The EC's Contribution to Peace and Prosperity in the Mediterranean and the Middle East: Some Proposals." *Jerusalem Journal of International Relations* 14, 2 (March 1992): 123-132.

"Turkey in Europe: An Assessment of Turkey's Application to Join the EC" (1990). An Intelligence Digest Special Briefing Paper No. 133, U.K.

Official documents

Agreement Establishing an Association Between the EEC and Turkey, Official Journal of the European Communities L 217, December 29, 1963.

Commission's Opinion on Turkey's Request for Accession to the Community, Europe Documents, Europe, December 20, 1989.

Commission of the European Communities, The European Community and Cyprus, Europe Information, External Relations, April 1990.

Commission Communication on Strengthening Relations With Turkey, Information 39/90, June 6, 1990.

Appendix A1

Revealed Comparative Advantage of Israel And Turkey in Trade With the EC, 1988

SITC	Name of category	Israel	Turkey
00	Live animals other than division 03	-0.604	-0.936
01	Meat and meat preparations	0.690	0.095
02	Dairy products and birds' eggs	-0.422	-0.743
03	Fish, crustaceans and prep. thereof	-0.544	0.764
04	Cereals and cereal preparations	-0.861	-0.183
05	Vegetable and fruit	0.880	0.991
06	Sugar, sugar preparations and honey	-0.919	0.716
07	Coffee, tea, cocoa, spices and manuf.	-0.691	0.187
08	Feedstuff for animals (excluding unmilled cereals)	-0.606	-0.075
09	Misc. edible and preparations	0.120	-0.302
11	Beverages	-0.784	-0.576
12	Tobacco and tobacco manufactures	-0.907	0.838
21	Hides, skins and furskins, raw	-0.870	-0.944
22	Oil seeds and oleaginous fruit	0.507	0.815
23	Crude rubber	-0.939	-0.910
24	Cork and wood	-0.950	-0.834
25	Pulp and waste paper	-0.946	-0.998
26	Textile fibers and their wastes	0.544	0.268
27	Crude fertilizers other than div. 56 and crude minerals	0.694	0.866
28	Metalliferous ores and metal scrap	0.833	-0.219
29	Crude animal and veg. materials n.e.s	0.879	0.388
32	Coal, coke and briquettes	-0.795	-0.995
33	Petroleum, petr. products and related materials	0.077	0.918
34	Gas, natural and manufactured	-0.998	0.507
35	Electric current	0	0
41	Animal oils and fats	-0.121	0.898
42	Fixed veg. oils and fats, crude, refined or fractionated	-0.835	-0.966
43	Processed animal and veg. oils and fats	-0.988	-0.939
51	Organic chemicals	-0.060	0.717
52	Inorganic chemicals	0.602	-0.513
53	Dyeing, tanning and colouring materials	-0.948	-0.965
54	Medicinal and pharmac. products	-0.739	-0.810
55	Essential oils and perfume mater.	-0.744	-0.680

Appendix A1 (cont'd.)

56	Fertilizers other than group 272	0.936	0.164
57	Plastics in primary forms	-0.421	-0.752
58	Plastics in nonprimary forms	0.195	-0.862
59	Chemical materials and prod. n.e.s	-0.454	-0.977
61	Leather, leather manufactures and dressed furskins	-0.778	-0.885
62	Rubber manufactures n.e.s.	0.021	0.149
63	Cork and wood manufactures (exc. furniture)	0.098	-0.415
64	Paper and paper manufactures	0.622	-0.971
65	Textile yarn, fabrics and related products	-0.161	0.692
66	Nonmetallic mineral manufactures n.e.s	-0.436	0.046
67	Iron and steel	-0.941	-0.586
68	Nonferrous metals	-0.756	-0.527
69	Manufactures of metal n.e.s	-0.372	-0.530
71	Power-generating machinery and equipment	0.494	-0.855
72	Specialized machinery	0.763	0.965
73	Metal-working machinery	-0.475	-0.908
74	Other industrial machinery and parts	-0.613	-0.919
75	Office machines and ADP equip.	-0.060	-0.948
76	Telecommunication and sound-recording apparatus	0.573	-0.565
77	Electrical machinery, apparatus and appliances, n.e.s.	-0.193	-0.808
78	Road vehicles	-0.966	-0.835
79	Other transport equipment	-0.045	-0.952
81	Prefabricated buildings, sanitary heating and lighting fixtures, n.d.a	-0.943	-0.142
82	Furniture and parts thereof	-0.435	-0.425
83	Travel goods, handbags, etc.	-0.279	0.896
84	Articles of apparel and clothing accessories	0.733	0.981
85	Footwear	-0.505	-0.030
87	Professional and scientific instruments n.e.s.	0.002	-0.810
88	Photo apparatus, optical goods, watches and clocks	-0.653	-0.980
89	Misc. manuf. articles n.e.s.	-0.257	-0.509

Source: *OECD Foreign Trade by Commodities 1988*, vol. 5 (Paris, 1991).

Appendix A2

Revealed Comparative Advantage of Israel And Turkey in Trade With the EC, 1983

SITC	Name of category	Israel	Turkey
00	Live animals other than division 03	-0.626	-0.721
01	Meat and meat preparations	0.267	0.705
02	Dairy products and birds' eggs	-0.989	-0.417
03	Fish, crustaceans and prep. thereof	-0.807	0.992
04	Cereals and cereal preparations	-0.402	0.408
05	Vegetable and fruit	0.928	0.989
06	Sugar, sugar preparations and honey	-0.953	0.484
07	Coffee, tea, cocoa, spices and manuf.	-0.717	0.815
08	Feedstuff for animals (excluding unmilled cereals)	-0.643	0.724
09	Misc. edible and preparations	0.688	0.843
11	Beverages	-0.926	-0.598
12	Tobacco and tobacco manufactures	-0.995	0.937
21	Hides, skins and furskins, raw	-0.523	-0.953
22	Oil seeds and oleaginous fruit	-0.993	0.997
23	Crude rubber	-0.989	-1.000
24	Cork and wood	-0.902	0.504
25	Pulp and waste paper	-1.000	-0.344
26	Textile fibers and their wastes	0.835	0.522
27	Crude fertilizers other than div. 56 and crude minerals	0.762	0.905
28	Metalliferous ores and metal scrap	0.782	0.087
29	Crude animal and veg. materials n.e.s	0.911	0.850
32	Coal, coke and briquettes	-1.000	-0.999
33	Petroleum, petr. products and related materials	0.765	0.836
34	Gas, natural and manufactured	-0.196	0.677
35	Electric current	0	0
41	Animal oils and fats	0.143	0.220
42	Fixed veg. oils and fats, crude, refined or fractionated	-0.967	-0.332
43	Processed animal and veg. oils and fats	-1.000	-0.993
51	Organic chemicals	-0.184	-0.964
52	Inorganic chemicals	0.530	-0.810
53	Dyeing, tanning and colouring materials	-0.957	-0.984
54	Medicinal and pharmac. products	-0.941	-0.900
55	Essential oils and perfume mater.	-0.815	-0.501
56	Fertilizers other than group 272	0.872	-0.999
57	Plastics in primary forms	-0.464	-0.905

Appendix A2 (cont'd.)

58	Plastics in nonprimary forms	-0.156	-0.870
59	Chemical materials and prod. n.e.s	-0.592	-0.988
61	Leather, leather manufactures and dressed furskins	-0.638	-0.554
62	Rubber manufactures n.e.s.	0.193	-0.396
63	Cork and wood manufactures (exc. furniture)	0.220	-0.022
64	Paper and paper manufactures	-0.848	-0.861
65	Textile yarn, fabrics and related products	-0.238	0.761
66	Nonmetallic mineral manufacturs n.e.s.	-0.206	-0.157
67	Iron and steel	-0.990	-0.860
68	Nonferrous metals	-0.806	-0.982
69	Manufactures of metal n.e.s	-0.669	-0.809
71	Power-generating machinery and equipment	-0.524	-0.810
72	Specialized machinery	-0.938	-0.988
73	Metal-working machinery	-0.850	-0.989
74	Other industrial machinery and parts	-0.816	-0.964
75	Office machines and ADP equip.	-0.422	-0.955
76	Telecommunication and sound-recording apparatus	-0.627	-0.973
77	Electrical machinery, apparatus and appliances, n.e.s.	-0.663	-0.960
78	Road vehicles	-0.985	-0.965
79	Other transport equipment	-0.512	-0.846
81	Prefabricated buildings, sanitary heating and lighting fixtures, n.d.a	-0.963	0.045
82	Furniture and parts thereof	-0.759	-0.445
83	Travel goods, handbags, etc.	-0.084	0.883
84	Articles of apparel and clothing accessories	0.760	0.977
85	Footwear	-0.716	0.110
87	Professional and scientific instruments n.e.s.	-0.088	-0.957
88	Photo apparatus, optical goods, watches and clocks	-0.777	-0.955
89	Misc. manuf. articles, n.e.s.	-0.333	-0.693

Source: *OECD Foreign Trade by Commodities 1988*, vol. 5 (Paris 1991).

Chapter 7

The European Community's Approach to Association: Applicability to the Case of Israel

J. REDMOND

The Nature of Association

Association with the European Community is provided for by articles 131-136 (Part IV association for countries that "have special relations" with EC members) and, more generally, by article 238 of the Treaty of Rome. Association agreements have been concluded with countries in three categories or parts of the world:

- Former colonies of the original EC Six engaged in Part IV association that subsequently developed into the Yaoundé and later the Lomé conventions. These agreements are arguably very special cases because of the unique historical relationship of the countries concerned with the EC.
- The Mediterranean, specifically, those countries in the north that qualify for EC membership on geographical grounds[1] but are currently unacceptable to the EC for economic and/or political reasons. However, not all potential and, in the case of Spain and Portugal, eventual members became associates and only some association agreements make a specific reference to eventual membership.
- Those countries in Central and Eastern Europe that were until recently part of the Soviet bloc. In these cases, association takes the form of "Europe Agreements" that have been agreed with Poland, Hungary, and Czechoslovakia, are in the process of being completed with Rumania and Bulgaria, and may be extended beyond these countries in due course.

Thus association has tended to be reserved for those countries that might legitimately aspire to become members of the "European club" and, more pragmatically, of the "European Economic Space" (generally defined), either by dint of geography (countries in Central, Eastern, or Mediterranean Europe) or of their former colonial status and hence strong economic and political links—even to the point of economic dependency—with the "motherland." Associates also tend to be relatively (to the EC) poor countries.

What constitutes association? In practice, it appears to fall somewhere between a mere trade agreement and membership in the forthcoming European Economic Area and can perhaps be generally described as a "trade agreement plus." However, it is not possible to be much more precise in general terms since the Treaty of Rome is itself vague on the definition of association. Article 238 refers to "creating reciprocal rights and obligations, joint actions and special procedures"—but this could mean anything from a mere trade agreement to a relationship verging on full membership. Consequently, association has effectively been defined by practice but even on this basis it is not possible to be definitive. The trade agreement aspect of "association" with the Lomé countries means the EC grants nonreciprocal concessions, in Eastern and Central Europe it denotes a free trade area, but in the Mediterranean it implies a customs union. Of course, association for a new associate (such as Israel) could include any or none of these and still conceivably remain within article 238. However, pragmatically speaking, an association agreement would seem to imply most, but not necessarily all, of the following:

1. Either (a) a free trade area or (b) a customs union
2. A financial protocol (EC financial aid)
3. Harmonization or alignment of economic and related policies
4. Association institutions at Council and Parliament level
5. Political dialogue
6. Cultural dialogue

Association in the Mediterranean appears to have originally consisted of 1(b), 2, 3 and 4, with 5 and 6 being increasingly included more recently. However, as association has only been given to countries that are eligible for full EC membership (Greece, Turkey, Malta, and Cyprus), it is not certain that association for "noneligible" countries in the eastern and southern Mediterranean would take precisely the same form.

Having examined the nature and geographical coverage of association, the rest of this chapter falls into three parts. The next section focuses on the Mediterranean and sets association in the context of the EC's approach to the region by outlining the development of the Global Mediterranean Policy (GMP). The third section looks at the EC's approach to association both in general terms and, more specifically, by examining four Mediterranean examples—Greece, Turkey, Cyprus, and Malta—in more detail. The final section explores the prospect of an association agreement for Israel, discussing the possible benefits and drawbacks of such an arrangement and offering some conclusions.

Association in the Mediterranean Context

The EC's interest in the Mediterranean is longstanding and, indeed, dates back to its very beginnings when it was faced with the issues of accommodating the Maghreb countries—Algeria was actually still part of France in 1957, and Morocco and Tunisia, although independent, retained close links with France—and dealing with Greek and Turkish aspirations. The fact that different agreements were negotiated for different countries set the pattern for the future development of the EC's policy toward the Mediterranean. The reasons that the Community sought involvement in the region are clear enough—it perceived it as a politically and strategically important area in its own backyard—and this is equally true of the EC's objective: "the aim ... is the creation of a sphere of influence."[2] Moreover, although the Soviet threat has disappeared, the Gulf War and the Yugoslavian crisis have ensured the continuation of the strategic and political importance of the Mediterranean. For the Mediterranean countries' part, they see little alternative to a close relationship with the only significant politico-economic power in their vicinity. Consequently, it is not surprising that the EC has emerged as their major trading partner and the most obvious source of financial assistance and that virtually all Mediterranean states have negotiated agreements of some kind with the EC.[3]

In fact, despite its essentially political motivation there are also economic reasons for EC interest: overall the Mediterranean countries constitute a significant market and trading partner even now (and this was obviously even more the case before Greece, Spain, and Portugal joined in the 1980s); tourism and oil also feature in EC-Mediterranean relations. Moreover, since the EC's competence has been principally in economic matters, its agreements with Mediterranean countries have been largely concerned with preferential trading arrangements, financial and technical assistance, and, in some cases, institutional arrangements. Indeed, this has suited the Mediterranean countries because it is the economic aspects of the relationship that interest them, particularly the prospect of improved access to EC markets for their exports, which, together with financial assistance from the EC, could accelerate their industrialization; the prospect of free access to EC labor markets for their workforce is also attractive. It is true that, in some cases, the impetus has been political in part—for example, the perception in Greece, Spain, and Portugal in the past (and, to some extent, Turkey today) that a closer relationship with the EC would enhance the prospects of their democracies continuing—but economics remains the more fundamental motivation.

However, in spite of the EC's obvious need for a relationship with its Mediterranean "hinterland," because of internal preoccupations with the first phase of integration this issue was not taken up seriously until the 1969-1972 period when there was a rush of agreements. Unfortunately, they were negotiated independently with different contents and expiry dates and this combined with the introduction of the EC's Generalized System of Preferences (GSP) in 1971 and the impending 1973 enlargement to create a haphazard and changing pattern of net discrimination (by the EC) not only in terms of the position of the Mediterranean compared with the rest of the world but also between different countries within the Mediterranean itself. The result was clearly arbitrary and illogical. The Community's response was to instigate its Global Mediterranean Policy (GMP)[4] in 1972, with which it intended to restore order to the situation by standardizing its agreements with the different Mediterranean countries to consist of a free trade area in manufactures (to be introduced by the Community in 1977 and by each Mediterranean country as and when its level of development permitted) together with agricultural trade concessions and financial assistance. The current and past network of the EC's relations with the Mediterranean is indicated in Table 1.

Table 1
Agreements Between the EC and Mediterranean Countries

Full EC Membership:	*Greece, 1981; Spain, 1986; Portugal, 1986*
Association under article 238:	(Greece, 1961);[1] *Turkey, 1963*; (Morocco, 1969); (Tunisia, 1969); *Malta, 1970; Cyprus, 1972*
Cooperation agreements:	*Israel, 1975; Maghreb: Algeria, Morocco, and Tunisia, 1976; Mashrek: Egypt, Lebanon, Jordan, and Syria, 1977; Yugoslavia, 1980*
Preferential trade agreements:	(Spain, 1970); (Israel, 1970); (Egypt, 1972); (Lebanon, 1972); (Portugal, 1972)
Nonpreferential trade agreements:	(Israel, 1964); (Lebanon, 1965); (Yugoslavia, 1970 and 1973)

Source: Adapted from K. Featherstone, "The Mediterranean Challenge," in J. Lodge, ed., *The European Community and the Challenge of the Future* (London: Macmillan, 1984, p. 187).

[1]Agreements in parentheses have been superseded by the current agreements (which are in italics).

However, the theoretical logic and tidiness of the GMP were not converted into practice, except in a very specific and unintentional way, so that what emerged by the late 1970s was not so much a "global" policy but rather a "common approach to various groups of Mediterranean countries,"[5] ranging from the (least favored) nonpreferential agreement group (in fact, just Yugoslavia) to the (most favored) group with association agreements leading to membership (Greece and Turkey). Although the agreements did have the common element of substantially improved access to the EC market for manufactures and marginal improvements for agricultural products and, furthermore, the GMP did allow countries to move up the hierarchy of agreements so that all of them had either a cooperation or association agreement with the EC, there were problems. Indeed, the principal deficiencies were pointed out by the Commission itself. The EC's concessions on manufactures had not led to increased exports from the Mediterranean countries to the EC, not least because the latter had felt it necessary to protect various "sensitive" sectors (such as textiles and steel) and consequently the projected increase in the rate of industrial development in the Mediterranean had not taken place. Similarly, the EC had not extended its agricultural concessions and the result of all this was increased trade deficits for the EC's Mediterranean partners forcing them to curb their imports from the EC.[6]

This recognition of failure (together with the Mediterranean enlargement of the Community) prompted a "relaunch" of the EC's Mediterranean policy in 1982[7] and a "redirection" in 1990.[8] However, the former did not amount to much more than a restatement of the obvious objectives of improving access to the EC market for the Mediterranean partners and helping to promote their economic development. Similarly, the "redirection" has only three substantial aspects:

- A renewal of the financial protocols with the Maghreb and Mashreq countries, and Israel for the period 1991-1996 with the funds available increased by an extra 30% over the previous protocols (to a total of ECU 2,075 million)
- The provision of ECU 2,030 million for "horizontal" financial cooperation; this is available to all Mediterranean countries with agreements with the EC and is to be used for regional projects of relevance to the Community, notably for environmental protection
- Improved trade concessions from the Community allied with ECU 300 million of financial support to the Maghreb and Mashreq countries to support structural reform programs

Thus the EC has a Mediterranean policy but it is certainly not "global" and probably not common either, and the jibe that it represents "an unplanned accident,"[9] directed at the period before 1972, may be little less true today. Moreover, even the minimalist "redirection" described above has been fraught with difficulties. Greece blocked the horizontal financing component because Turkey was one of the beneficiaries, and this also delayed the implementation of some of the trade concessions. It was only when the Greeks lifted their reservations in June 1992 that the redirected Mediterranean policy became fully operational.

In light of the continuing inadequacies of the EC's Mediterranean policy, it is hardly surprising that those countries in the region that feel they are in a position to seek a much more integrated relationship with the EC (membership) are doing so, and those that cannot are simply accepting the status quo or turning inward. In fact, the GMP has long been overtaken by events as the Mediterranean has really divided into two broad camps. The "associates" in the north who, because of geography, are eligible to apply for full EC membership have done just that, beginning with Greece; the applications of Turkey, Cyprus, and Malta represent a continuation of this trend. The remainder, in the south and east, in the face of a continued erosion of their trade preferences in the EC market, appear to be confronted with a choice of accepting a continuation of the current relationship, turning away from the EC and promoting their own regional cooperation schemes (which appears to be happening in North Africa),[10] or seeking to strengthen relations with the Community, possibly through association. The latter may look inviting, but other than as a channel through which an application for full EC membership can be made, past experience suggests that article 238 association is of dubious benefit.

The EC's Approach to Association

The most striking feature of the EC's association agreements is that they have all run into difficulties, in particular those with Mediterranean countries. The relationship with former colonies—currently through the Lomé Conventions—is perhaps more controversial. The Community would argue that Part IV association and the subsequent arrangements have been reasonably successful, but critics would take a different view. In particular, they would point to the deterioration of the trade balance of the Lomé countries, the insufficient funding of the commodity export support programs (STABEX and SYSMIN), the relatively ungenerous levels of EC aid through the European Development Fund (EDF), and the failure of the "partnership" concept (and de facto continuation of dependence on the EC of its former colonies). The "European Agreements" with the ex-Soviet-bloc countries are too new to assess, but the delay caused by French objections to Hungarian and Polish agricultural exports seems to suggest that the trend established by Part IV association is being continued.

Although the difficulties of EC association with former colonies and Eastern-Central Europe perhaps arise principally on the EC side, association agreements with Mediterranean countries have been held back by developments within the EC's partner countries. These have taken the form of military interventions (Greece and Turkey), internal political division (Cyprus), and the election of an uncooperative, anti-EC government (Malta). Although economic factors also come into play, it is significant that it is political factors that have brought association, essentially an exercise in economic integration, to a halt. However, all four Mediterranean associates have, nevertheless, gone on to apply for full EC membership as soon as they regarded it as feasible to do so, at least in part because they felt that association was an inadequate form of relationship with the EC. On the one hand, this suggests that association has clearly been a failure because it was inadequate; but on the other, it could be interpreted as having succeeded in that it created a platform for an attempt to achieve a much closer relationship with the Community (full membership).

The only associate that has managed to become a full EC member so far is Greece, and in economic (and possibly other) terms this accession has hardly been a success. Indeed, in 1992 Jacques Delors, the president of the EC Commission, was moved to describe Greek membership in the Community as an economic failure, noting that "Greece has not taken part in the general movement either in macroeconomic convergence or structural remediation."[11] Greece was the first country to apply for EC association and did so as early as 1959, although the agreement was not eventually signed until 1961 (effective 1962). It set the pattern for future article 238 associations in the Mediterranean and had five main elements:

- The progressive creation of a customs union between the EC and Greece, with tariffs to be removed over a 22-year transition period (12 years for some products)
- The harmonization of Greek and EC policies in a variety of areas, most importantly agriculture but also free movement of labor, transport, taxation, competition rules, and economic policy
- Financial assistance from the Community to encourage thedevelopment of Greek industry, agriculture, infrastructure, and the economy in general
- The creation of appropriate institutions—an Association Council at ministerial level to supervise the agreement and, at parliamentary level, an advisory committee drawn from members of the Greek and European parliaments
- The provision for a Greek application for full membership at the end of the transition period, which was considered, to some extent, to be a preparation for membership; however, Greek accession was not automatic—the commit-

ment was merely to allow and encourage an application to join the Community

Association worked well enough for the first five years but then, in 1967 following the military coup, the EC suspended the agreement as Greece ceased to be a democracy. However, contact with democratic elements in Greece continued throughout the period of military dictatorship, and the timetable for an industrial customs union continued on schedule so that in 1974, following the return to democracy, Greece was able to abolish on time all duties on those goods subject to a 12-year transition period. However, progress with respect to other elements of association—particularly the harmonization of policies—was minimal, and even the financial provisions ran into difficulty so that it proved impossible to negotiate a second financial protocol until early 1977. In short, association, for Greece, amounted to little more than a trade and aid ("cooperation") agreement of the type beginning to be widely negotiated by the EC in the Mediterranean and elsewhere. The Greeks felt that association was no longer the appropriate framework within which to conduct their relations with the EC and promptly applied for full membership in 1976. In view of the substantial difficulties experienced by Greece during its EC membership, it seems likely that association was of limited benefit.

The second association agreement was with Turkey,[12] which asked for such an arrangement within weeks of the Greek request but had to wait rather longer because of the subsequent military intervention (the anti-Menderes coup). The Ankara Agreement was eventually signed in 1963 (effective 1964) with much of the detail filled out by the Additional Protocol, signed in 1970 (effective 1973).[13] The arrangement mirrored the Athens Agreement in that it included a gradual transition to a customs union and toward free movement of labor (and capital), "closer alignment of economic policies" (with specific references to competition policy, taxation, and economic policy in general), EC financial assistance to Turkey, and the standard institutional framework. However, there are two key differences: first, the transitional stage was preceded by a preparatory stage during which the EC would make unilateral tariff concessions and give financial aid while Turkey strengthened its economy in readiness for the transitional stage; second, the commitment to the ultimate objective of EC membership was rather weaker and, indeed, marked the last reference to such an objective in association agreements (until very recently when, after much pressure from the Visegrad countries, a reference to the possibility of membership was included in the preambles of the Europe Agreements with Poland, Hungary, and Czechoslovakia.)

Unfortunately, Turkish association with the EC proved to be a nearly complete failure. The fundamental reason for this was the failure, on both sides, to comprehend fully what such a commitment entailed. Turkey approached the EC on the basis of vague feelings that EC association would confirm its European identity, with apparently little conception of the extent of economic adaptation that would be required nor of the need for a liberal, free-trade-oriented economic strategy. Indeed, in the 1970s it pursued a wholly incompatible policy based on a rigid import substitution plan and the consequent inward-looking Turkish policy toward the end of that decade actually contradicted any intention of a closer relationship with the EC. Similarly, the EC's approach lacked consistency as it blew hot and cold on Turkey according to its own needs, seeming to have little idea of where its relationship with Turkey was going or where it wished it to go, beyond acting as a means of securing the continuation of Turkish political support for NATO and the West. In fact the EC paid scant attention to its obligations, as illustrated by its failure to maintain all its commercial concessions to Turkey in the face of the increased competition for its own producers.

The relationship ground to a halt with the 1980 military intervention—although it had failed economically well before then—and the subsequent reestablishment of a democracy that has pursued a more liberal (and hence appropriate) economic policy has done little to improve matters. In the 1980s, a further hindrance was created by Greek accession to the Community and the implacable Greek hostility to any EC concessions to Turkey that has ensued ever since. In 1987 Turkey chose the Greek route and, in the face of an unsatisfactory association agreement, applied for full EC membership. A rebuff was never really in doubt, although the politics and diplomacy of the issue meant that the (heavily qualified) rejection did not appear until the end of 1989. The Community subsequently offered what amounted to a reactivated association agreement,[14] which still remains on the table.

Malta's association agreement with the EC has a rather curious history in that it was negotiated by a (broadly) "pro-EC" Nationalist government but then implemented or, perhaps better, tolerated by a (broadly) "anti-EC" Labor government for the next sixteen years. Once Britain decided to seek EC membership the need for Malta to have a close relationship with the Community became inevitable, and an association agreement was signed in 1970 (effective 1971). The centerpiece of the agreement was a customs union to be achieved in two five-year phases, although only the first of these was spelled out in any detail. The usual financial and institutional arrangements were also included, but unlike the Greek and Turkish agreements there was no reference to future membership in the EC. However, in the face of EC restrictions on Maltese textile exports (via a safeguard clause) and the anti-Western and pro-Libyan posturing of the Maltese Labor government, the association agreement did not prosper. It was modified by additional protocols, and the first stage was extended in 1976 and again in 1977. The agreement eventually lapsed in 1980 and was then extended unilaterally by the EC until 1988, when a supplementary protocol was agreed with the new Nationalist government that extended the first stage again (until 1990) and put EC-Maltese relations on a contractual basis once more. In 1990, following the Maltese application to join the EC, it was decided that the first stage should automatically be extended annually until the membership issue is resolved.

Whether association has benefited Malta is a debatable point. Those in Malta in favor of joining the Community would point to the massive increase in EC-Malta trade, the three EC-Malta financial protocols, the explosive growth in the numbers of (mainly EC) tourists, and the increase in foreign investment, much of it from the EC, coming to Malta. There is also evidence that "the 1970 association agreement with the EEC inaugurated a period of rapid manufactured export expansion, based on industries whose growth was fuelled by foreign investment."[15] Thus association was good for manufacturing, good for exports, and good for foreign investment. However, the doubters would point to the huge trade imbalance, the use by the EC of safeguards to protect its textile producers, the unbalanced nature of Maltese restructuring with exports concentrated in a few (often foreign-owned) companies and sectors, the unsatisfactory treatment by the EC of Maltese agricultural exports, and the EC's lack of generosity in this respect. Moreover, as the EC has gradually introduced more general trade concessions (such as its GSP) and negotiated concessionary agreements with other countries (most recently Hungary, Czechoslovakia, and Poland), the value of association has been eroded, compared to what Malta could have obtained via a less extensive agreement.

The final Mediterranean associate is Cyprus. Even more so than with Malta, the economic dependence on Britain meant that a necessity for a close relationship with the EC was sure to follow any successful British bid for EC membership. The EC-Cyprus association agreement therefore paralleled British accession; it was signed in 1972 and became effective in 1973. As with Malta it consisted of a two-stage, ten-year transition to a customs union with the EC, but only the details of the first stage were specified in detail, together with a financial protocol and association institutions (but with no reference to EC membership). Dissatisfaction with the EC's trade concessions soon emerged on the Cypriot side, and any lingering hopes that there might be a smooth progression to the second stage were dashed by the Turkish invasion of the island in 1974 and de facto division of the territory thereafter. This made further progress impossible for two reasons. In the first place, it created a highly charged political situation in which a move to the second stage of association might have been construed as the EC favoring the Greek Cypriots. Second, the division of the island caused substantial economic dislocation, which raised major doubts as to whether the Cypriot economy could withstand even a gradual move to a customs union with the EC.

Over the next ten years there were repeated extensions of the first stage, with minor modifications until, in 1987, agreement was reached to move to the second stage (effective 1988), which will lead to a full customs union. The first phase is to last ten years; however, progression to the (five- year) second phase is not automatic but requires a decision by the Association Council. The Turkish Cypriots officially oppose the agreement (and the subsequent membership bid), but the EC operates on the principle that the concessions and financial aid that it offers are available to the whole of Cyprus. The agreement also requires Cyprus to apply various accompanying EC policies relating to the approximation of laws, competition policy, state aids, and agricultural policy. The Cypriot decision to apply for full EC membership in July 1990 was essentially a natural development of the evolution of EC-Cyprus relations and was probably inevitable sooner or later once Greece had joined the Community. However, it is more indicative of expectations of future benefits of EC membership than of any sense of satisfaction with EC association, which in many ways has been untested as much as unsuccessful.

In the light of the peculiarities—uniqueness even—of the four examples of Mediterranean association described above, it may seem difficult to draw any general conclusions or lessons for any future Israeli case. Indeed, military interventions from within (Greece) or without (Cyprus) or local quirks (Malta and Turkey) have arguably prevented the principle of association from being adequately tested in practice. Nevertheless, the EC side has not been affected by such events and so it is possible to discern some features of the Community's attitude toward association, in particular:

- The Community appears to reserve association for countries that it regards in some sense as special cases. The Greeks applied at a time when the EC was looking for diplomatic success, and the fact that Greece had "chosen" the EC rather than the "rival" European Free Trade Area (EFTA) ensured a warm welcome. Moreover, the Americans were very keen that the EC should assist an exposed NATO member. The Turks were offered association because of their very early application, (shortly after that of the Greeks), the desire to treat the Greeks and the Turks even-handedly, and Turkey's strategic importance. Malta and Cyprus were eligible for association because of their close economic dependence on Britain and the need to accommodate them when Britain became a member of the Community.
- The Community's enthusiasm for association agreements appears to have waned over time. (The recent agreements with Poland, Hungary, and Czechoslovakia are very special cases and were, to some extent, given grudgingly.) Greek association was negotiated at the height of the EC's initial outward-looking phase of development, so that Greece's agreement was relatively generous. However, negotiations with Turkey were delayed by the anti-Menderes coup and by the time they began the EC had become, under

Gaullist pressure, much more inward-looking and this, together with growing Italian and French self-interest, led to a less generous form of association for Turkey. The Maltese and Cypriot association agreements were similarly ungenerous in certain respects, and in any case their value had been eroded by the more general trade concessions the EC offered to nonassociates. The reference to future accession contained in the Greek and Turkish agreements was also dropped. In essence, association has become outdated.

- Association does not appear to lead to access to the EC market beyond that available to nonassociates through trade agreements and the EC's GSP (Generalized System of Preferences). Indeed, the extent of the criticism of the four Mediterranean associates is such that it might be questioned whether association would have been successful even in the absence of exogenous obstructions. All the familiar criticisms of EC trade policy and EC trade concessions are there. First, it is charged that the EC uses safeguard clauses to exclude imports of "sensitive" industrial products (such as textiles), or, more generally, that it is "quite hypocritical, in that it [is] prepared to allow free entry for all industrial products except those in which [the associate is] fully competitive."[16] Second, there are complaints that the value of the concessions given to the associates is steadily eroded by the succession of agreements negotiated by the EC that give similar concessions—the GSP, the agreements with nonassociates that make up the rest of the GMP, and, of course, enlargement of the EC, particularly the accession of Greece, Spain, and Portugal. Indeed, there was a very perverse example in the early 1970s where the tariff concession on EC industrial imports being given as part of the EC's GSP (100%) was actually greater than that being given to Cyprus and Malta as part of their association agreements (70%). Third, the greatest vitriol is, of course, reserved for the EC's agricultural regime. EC agricultural concessions are small in size, hedged by quotas for any product that may threaten indigenous EC producers, arbitrary in that they vary between countries for similar products[17] and cover a limited number of products, and finally, and perhaps more damaging, they drive countries to produce those products that the EC is prepared to import rather than those that ought to be produced according to comparative advantage or some other rational criterion. Indeed, instinctive French and Italian tendencies to protect their farmers have become a permanent obstacle to the Mediterranean associates' efforts to extract agricultural concessions from the EC.

There are also a whole range of complaints about specific products and about the strictness of EC rules of origin.

- Association does not appear to lead to a significantly better trade balance with the EC than that achieved by countries with lesser forms of agreement. Some comparative data for Mediterranean countries is given in Table 2. Although it is difficult to be precise, since trade is dependent on many other factors besides trade agreements with the EC, the story seems to be much the same for all countries in the Mediterranean: growing trade deficits with the EC. Equally, association does not appear to lead to an especially enhanced aid element. Table 3 indicates the amounts made available to Mediterranean countries under the financial protocols currently in force, and there is no suggestion that the associates receive a particularly generous allocation. Indeed, it is perhaps not unreasonable to assert that they would have been given much the same if they had only had cooperation agreements.

Table 2
GNP and Trade Statistics of Mediterranean Countries

	(1)	(2)	(3)
Yugoslavia	3060	56.0	100
Turkey	1630	50.8	102
Algeria	2060	67.7	81
Morocco	950	67.8	121
Tunisia	1420	73.8	128
Egypt	600	28.3	155
Jordan	1240	3.1	879
Lebanon	n.a.	22.7	823
Syria	990	45.7	102
Israel	10970	34.4	159
Malta	6630	71.8	186
Cyprus	8040	44.1	272

Key:

(1) GNP per capita, 1990, thousands of $US (*World Bank Atlas*, 1991).

(2) Exports to the EC as a percentage of total exports, 1991 (IMF, *Direction of Trade Statistics Yearbook*, 1992).

(3) Imports from the EC as a percentage of exports to the EC (EC Eurostat, *External Trade Statistical Yearbook*, 1990).

Table 3
Financial Protocols Currently in Operation
(millions of ECU)

Country	Agreement (FP) (Financial Protocol)	Duration	Loans	Grants	Total
Yugoslavia	Third FP	1991-96	730	77	807
Turkey	Fourth FP	awaiting signature	550	50	600
Algeria	Fourth FP	1991-96	298	52	300
Morocco	Fourth FP	1991-96	245	193	438
Tunisia	Fourth FP	1991-96	183	101	284
Egypt	Fourth FP	1991-96	326	242	568
Jordan	Fourth FP	1991-96	82	44	126
Lebanon	Fourth FP	1991-96	47	22	69
Syria	Fourth FP	1991-96	117	41	158
Israel	Fourth FP	1991-96	82	—	82
Malta	Third FP	1988-93	25.5	12.5	38
Cyprus	Third FP	1988-93	49	13	62

Source: *EIB* (European Investment Bank) *Information*, no. 70, November 1991, p. 1.

- The omission of a clause relating to future membership in the EC from all but the very first association agreements raises questions about the EC's perception of the purpose of association. The contention that association facilitates accession to the EC is at best unproved and, indeed, the opposite may be true. The Mediterranean associates would probably have applied to join the EC anyway. Moreover, the concept of association or "associate membership" might be used to provide a convenient alternative to full EC membership that the EC can offer to countries that it does not wish to admit. Turkey, Cyprus, and even Malta may all find themselves in this category—Greece was a special case and, in the light of Delors's recent comments, possibly a mistake. In any case, it should be remembered that Spain and Portugal did not need association as a staging post on the way to full EC membership.

Ultimately, although the content of the concept of association has been defined over time, its purpose remains unclear and it is not easy to clarify what the authors of the Treaty of Rome intended association to be. In practice, the Community appears to have allowed it to lapse into a form of extended cooperation agreement, setting targets that seem to have as much to do with politics as economics.

Moreover, it is very difficult to see much practical difference between association and cooperation agreements since no associate has come close to achieving the elements that differentiate the former, notably a customs union and an alignment of competition, taxation, and other economic policies with the EC. Even the association institutions have been of limited value, since in many cases they have met very infrequently and have been largely unable to break the deadlocks that have plagued the association agreements in the Mediterranean. It is therefore difficult not to conclude that association has been a failure in the Mediterranean in the sense that it offers no more in practice than a cooperation agreement. Furthermore, there appears to have been a lack of the coherence, reality, and goodwill that are needed on both sides if association is to be successful. Some of the EC's shortcomings have already been described, but there have also been problems on the side of the EC's partners. Unrealistic expectations constitute an obvious problem, but a more specific example is provided by the Turks' pursuit in the 1970s of an inward-looking economic policy based on import substitution that was simply incompatible with EC association. Similarly, the actions and attitudes of the Maltese Labor government in the 1971-1987 period were frequently incompatible, leading one frustrated Commission official, ostensibly in Malta to discuss security issues, to comment: "They were only interested in money."[18]

An Association Agreement for Israel?

Turning to an Israeli perspective and the applicability of association to the Israeli case, there are two questions that immediately come to mind: first, is Israel eligible for association; and second, would it be beneficial to have such an agreement? Logically speaking, Israel might be interested in association as a bridge to full EC membership, or, if that concept is too incredible, then as a bridge to membership in the EC-EFTA European Economic Area or to a lower-tier form of EC membership if the EC evolves into a multitier arrangement, a "Europe of concentric circles." (Arguably, being an associate "member" is already a form of lower-tier, albeit much lower-tier, EC membership.) The prospect of EC membership is perhaps not that outlandish given Israel's participation in some "European" activities, the Turkish parallel, and the possibility that "membership" may not have to mean full membership. However, the eligibility issue would seem to be resolved by the fact that it is quite possible to have an association agreement with no reference to membership. The important consideration then becomes whether the EC would regard Israel as falling into the category of ("special case") countries that merit association or whether it would be prepared to extend that category to include countries that were not geographically "European" and with which it did not have former colonial links.

However, the more substantial question concerns the potential value of association to Israel. This has to be set in the context of the applicability of the experience of the EC's Mediterranean associates to Israel and the existing EC-Israel trade agreement. The ultimate question is whether anything would change; and that would hinge on whether the elements of association in the Mediterranean region that go beyond a cooperation agreement—a customs union, policy harmonization, and joint institutions— could actually be achieved. In general terms, it is quite clear that the geopolitical situation of Israel is such that it offers ample scope for exogenous factors to disrupt association in an all too familiar way.

More specifically, it is not entirely clear what benefits a full customs union will bring and why it should be desirable other than as a staging post on the way to full participation in the EC's internal market or even accession. Indeed, the existing associates have, in a sense, already realized this and by opting to apply for immediate EC membership have decided that they wish to miss the customs-union phase-out. For example, in Malta, although the two major political parties are divided as to whether they want to join the EC now (the Nationalists) or to negotiate a special arrangement that would leave membership an option in the future (the Labor Party), they are in agreement on one thing: they do not want a customs union as envisaged in the association agreement. They see a customs union as a halfway house that provides all the pain of membership (competition from the EC) with none of the gain (access to the EC's structural funds). More generally, a customs union clearly offers a subordinate status since the partner country effectively (and completely) cedes sovereignty over its commercial policy to the EC. (A free trade area would seem more advantageous, providing the benefits of a customs union without the same loss of sovereignty.)

Similarly, it is not entirely clear what would be achieved by policy harmonization in the context of association. This would have to be on the EC's terms—i.e., Israel aligning its policies to those of the EC and not vice versa—and would entail a significant loss of Israeli sovereignty. The gain might take the form of the EC being more generous with a country that seeks to provide a level playing field for EC competitors—through adopting a parallel competition policy, for example; however, given the EC's past and present trade policies it is difficult not to be more than a little skeptical. Finally, it is hard to see what an Association Council could achieve over and above what is already achieved by the Cooperation Council. The "extras" provided by association would therefore seem of dubious value to Israel. Consequently, the next question becomes whether the cooperation elements (trade and aid) of an association agreement are likely to be any better than those already available through Israel's present agreement with the EC. The contents of Tables 2 and 3 would seem to suggest that this is highly unlikely.

Ultimately, association does not seem the optimal way forward for Israel. Not only is this type of agreement inappropriate in light of Israel's geographical location as well as level of GDP per capita—association is mainly for relatively poor countries—but the concept has arguably become outdated anyway. Part IV association has given way to the Lomé Convention, and article 238 association has proved largely unsatisfactory in practice and has been rejected by the associates in favor of full EC membership. The only possible purpose that association could serve would be as a halfway house to somewhere else, presumably the European Economic Area (EEA) in the case of Israel, and it would make far more sense for Israel to try and get there directly in the current negotiations to update the 1975 EC-Israel agreement. It is, of course, possible that the Community may not offer direct membership in the EEA because "Israel's case is untypical [with its] European-type industrial dimension [and] Middle Eastern type economical dimension."[19] Consequently, a specific form of relationship between the EC and Israel may have to be found. This might be called association, but it would differ from and be more extensive than past versions of association in the Mediterranean and would not really be the same thing.

Notes

1. Morocco and Tunisia did also temporarily have association agreements in the 1969-1974 period, but these were subsequently replaced by a trade and cooperation agreement within the Maghreb framework.

2. H. Corbet, Preface to R. Pomfret, *The Mediterranean Policy of the European Community* (London: Macmillan, 1986), p. xii.

3. Following Albanian overtures to the Community, the only exception is now Lybia.

4. Instructive accounts of the establishment of the GMP are provided in: R. Pomfret and A. Tovias, "The Global Mediterranean Policy of the EEC," in H. Giersch, ed., *The Economic Integration of Israel in the EEC* (Tubingen: Mohr, 1980); Pomfret, *Mediterranean Policy*; A. Tovias, *Tariff Preferences in Mediterranean Diplomacy* (London: Macmillan, 1977).

5. Pomfret, *Mediterranean Policy*, p. 23; Tovias, *Tariff Preferences*, p. 12.

6. Commission of the ECs, "The Community and the Countries and Regions of the Mediterranean," *European File*, no. 19, 1982, p. 3.

7. Commission of the ECs, Communication From the Commission to the Council of Ministers: A Mediterranean Policy for the Enlarged Community (Brussels, 1982).

8. Commission of the ECs, Communication From the Commission to the Council of

Ministers: Redirecting the Community's Mediterranean Policy (Brussels, 1990).

9. G. Curzon, Introduction to Tovias, *Tariff Preferences*, p. xvii.

10. A useful summary of this development is provided by R. Pomfret, "The European Community's Relations With the Mediterranean Countries," in J. Redmond, ed., *The External Relations of the European Community* (London: Macmillan, 1992), pp. 86-88.

11. Jacques Delors, speech to the General Assembly of Greek Industry, Athens, May 26, 1992, reported in *Europe*, no. 5738, May 27, 1992, pp. 7-8.

12. The history, current status, and likely future development of the relationships of Turkey, Cyprus, and Malta with the European Community are examined in detail in J. Redmond, *The Next Mediterranean Enlargement: Turkey, Cyprus, and Malta?* (Aldershot: Dartmouth, 1993).

13. For more detail, see Commission of the ECs, "Agreement establishing an Association between the European Economic Community and Turkey" (1963), and Commission of the ECs, "Additional Protocol" (1970), both published in English in *Official Journal of the ECs*, vol. 16, no. C113, December 24, 1973.

14. Commission of the ECs, Communication from the Commission to the Council on relations With Turkey and proposal for a Council Decision on the conclusion of the fourth financial protocol, SEC(90) 1017 final, Brussels.

15. R. Pomfret, "Trade Preferences and Foreign Investment in Malta," *Journal of World Trade Law* 16 (1982): 241.

16. W. Hale, *The Political and Economic Development of Modern Turkey* (London: Croom Helm, 1981). Many other countries with commercial agreements with the EC—for example, the ACP (African, Caribbean, and Pacific) signatories to the Lomé Conventions—are all too familiar with this particular aspect of Community policy.

17. For example, the degree of preference given by the EC to citrus fruit from Cyprus under the association agreement was on a par with that given to Spain and Israel but less than that given to the Maghreb countries and Greece.

18. R. Pace, "Malta-EC Association: Back to the Spirit of the Origins," *Sunday Times* (of Malta), March 31, 1985, p. 16.

19. Jacques Delors, meeting with Shimon Peres, October 2, 1992, reported in *Europe*, no. 5828, October 3, 1992, p. 7.

Chapter 8

Trade Blocs and the Stranded Countries[1]

LUIS DE SEBASTIÁN

Introduction

The issue is whether the formation of several trade blocs such as the European Single Market endangers or rather favors the establishment of an open and free Global System of Trade and Investment. That kind of system does not yet exist as a fully-fledged reality, but it is considered desirable from the point of view of world welfare, and as such it is duly promoted by institutions such as GATT. In this chapter it will be referred to as the GATT-System.

The urgency arises not so much from the inception of the European Single Market, which has been in the making for a long time, as from the signing of the North America Free Trade Agreement, NAFTA (with 363 million potential consumers), between the United States, Canada, and Mexico. The former gives rise to fears of a Fortress Europe; the latter could be regarded—and has been by many, including *The Economist*—as the second important step toward the alignment of all economic powers in trade blocs.[2] This development appears more serious in view of both the difficulties of the leading countries of the world in clinching the Uruguay Round of trade negotiations, and a certain disappointment with multilateral thinking, which could give a new and necessary impetus to the GATT-inspired trade relations.[3]

It is feared that if the fragmentation of the world economy occurs, it will mean the end of the multilateral, open, and free trade system that the international community has been striving to establish since the end of World War II, and that, although imperfect, has contributed a great deal to the prosperity of the postwar world. Furthermore, there seem to be reasons to fear that the coexistence of large economic blocs will not be a peaceful affair nor its outward behavior cooperative, and that trade wars will devastate rich and poor economies alike. World solidarity will also suffer, as one portion—accounting for 18% of the population and three-fourths of the production—will be rich, organized, and self-enclosed though not free from trade disputes; and another portion—with 82% of the world population and one-fourth of world production—poor, disunited (with countries fighting each other), and left to its own destiny. In this chapter, the term stranded countries will refer to those countries that are not likely to be members of any trade bloc whether existing or in formation.

From the viewpoint of a small country such as Israel, which is not party to any of the existing trade blocs, the problem is whether the configuration of the world trading system in somehow closed blocs will mean the end both of the free access to its export markets and of the export-led development strategy.

On the other hand, some believe that moving toward a world of free trade blocs (with or without monetary union) is a necessary prerequisite under present circumstances for arriving at an open and free trading system, which they also regard as the ideal way of organizing international exchanges.

The purpose of this chapter, then, is to explore whether regional free trade arrangements are "building blocks or stumbling blocks"[4] for the GATT-System and for the stranded countries in particular. This will be done by considering the conditions that could cause one or the other outcome to occur. In the course of the discussion it is hoped that several issues, which make up the main body of the literature on the subject, will be clarified:

- The definition of a GATT-unfriendly trade bloc
- The empirical contrast of the proposition that the world is going to divide into several trade blocs
- The advantages and drawbacks of trade blocs, as compared with the GATT-System, under present circumstances
- An assessment of the actual effect on the trade system if these blocs are formed in the immediate future

In the next section, after attempting a definition of trade blocs, their relations with the GATT-System and their status in it are discussed. In the succeeding section, the conditions for bringing about either a free-trade-promoting bloc or a free-trade-damaging one will be explored. Finally, the path to confrontation and the path to cooperation will be made explicit, and some informed guesses about the most likely outcomes will be offered.

Trade Blocs and Their Role Today

What Is a Trade Bloc?[5]

"Trade bloc" is a new term for an old thing. *The Economist* associates the term with the formation of free trade areas, in particular NAFTA. According to current usage, a trade bloc is any of the forms of economic integration, ranging from the looser free trade area to the more integrated Single Market. Frankel has proposed a precise definition: "a group of countries who are concentrating their trade and financial relationships with each other, in preference to the rest of the world."[6] Frankel adds to the definition the criterion that this concentration is the outcome of policy rather of common language or culture. This definition is adopted in the following pages.

For the purposes of this chapter, which discusses the issue of a possible breakup of the GATT-System through the proliferation of regional integration projects, only those regional trade arrangements that can in fact represent a threat to the GATT-System will be considered. One question is: *which type of trade bloc represents a potential threat to the Free Trade System?*—i.e., all of them, or only certain types? The next question is: *how many of the threatening types have the capacity to cause real harm to the GATT-System?* One type would certainly not suffice, but would two or three?

With respect to types, we may note the following:

a. For one thing, to pose a threat, a bloc must be made up of large and medium-size industrial countries. For example, if MERCOSUR (composed of Argentina, Uruguay, Paraguay, and Brazil) were to develop into an exclusionary trade bloc, it would be a nuisance, but would hardly represent a threat to the system.[7]

The ASEAN countries are taking steps in the direction of turning what used to be a regional security group into a free trade area. But when the West worries about a trade bloc forming in Asia, it is not ASEAN that concerns it but the possibility of Japan joining in an Asian trade bloc. In the present discussion, therefore, it is assumed that the member countries are medium-size industrial countries with at least one big economy (U.S., Germany, Japan).

It is true that small, less developed countries have played havoc with the world economy by coalescing in OPEC and raising oil prices ten times in five years (1970-1975). However, OPEC is not a trade bloc, but rather a "commodity bloc" that owes its relative success to the fact that oil is the single most important commodity in world trade. Fuel imports represented 20% of Japan's total imports in 1970, and 11% of all OECD imports. Commodity power was used up with oil, and today it is not likely that any other producers association, or commodity bloc, be it of bananas, coffee, tin, or oranges, could influence the world trade system in the way OPEC did.

b. Trade arrangements leading to the formation of a trade bloc must be capable of carrying out an effective and substantial discrimination against nonmember countries. A payments union, for instance, or a trade agreement that includes the Most Favored Nation clause (as do many trade pacts that the U.S. signed in the 1930s),[8] will, by virtue of the arrangements themselves, be insufficient to discriminate against third parties.[9]

The question now is whether a free trade area with no external common tariff or common commercial policy will be capable of discriminating against nonmember countries as a Single Market is empowered to do. The question arises when there exists the possibility of importing into the area through the country with the lowest tariff and circulating the imported goods freely among the member countries. To prevent this from happening, "rules of origin" and other regulations have been established.[10] Both have the capacity to discriminate, but in common markets discrimination—and therefore liberalization—can be more consistent and effective because of the common external tariff.

c. In order to be really exclusionary, the bloc would have to concentrate trade between the member countries. In the EC, as of 1989, 59.60% of exports and 58.12% of imports were intra-EC.[11] The situation in NAFTA is totally different: roughly 75% of U.S. trade is non-NAFTA trade!

U.S. Trade 1990

	Imports from	Exports to
Japan	17.82%	12.20%
EC	21.80%	28.31%
Canada	18.82%	21.82%
Mexico	5.00%	6.00%

Source: "The Economic Report of the President 1991," p. 254.

American trade flows would have to change a great deal for NAFTA to achieve a degree of intrabloc trade concentration similar to that of Europe. If the convenience of trade bloc formation were measured by the criterion of intrabloc trade concentration, it would make no difference if the United States formed a trade bloc with the EC or with Canada and Mexico!

All this begs the question of what is the minimal degree of trade concentration—the exclusion potential—for the trade bloc to become GATT-threatening. It could be assumed that a figure of 25% at the start is already enough to create severe disruptions of the trade flows with a great deal of trade-diverting effect.

d. A trade bloc must represent the outcome of purposeful political initiatives of several governments (commercial agreement; treaties with definite economic content, such as the Maastricht treaty, etc.), in their attempts to organize external trade flows in a certain patten consistent with their design of international relations.

How Many Trade Blocs Are There?

To put it briefly, at present there is only one trade bloc, the EC—which, by the way, is already creating problems for the GATT-System (for instance, in the Uruguay Round negotiations!) and producing significant effects of trade diversion in agricultural products. Only this bloc satisfies the four above criteria.

NAFTA is just now forming; it has the potential to become a trade bloc, but commercial flows between the United States, Canada, and Mexico must still grow a great deal to satisfy the concentration criterion. With time other Latin American countries may join the bloc: Chile, which already has a broad trade treaty with Mexico and does not want to join MERCOSUR; Venezuela, Colombia, and eventually the countries of MERCOSUR, although this eventuality, in view of the Brazilian situation, is still many years away.

The consolidation of NAFTA is a political problem that has to do both with the results of the Uruguay Round of negotiations and with the commercial policy of the United States. The troubles in Canadian politics, aggravated by economic recession, have reactivated the opposition to NAFTA there. It will take at least another year for NAFTA to be operative; by then, barring setbacks in the ratification of the Maastricht treaty, the European Single Market will be in full swing.

In the Pacific Rim there are schemes and moves, but little substance as yet. Japan maintains diversified trade flows with all important markets. Japan's trade, indeed, is somehow concentrated in Asia, but it is equally concentrated on the United States: Japan's exports to NAFTA represent 35% of the total, more than to the whole of Asia. For Japan it would probably be more profitable, if it were politically feasible, to go into a trade bloc with the North American countries. It is true that trade as measured by exports to Asian countries grew in the period 1984-1990, whereas exports to the United States in the same period decreased, but exports to Europe also increased. It is difficult to see some Asian NICs liberalizing their exchanges vis-à-vis Japan. Japan's surplus with Southeast Asia has jumped from U.S. $12 billion in 1986 to a massive $47 billion in 1992. The loudest complaints about Japanese exports should logically come from Asia itself.[12] In addition, many observers stress cultural barriers to a project of Asian integration, although it has also been observed that integration in Asia will proceed not by treaties as in the West, but through market forces, as is already happening.[13]

The Trade Blocs in the GATT-System

The GATT-System is basically a nondiscriminatory system of trade, which extends to all its members whatever tariff reduction or other trade concession may be agreed between any two member countries through the automatic and universal application of the Most Favored Nation clause. But the GATT allows for the formation of regional integration projects (trade areas and customs unions), which, obviously, are discriminatory by nature. Regional integration projects are contemplated in article XXIV of the Agreement. It is clear from the wording of article XXIV that both its spirit and its letter point to the instrumentality of integration, and therefore trade blocs, in promoting universal free trade: "The contracting parties recognize the desirability of increasing freedom of trade by the development, through voluntary agreements, of closer integration between the economies of the countries parties to such agreements" (article XXIV, 4). This instrumentality is stressed by the proviso that in its trade relations with third parties the regional project does not increase the level of protection that each member had individually before the integration: "[The contracting parties] also recognize that the purpose of a customs union or a free-trade area should be to facilitate trade between the constituent territories and *not to raise barriers to the trade of other contracting parties with such territories*" (emphasis added). Thus "trade blocs can be GATT-consistent," as Bhagwati puts it, "even if they may be considered threatening to GATT's basic conception of the world trading system."[14] This is a view that will be discussed later.

In principle, the common protection level of a customs union should be kept at the level that the lowest-tariff member had before joining it. But the GATT is vaguer on this point: "the duties and other regulations of commerce . . . shall not on the whole be higher or more restrictive than *the general incidence of the duties and regulations of commerce* applicable in the constituent territories prior to the formation of such unions" (emphasis added) (5a). For the free trade areas the rule is that the "duties and other regulations of commerce" are not to be "higher or more restrictive" than those previously in effect.

It is necessary to recall that GATT is itself a huge regional trade bloc of discriminatory nature, as it does not apply the Most Favored Nation clause to nonmembers. But these consist of a few trading nations of not very significant weight in world trade. Furthermore, GATT is open to new membership, so long as the applicants meet the criteria for admission, and in fact it has been inclusive rather than exclusive. It began in 1947 with 23 countries and has now been subscribed to by 108.

Certain features of GATT—that it must (a) be open to new members (i.e., inclusive rather than exclusive), (b) maintain or reduce the level of protection vis-à-vis nonmembers (not increase discrimination), (c) be committed to the gradual elimination of all kinds of protection, and (d) promote international cooperation in trade matters—are probably the four criteria that trade blocs must fulfill in order to be GATT-friendly and to lead to a free and open trade system. These four GATT-like characteristics constitute the litmus test for trade blocs.

Israel's Trade Relations

Israel is not party to any of the existing blocs, but it has free trade arrangements with the EC (since 1977), the United States (since 1985) and, since January 1, 1993, with the EFTA countries. By 1995, some 85% of all goods imported into Israel will be covered by free trade agreements. *Liberalization is thus an integral part of Israeli trade policy.* This is precisely the reason why Israel needs to have access to markets in industrial countries, in order to make liberalization possible and meaningful. Free trade agreements are an important means of obtaining this access, but they can be undermined by restrictive trade bloc policies. Israel is hardly a commercially "stranded" country, but it can also suffer from the wrong kind of trade bloc formation.

Bilateral arrangements are not without difficulties on both sides (remember the teabag dispute!). It seems that the United States has emerged as the major beneficiary of the Israel-U.S. Free Trade Agreement. From 1980 to 1984 imports from the U.S. grew by 11%, but from 1985 to 1989 they grew by 38%. In other words, the growth rate in imports from the U.S. almost tripled from the signing of the agreement. On the other hand, Israeli exports to the U.S. did not sustain the same growth rate as imports from the U.S. In fact, the growth rate in Israeli exports to the U.S., excluding diamonds, declined from 113% in 1980-1984 to 49.5% in 1985-1989.[15] In 1990-1991 imports from the U.S. grew by 19%, whereas exports to the U.S. decreased by 0.45%.[16] Because of bilateral trade disputes and the presence of asymmetries in the sharing of benefits, in most cases bilateral agreements are not good substitutes for free access to markets under the GATT-System.

In regard to a country such as Israel, Krugman's geography-based contributions to the subject warrant discussion. As the leading theorist of international trade, Krugman could not ignore the question of trade blocs. In fact, he is the first to present a formal model for making predictions about the welfare effect of the formation of trade blocs. Working with an ad hoc model, Krugman arrives at two equilibrium equations: the first states that the optimal tariff of the trade bloc is increasing in the share of the trade bloc's exports in the rest-of-the-world expenditure (with a minimum value for a share equal to zero), so that the larger the share the higher the tariff that can be charged; the second equation places the share of the bloc's exports in inverse relation to the tariff rate and the number of blocs. The interaction of the two equations simultaneously determines the bloc's tariff rate and its share of exports, given a number of trade blocs. A reduction of the number of blocs shifts the second relation up and to the right, thus increasing both the tariff rate and the bloc's share in the world exports. This result will reduce the amount of trade between any two countries that are in different blocs. The model thus "suggests that there is something in the concern of trade specialists that bilateral trade pacts may impair multilateral trade."[17]

To ascertain whether this result is good or bad for welfare, Krugman arrives at a function defining the level of world welfare in terms of the number of trade blocs. In his model world, welfare is maximized if the number of blocs, $B = 1$, that is, if the whole world constitutes a single bloc, a situation of multilateral and free trade. Given the particular form of the welfare function, *three trade blocs is the number that minimizes world welfare.*[18] If after that the number of trade blocs increases, so will the world welfare level. In this way Krugman has given formal proof of the intuitive proposition, which some free traders defend as a dogma, that a world split into three big trade blocs would be disastrous for global welfare.

Krugman qualifies this result by introducing the concept of "natural trade blocs." These result from including transportation costs (which take Samuelson's "iceberg form" $1-a$) in a context of continental trade. The extent of natural regionalism is determined by the rate of transportation costs a. If a nears unity, transportation costs make trade between blocs prohibitive. The smaller a becomes, the more "natural" regional arrangements will be. The assessment of regional trading arrangements depends on whether there is enough inherent regionalism in the structure of transportation costs.[19]

At the Jackson Hole Conference on Trade Zones, Krugman[20] returned to the subject in order to buttress the concept of natural trade blocs, already outlined in his previous paper. The gains from freeing intraregional trade will be larger, and the costs of reducing interregional[21] trade smaller, than a geography-free model suggests. The reason is that proximity has led to trade concentration, and this to forming trade blocs. In this case, bloc formation results in greater trade creation than trade diversion. Krugman's argument assumes, of course, the empirical proposition that the countries forming trade blocs had a high degree of trade concentration among themselves before setting up this arrangement.[22] Sheer geographic proximity does not warrant significant trade flows between neighbors, as has been repeatedly observed in underdeveloped countries. This is also the experience of the state of Israel.

Krugman admits that trade blocs will somehow damage the drive to improve the multilateral system that GATT has in the past helped to establish; in practice they will not be very damaging to world welfare (even if theoretically they could be nondesirable because of trade diversion), for they are and will be "natural trade blocs." Above all, the alternative to the existence of trade blocs—a further development of GATT—is so problematic and difficult to visualize that it is better to have regional free trade agreements than to have none at all. We can revert to Viner's basic intuition: economic integration schemes are theoretically "second best," but they are the only way to advance toward free trade in an increasingly complex world.

The existence of "natural trade blocs" in all areas of the world becomes doubtful if we consider both the lack of correlation between geographical proximity and trade concentration in certain areas and the degree of trade concentration among some distant countries. Consider South Korea, Taiwan, and the other "tigers": their trade with far-off America and Europe is more significant than that with neighboring countries. *This is also the case for Israel.*

Some Conclusions

Not much more can be said on an analytical, a priori level about the desirability or otherwise of trade blocs. Whether the enlarged EC, NAFTA, the Asiatic bloc, MERCOSUR, or whatever—i.e., the trade blocs already formed or in formation—will promote freer trade or bring about a more protectionist world is an empirical question whose solution is reserved for future observers.

Nevertheless, given that the energies that governments and societies devote to arranging trade matters seem to be in limited supply, we can suspect that if much of their energy is consumed in forming and administering regional groupings, there will be less energy left for multilateral, worldwide concerns. By the same token, if the big multinational firms find that their conflicting interests can be adequately balanced on a regional basis, they will not go in for multilateral negotiations, which consume a great amount of time and energy. The suspicion that on the whole the rise and consolidation of regional trade blocs will scale down the importance of a multilateral trade system as it has been known in the past is well grounded.

The question is whether there is a real alternative to bloc formation. Although economists such as Bhagwati and Bergsten, publications such as *The Economist*, and the pro-GATT lobby have suggested that the alternative (the Uruguay Round) should be fully developed, most trade practitioners and observers believe that

GATT, at best, is much slower, ineffective, and politically limited to tackling new issues and problems rather than regional trade pacts. There is always the possibility that people will soon become disappointed with and tired of trade blocs, as they have become of GATT, because of the difficulty in reconciling an increasing number of powerful opposing interests in the international trade arena. Nevertheless, they deserve to be given a chance.

Attention should be paid to those countries that, for whatever reason, will remain outside trade blocs and may be cut off from major world markets. They are likely to be emerging countries and/or export sectors of developing countries striving to achieve better standards of living through trade, as the developed countries have taught them to do. It is somehow ironic that at a time when developing nations have finally been convinced to take part in GATT and bring their complaints there, instead of taking them to UNCTAD or other demagogic fora in the United Nations, the developed world seems to have lost interest in GATT. Thus emerging countries that have opted for an export-led development process are the most convinced defenders of the open, multilateral trading system that GATT is supposed to promote. Defending GATT has become a concern of those who care for the well-being of the Third World.[23] For this reason, trade blocs will have to include something like a system of preferences of some kind to take into account the needs of stranded countries.

The million-dollar question is whether trade blocs will be GATT-friendly, in the sense of article XXIV, and therefore develop a cooperative strategy toward nonmembers in general and members of the other blocs in particular, or rather trade-war-friendly with noncooperative behavior. Here it will be appropriate to spell out the conditions that determine the path to cooperation and the path to confrontation, respectively, and finally to take another look at empirical studies and evaluations about the observed behavior of the main agents.

The Path to Cooperation

There are three scenarios to be considered, according to the number of consolidated trade blocs in the world: (1) one in which there are only two trade blocs, the enlarged EC and NAFTA, but no Asiatic bloc; (2) one in which there are three trade blocs, the EC, NAFTA, and an Asiatic bloc in which Japan has the leading role; and (3) one in which there are more than three trade blocs. It is difficult to see how any trade bloc in which none of the trade giants, the United States, Germany, and Japan, is present can have a significant impact on the world trade system. In terms of evaluating the impact of alternative strategies on world welfare, the third scenario would be equivalent to the second. On the other hand, in the first scenario an understanding between Europe and America could easily result in some sort of alliance against Japan. Europe and America would cooperate against Japan to open up the Japanese market to their exports, but Japan would be pushed into forming an Asiatic or Pacific (with Australia and New Zealand) bloc, thus developing a tripolar world. In fact, only a tripolar world will be stable in a system of trade blocs. For if the two trade blocs, the European Single Market and NAFTA, fight against each other, each of them will seek the support of Japan against the other, and if Japan aligns itself with any of the blocs, the confrontation will be extended to the whole world. It seems plausible that only the second scenario (or, by equivalence, the third) would be stable, as it alone will offer a system of trilateral checks and balances to prevent worldwide confrontation. Accordingly, there can be a meaningful discussion about cooperation only if it is assumed that there are three trade blocs, corresponding to the trade hegemony of the Triad.[24]

For the trade blocs to be cooperative, it will be necessary that they jointly agree to:

- Be open, in the sense that the admission of new members is not excluded and is in fact practiced when the requisites for admission are fulfilled. For the 12-member EC, the test would be the admission of willing EFTA members, East European countries, and eventually Turkey, Malta, Cyprus, and so on. For NAFTA, it would be the incorporation of Chile, Venezuela, Central America, and so on.
- Unify external tariff levels in a common external tariff, thus turning free trade areas into true Common Markets, which do not increase the average level of previous protection.
- Gradually reduce the existing levels of protection through both tariffs and nontariff barriers vis-à-vis nonmember countries, "external liberalization," and joint discussions and negotiations to that end.
- Take responsibility for the further development and institutional transformation of GATT, and for the eventual resuscitation of the stillborn International Trade Office,[25] as a forum for discussing and solving multilateral—and interbloc—issues and conflicts.
- Avoid the use of commercial arrangements as substitutes for internal adjustments in declining industries.
- Have concern for the special needs of the export-led development strategies of emerging countries. A generous revision of the Multifibre Agreements will set a good example.
- Promote cross-bloc direct investments in manufacturing and services, and protect the results of such endeavors, as knowledge-intensive products (software), patents and royalties, copyrights, and so on.

- Refrain from using "rules of origin" legislation to discriminate against foreign producers within the bloc; and accord them the treatment of "national industry."

As a result of such cooperation, a situation can be envisaged in which free trade, flowing from the big pools of regionally integrated markets, will end up by encompassing the whole world with its beneficial influences.

The Path to Confrontation

The way to confrontation, with trade blocs or without, will start with the failure of the Uruguay Round, which will deal GATT a severe blow. From then on GATT could well enter a process of losing credibility that would leave the world economy without a mechanism—however imperfect—for settling trade disputes, and international trade could become an activity subject to no agreed rules (legality), but to the law of the strongest contenders (bilateral reciprocity). In theory the failure of the Uruguay Round should not have these adverse effects, but the probability that the United States will continue its past support to GATT after a failure of the Uruguay Round is very slim. If the Round fails, Lester Thurow can be proved to be right.

Let us assume, however, that the Uruguay Round registers a moderate success, enough to keep GATT going. Even in this case, the formation of trade blocs will lead to confrontation, increased protectionism, trade wars, and the eventual reduction of international trade, if all or any of the blocs:

- lose interest in the multilateral process of negotiation and problem solving
- become a closed arrangement that systematically excludes would-be candidates
- maintain or increase the average level of protection against nonmembers
- resort to bilateral reciprocity for the granting of trade concessions
- impose unilaterally countervailing duties or other retaliatory measures and resort to bilateral threats
- restrict direct investments in specific areas
- discriminate against foreign producers within the bloc
- impede the political process whereby the executive branch can quickly and effectively negotiate trade arrangements (the "fast track" procedure) in the United States

The European Record

How the trade blocs will behave remains to be seen, once they come to full operation. Meanwhile some hypotheses can be formulated from the experience accumulated by the first, and so far only, functioning trade bloc, the European Community. According to most authors cited in this chapter, Europe's international behavior in regard to agriculture is the supreme example of a commercial policy that will turn trade blocs into an utter disaster. Some 80% of GATT actions initiated by the United States against the EC have affected agriculture and fisheries, and the great majority of actions were triggered by nontariff barriers and subsidies.[26]

The question for Europe-watchers is whether the political economy criteria that led to the Common Agricultural Policy are still the relevant ones on every other trade issue, or if they are instead confined to the agricultural sector as a vital and strategic field.[27] That would be better; but even if it were the case, there is always the suspicion that such "vital and strategic" fields could pop up every time that there are important industrial issues at stake such as, say, commercial airplanes or high-definition television.

Furthermore, if these special issues arise, will they be dealt with in the same way as agriculture? If the answer were affirmative, further European integration would actualize the worst fears of the international community. For the sake of the tranquillity of the world, Europe has to assert that agriculture is indeed a special case that will not be repeated in the future. By the same token, every concession on agriculture the Community makes in the current trade negotiations will contribute toward dispelling the mistrust of outsiders toward the European Single Market, as much as every refusal to make progress on the subsidies question accumulates prejudice against it.

The Community economists have taken great pains to show that the European Single Market is meant to be liberal with nonmembers, that external liberalization has made great strides, that agricultural policy is indeed an oddity in the EC commercial policy, and that further progress in integration will not mean greater protectionism (in the spirit of GATT's article XXIV). Winters, for instance, has shown that the two stumbling blocks of EC external trade—agriculture and anti-dumping policy—have not worsened because of the measures leading to the completion of the Single Market.[28] Neven and Röller have found that, for industrial products, the elimination of intra-EC barriers should increase extra-EC imports more than intra-EC imports.[29] And not only Europeans have stressed positive facts; basing his figures on Emerson's calculations,[30] an American, Hufbauer, estimates that "Europe-1992" (as it was then called) will generate a \$6.4 billion increase in U.S. exports.[31]

Nowadays, high technology has appeared as another field that raises doubts about the ability of the Single Market to liberalize the European trade bloc. The Americans usually mention different protectionist practices, such as: resisting common international technical standards; refusing admission of foreign firms into European consortia; favoring European firms in public procurement of high-technology products; subsidizing high-technology production, as it is practiced on a great scale with Airbus; and tolerating anticompetitive behavior within the EC market in order to promote the extra-EC capacity to compete.[32] This may be an American vision of things, more or less founded on reality, but unless it is somehow mitigated or changed, cooperation between the two trade blocs and with many other nonbloc countries will be very difficult. With respect both to agriculture and high-technology products, European declarations of practicing an open, liberal trade policy are not quite credible in the world at large.

The lack of interest in the current GATT negotiations is something that troubles the pro-GATT lobby. At the meeting of Community chiefs of government in Edinburgh in December 1992, "the 12 leaders ignored GATT" according to *The Economist*.[33] At the meeting, the agreement with the Americans to reduce the EC's subsidized farm exports and oilseed output in particular provoked severe tensions between the British and the French and was left to further discussions in order to reach "global and balanced agreement," as the French desire.

The American Record

As far as NAFTA is concerned, there are also many worries among Europeans, Japanese, and the Americans themselves. As Krueger, a champion of free trade, has put it:

> The regional integration move contrasts with increasing protection through administered measures on a global scale. That explanation is certainly in line with other U.S. trade policy actions, including the negotiation of bilateral voluntary export restraints, intellectual property concerns, threats of "super-301" penalties, and insistence on bilateral bargaining for telecommunications. All of these measures contribute to the weakening of the GATT system. . . . It seems clear that the U.S. self-interest lies not in an exclusive trade bloc, but rather in an open multilateral system. Why, then, do so many U.S. policies seem to conduce toward bilateral rather than multilateral arrangements? The answer can only be that the special interests seeking protection have "captured" trade policy and moved it away from the domain of the public good.[34]

Those acquainted with the politics of international trade in America[35] have shown that the evolution of the political process through which trade policy is shaped moved in the 1980s away from free and multilateral trade toward protectionism and bilateralism. By increasing its involvement in international trade matters, the U.S. Congress has made itself more accessible and more sensitive to the lobby of special groups (steel, sugar, semiconductors, textiles and apparel, farm products, etc.). Congressional power has succeeded in forcing the executive branch to violate provisions of GATT through amendments to trade acts, defining U.S. standards and procedures in the application of tariffs and other trade restrictions in terms that are inconsistent with GATT,[36] among them, for instance, the application of the "escape clause" allowed for in GATT. The escape clause applies to those domestic producers who are suffering "serious injury" as a result of trade concessions and unforeseen events. The legislative process has come to interpret injury as including unemployment, idling factories, and growing inventories (the sign of intense competition), and in recent times "significant" has replaced "serious." A similar process of enlarging the scope for application of antidumping provisions, penalties against the use of subsidies, and the use of bilateral threats has taken place in the United States. All these developments make any impartial onlooker wonder "how much evidence existed to support the widespread U.S. perception that the country's policy still stood for non-discrimination and lowered trade barriers. At that point the exceptions seem to have gained an importance equal to the avowed principles."[37]

Throughout this period, however, both Presidents Reagan and Bush continued to declare that the preservation and strengthening of GATT was a top American priority. In his 1991 Economic Report, Bush told Congress: "My administration's top trade policy priority continues to be the successful completion of the Uruguay Round negotiations of the General Agreement on Tariffs and Trade";[38] he added in the next paragraph: "my administration has moved to pave the way toward a hemispheric zone of free trade. We have announced our intention to begin negotiations on a free-trade agreement with Mexico," which he completed a year later. It is quite obvious that the Council of Economic Advisers does not see any contradiction between "strengthening the GATT" and "paving the way to regional free trade agreements." Perhaps it is easier than economists believe.

News of fresh restrictions imposed by the United States on two varieties of steel imports, severely damaging EC interests, cast a new shadow over the GATT negotiations.[39] The EC, already undergoing a severe crisis in the steel sector and having promulgated a restructuring plan, could not take the new American move passively, and retaliation is certain. If this is an example of the "defensive trade and domestic policy" that Laura D'Andrea Tysson, the head of the Council of

Economic Advisers, advocated,[40] and "toughness" in trade relations is to characterize President Clinton's commercial policy, then there is no doubt that the two blocs are moving away from an agreement within the framework of GATT, and the world is heading for a reduction in trade.

Overall it would seem that the trade bloc system, as it is taking shape before our eyes, *has a slightly greater tendency to confrontation than to cooperation.* The survival of the GATT, and its strengthening, could be a guarantee for cooperation. But with GATT or without it, the governments of the countries entering into trade blocs must be aware of the dangers they face, for themselves and for the world economy. With this awareness and a great deal of prudence the dangers can be avoided, but it will require a clear vision of the forces that shape trade policy and the political will to resist the pressures of special interest groups, which are bent on optimizing their own advantages without any regard to the common efforts to maintain an open, nondiscriminatory, multilateral trading system.

A Strategy for Stranded Countries: Polilateralism

Israel is not an underdeveloped nor a "stranded" country, but being small it needs to maintain its export markets for economic survival. An open trading system as promoted by GATT would offer the best economic environment for further development of its export sector. What will Israel be able to do, however, if worse comes to worst and the big industrial countries practically restrict their markets to bloc members? I would suggest two different approaches, which are somewhat obvious. First, Israel must find new markets in nonbloc countries, particularly in Asia, South America, and Africa, by taking advantage of its developments in intermediate technology that could prove most appropriate for those countries. Second, Israel should reinforce the bilateral agreements that it has signed with trade blocs and single countries, and negotiate new ones with future blocs. We cannot assume that the blocs will be so locked into themselves as to invalidate existing bilateral trade arrangements and/or exclude advantageous new ones. I have coined the term polilateralism to describe precisely Israel's trade policy of having *many bilateral trade agreements with a variety of key countries*. Thus it seems that through its polilateralism Israel is preparing itself, in trade relations as in other fields, for the worst possible case.

Notes

1. This chapter was completed on February 29, 1993.

2. Its formation has not gone without protests; see "China Condemns NAFTA as a Threat to Global Trade," *Financial Times*, February 2, 1993, p. 5.

3. *The Economist*, December 26, 1992, pp. 86, 88.

4. R. Lawrence, "The Emerging Regional Arrangements: Building Block or Stumbling Block?" in R. O'Brien, ed., *Finance and the International Economy* (London: Oxford University Press, 1991).

5. Lester Thurow uses the term "quasi-trading blocs," because trading blocs are for him the economic-political-military arrangements imposed by the big powers in the imperialistic past: the British Empire, La Union Francaise, the Co-prosperity Sphere of Japan, Das Dritte Reich, the Monroe Doctrine (?) (*Head to Head: The Coming Economic Battle Among Japan, Europe and America*, New York: William Morrow, 1992).

6. J. Frankel, "Is Japan Creating a Yen Bloc in the East Asia and Pacific?," National Bureau of Economic Research, Working Paper no. 4050, Cambridge, Massachusetts, 1992.

7. MERCOSUR embraces a population of 190 million with a gross domestic product of 427 million, but the intrabloc trade is only 4.9 billion, which is a small fraction of the total. This arrangement can hardly be compared to the disruptive potential of the EC, NAFTA, or a possible Asiatic bloc. See "The New World's Newest Trade Bloc," *International Business Week*, May 4, 1992, pp. 16-17.

8. A. Tovias, "Trade Discrimination in the Thirties and Eighties," *The World Economy* 4 (1988): 501-514.

9. A country determined to discriminate against other countries can do so without any international legal instrument. It can be done by the sovereign will of the government. We refer here to actions or results obtained by the normal functioning of the trade arrangements.

10. But if these rules are somehow circumvented, the discrimination will be at the lowest tariff rate existing in the FTA, and it could happen that, in a world of generally low tariffs, the lowest tariff of the FTA would not be very substantial. This leads to the lesser-evil argument that, if the blocs take the form of FTAs in the strict sense and set up an external tariff at the level of the lowest rate existing in the area, the welfare lost will be substantially less than if the bloc takes the form of a Common Market. But, as we shall see later, FTAs could be worse than Common Markets.

11. EUROSTAT, *Estadísticas Básicas de la Comunidad*, 27a ed. (Luxembourg, 1990), p. 32.

12. "Japan's Trade Surplus Returns to Haunt It," *The Economist*, January 30, 1993, p. 66.

13. "Will Japan Rule a New Trade Bloc?," *Fortune*, October 5, 1992, pp. 47-48.

14. J. Bhagwati, *The World Trading System at Risk* (London: Harvester & Wheatsheaf, 1991), p. 58.

15. "US-Israel Trade Remains Far From Free," *Journal of Commerce*, November 19, 1990, p. 4A.

16. IMF, *Direction of Trade Statistics Yearbook 1992* (Washington, D.C., 1992), p. 233.

17. P. Krugman, "Is Bilateralism Bad?," in E. Helpman and A. Razin, eds., *International Trade and Trade Policy* (London: MIT Press, 1991), pp. 9-23, at p. 18.

18. Ibid., p. 21.

19. "If trade arrangements follow the lines of natural trading regions, they will have a much better chance of improving welfare than trade arrangements between 'unnatural' partners" (ibid.,

p. 22).

20. P. Krugman, "The Move Toward Free Trade Zones," *Federal Reserve Bank of Kansas Economic Review*, November/December 1991.

21. Krugman is talking about a region with many independent countries, such as Western Europe or North America.

22. Alternatively, it could be said that this normally applies to advanced, industrial countries.

23. L. de Sebastián, *Mundo Rici, Mundo Probe* (Santander: Sal Terrae, 1992), p. 63.

24. F. C. Bergsten, "The World Economy After the Cold War," *Foreign Affairs*, Summer 1990.

25. Although one must remember the Latin dictum "entia non sunt multiplicanda sine necessitate" (entities must not be multiplied without a good cause).

26. G. C. Hufbauer, ed., *Europe 1992: An American Perspective* (Washington, D.C.: Brookings Institution, 1990), p. 29.

27. For the United States, agriculture was also a special case left out of the original GATT negotiations.

28. L. A. Winters, "The Welfare and Policy Implications of the International Trade Consequences of 1992," *American Economic Review* 82 (May 1992): 107.

29. D. Neven and L. Röller, "European Integration and Trade Flows," CEPR Discussion Paper no. 367, London, 1990.

30. M. Emerson et al., "The Economics of 1992: An Assessment of the Potential Economic Effects of Completing the Internal Market of the European Economy," *European Economy* (Luxembourg) 35; M. Emerson and D. Alii, "The Economics of 1992," *European Economy* (Luxembourg) 35.

31. Hufbauer, *Europe 1992*.

32. Ibid., p. 31.

33. "The European Community: A Rough Year," *The Economist*, December 9, 1992, p. 19.

34. A. O. Krueger, "Government, Trade, and Economic Integration," *American Economic Review: Papers and Proceedings*, May 1992, pp. 109-114, at pp. 113-114.

35. R. Vernon and D. Spar, *Beyond Globalism: Remaking American Foreign Economic Policy* (London: Free Press/Collier-Macmillan, 1989); R. Gilpin, *The Political Economy of International Relations* (Princeton: Princeton University Press, 1987).

36. Vernon and Spar, *Beyond Globalism*, p. 59.

37. Ibid., p. 67.

38. EROP, 1991, p. 7.

39. "Estados Unidos impone nuevas sanciones arancelarias al acero procedente de Europa," *El Pais*, 28 de enero, 1993, p. 47.

40. L. D. Tysson, *Who's Bashing Whom? Trade Conflict in High Technology* (Institute for International Economics, 1992).

Chapter 9

Europe and Israel: The Effects of EMU on Development and Growth

ELISE S. BREZIS

Introduction

The decision to set up a monetary union in Europe was adopted at a time when the main target of economic policy was to keep inflation at a low level. The exchange-rate mechanism (ERM) led to a reduction in the inflation rate of the EC countries and to a convergence of the inflation rates with the German one. The European Monetary Union (EMU) was perceived as a natural continuation of the ERM agreement by "tying one's hand" into a single currency. It was an elaboration of a system adapted to fight a problem that was already passé; the problem we face today is no longer inflation, but the long-term growth of countries. The long-term effects of EMU on development and growth were not an aspect of the debate during the deliberations on the Maastricht treaty. The economic debate focused on the monetary and financial aspects of the economy. However, there is no dichotomy between the monetary side and the real side of the economy; a common currency will affect the rate of growth of nations. The passage from national currencies to a single currency can affect investment, the technology level, and the localization of new firms. The purpose of this chapter is to analyze the effects of EMU on the real side of the economy. The focus will be on European countries as well as on small countries trading with Europe.

The chapter first analyzes the implications of a monetary union for the European countries, and shows that a monetary union will affect the specialization of countries. It will also affect the technology race. All these effects lead to higher productivity and growth. The second part of the chapter analyzes the effects of European concentration on countries trading with Europe. The focus is only on small countries in the vicinity of Europe that have a high ratio of human capital to labor. Israel is a perfect example of such a country since its human capital is very high (see Table 1; years of schooling is a proxy for the stock of human capital). An important point is that in order to gain from the European Union, Israel should adopt policies that reduce the barriers with Europe.The economic implications of a political union are then examined, in light of the fact that the Maastricht treaty does not refer only to a monetary union but also to a political agenda.

Table 1
Average Years of Schooling in the Labor Force: Selected Countries

	1970	1985
Israel	6.2	10.1
Algeria	1.7	4.7
Egypt	5.7	
Morocco	1.2	3.5
Tunisia	2.0	5.7
Syria	3.1	6.6
Jordan	2.9	7.4
Malta		6.8
Turkey	2.7	6.3
Switzerland		7.3
Sweden	6.6	9.6
Austria		8.5
Belgium	8.1	9.3
France	8.6	9.6
Germany	9.1	10.3
Greece	6.3	8.4
Ireland	6.2	8.8
Italy	6.6	9.1
Luxembourg	4.5	6.9
Netherlands		9.5
Portugal	3.9	6.5
Spain	4.1	9.6
U.K	7.0	8.5
Denmark	6.5	6.9
Japan	7.2	9.5
U.S.	9.8	12.0

Sources: UNESCO; G. Kyriacou, "Level and Growth Effects of Human Capital," New York University, 1991 (mimeo).

Effects of EMU on the Growth of European Countries

From the creation of the ERM in 1979 until last year, the volatility of intra-European exchange rates has significantly diminished, but not disappeared; a monetary union should lead to a complete removal of this volatility. The disappearance of the exchange rate risk has numerous effects on the economy—specifically, on the cost of capital; productivity and competition; competition and technology; and on localization and specialization.

The Cost of Capital

The cost of capital faced by firms includes two components: the risk idiosyncratic to the firm as well as the return on the market portfolio. Firms trading internationally add to their risk, which is specific to their sector, the risk premium being related to exchange-rate movements. Under a monetary union, the risk premium disappears and therefore the cost of capital decreases.

The second component in the cost of capital is the return on the market portfolio. The unification of currencies results in a complete unification of capital markets. The appropriate market portfolio faced by companies will no longer be the home-country market portfolio but the European market one. Since a risk that is systemic in the context of the home country may well be diversified in the context of a European portfolio, the risk related to the market portfolio is therefore reduced. This greater portfolio diversification reduces the cost of capital. A reduction in the cost of capital faced by firms leads to more investment, a higher stock of capital, and therefore to a higher rate of growth of the European countries.

Nevertheless, investment and the stock of capital do not have the principal role as the "motor" for growth and economic development. Abramovitz, Solow,[1] and the new-growth economists have pointed out that only a small fraction of per capita growth was associated with an increase in the ratio of capital to labor. The main and central factor of growth is, in fact, an increase in productivity, also called total factor productivity.

Productivity and Competition

The single market has reduced the barriers that existed between European countries, which has resulted in increased competition between firms all over Europe. The monetary union is a continuation on the same path: a disappearance of the volatility of exchange rates between European countries leads to increased competition. Indeed, projects with large up-front and irreversible investments are very sensitive to risk; when the risk is reduced, firms do invest. The extrasensitivity to risk of firms with start-up costs is attributable to the fact that even when a project is profitable, i.e., with a positive Net Present Value (NPV), firms might, instead of investing immediately, decide to wait a while in order to get additional information on the elements affecting their decision. Thus, a reduction of risk due to a monetary union will promote cross-border investments and therefore cross-border competition.

Competition triggers development and productivity since it forces firms to improve, and to become more efficient. Porter emphasizes that through domestic rivalry, companies progress and increase their productivity:

> Among the strongest empirical findings from our research is the association between vigorous domestic rivalry and the creation and persistence of competitive advantage in an industry.... In global competition, successful firms compete vigorously at home and pressure each other to improve and innovate.... Rivalry has a direct role in stimulating improvement and innovation.[2]

A monetary union that ends up increasing competition can therefore lead to higher efficiency and productivity. This is not the only side effect of increased competition on productivity; competition can also affect the technology race and the adoption of new innovations.

Competition and Technology

We saw that EMU will lead to competition and to higher productivity. Technological progress may also affect productivity in two different ways: firms may adopt new and more efficient technologies, or firms may retain the same technology but, through learning-by-doing or through spillover effects from other sectors, the productivity may increase. Empirical research has shown that these effects are significant in the increase of total factor productivity.

The reduction of barriers in Europe means that know-how will circulate more rapidly between firms; there will be an increase in the general level of "knowledge." These positive spillover effects will result in an increase in the rate of growth of the European economies.

When firms adopt new technologies, the effect of competition on productivity is ambiguous. On the one hand, firms will try to innovate in order to gain the market; on the other, the product developed can become obsolete more rapidly when the rate of innovation increases. Therefore, prospects of competition can deter present research by threatening its outcome with rapid obsolescence. Decreasing monopoly power, i.e., increasing competition, decreases the amount of research in the steady state. The implications of EMU for the rate of technological progress are therefore unclear.

Concerning technical progress, even if the rate of innovation falls, it does not mean that a reduction in welfare will occur. Innovation creates gains but also losses by rendering obsolete old skills, goods, and manufacturing processes. It may be that the rapidity of obsolescence of techniques nowadays is already too high, that is, that the rate of innovation is already higher than the social optimum. It will be a Pareto improvement to reduce the rapidity in the adoption of new technologies. An increase in competition could then just do that, and therefore increase welfare.

Thus, the European Monetary Union could have wide effects on the real side of the economy—on the level of investment, the efficiency of the economy, and the technology race. The monetary union can also affect the geographic distribution of firms.

Localization and Specialization

International trade theories have stressed three reasons why countries and regions gain from being specialized in their production. First, by concentrating firms of the same sector in one place, it allows a formation of a pooled market with specialized skills. Second, an industrial center attracts the establishment of intermediate inputs linked to their production. Finally, because information flows more easily at the same location, concentration generates technological spillover.[3]

Since production displays economies of scale and spillover effects, firms from the same sector gain from being located in the same region; production should therefore be concentrated in one location. However, Europe is less specialized than the United States. From the size and the population of both, "one might expect that the degree of economic differentiation among U.S. regions and that among European nations might be roughly similar."[4] Yet they are not: the U.S. has a greater regional difference in production and has an industry that is far more localized. In Europe, barriers of tariffs, language, and cultural differences partly account for the lack of specialization. Another barrier is that each country in Europe has its own currency.

Indeed, because of exchange rate risks, firms have diversified their localization and do not concentrate production in one country. It must be recalled that foreign risk management has real effects on the allocation of capital and production despite the sophisticated financial development as future, forward, and options. A firm facing transaction exposure can hedge it; however, real operating transaction exposure cannot be hedged. The firm is left with the decision about the location of its plant. Long-term decisions cannot always be completely free of foreign risk exposure. The best example is the case of Japanese car producers who, while the dollar depreciated rapidly, preferred to reduce their risk by locating near the market, and started production in the United States.

The optimal localization of firms in a specific sector is therefore a resultant of two forces. On the one hand, increasing returns lead to localization of production in a single place. On the other, when facing multiple currencies, firms do not cluster in one location but diversify.

The consequence of a single currency is the disappearance of the need to diversify, which will eventually lead to specialization. This may be illustrated with a simple numerical example of how the European Monetary Union will remove one of these costs and lead to greater specialization.

Certain industries can locate either in Italy or Germany. In order to benefit from economies of scale, manufacturers prefer to produce in a single location. The simplest way to model increasing returns is in situations where there are high fixed setup costs (and constant marginal costs). For various historical reasons the production costs (including the fixed costs) are lower in Italy for the ceramic tiles industry, whereas chemical industries have lower production costs in Germany. We assume that computer software industries have the same fixed costs in both countries since they were started in the same way. Table 2 offers such an example. If firms are not localized in the same country, they do not enjoy the spillover effects of being clustered; therefore production costs are higher when production takes place in both countries.

Table 2
Industrial Location due to EMU

Localization of production	Production costs			Transaction cost (including exchange rate exposure)	
	Ceramic	Chemicals	Computers	Before EMU	After EMU
Italy only	6	10	5	10	3
Germany only	10	6	5	10	3
In both countries	12	12	8	0	0

In addition to production costs, firms face costs of exposure to exchange rate risks. To simplify, we assume that demand for every good is given and equal in every country. This example shows that when an exchange rate risk exists, it is optimal to produce all the goods everywhere. This explains the small amount of country specialization.

On the other hand, when the exchange rate risk is removed because of a single currency, we see a localization of production: Italy producing ceramic tiles and Germany chemical goods. In this example computer software is still produced in both countries. Concentration is increasing total factor productivity. However, it must be stressed that this effect depends crucially on some degree of economies of scale. The existence of economies of scale means that a large center of production is more efficient than a small one. This process of concentration, which will occur as a consequence of the adoption of a single currency, therefore enhances growth.

Overall, then, the removal of trade barriers between countries profoundly affects the economy. A monetary union leads to a removal of one more barrier: the use of national currencies. The use of a single currency will affect the pattern of trade, and allocation of capital will become efficient. Furthermore, there will be a process of concentration and the rate of innovation might decrease. The next section analyzes the implications of these effects for the economy of countries outside the EC.

Effects of EMU on the Rest of the World

A monetary union will promote growth in Europe by increasing the efficiency of factor of production and creating a lower cost of capital. During the period of adjustment to the new steady-state levels, it is quite foreseeable that Europe will attract foreign capital and that there will be greater inflows of capital into Europe. For given worldwide savings, this could be harmful to the less developed countries. However, this effect is only a consequence of a partial equilibrium, and should not be exaggerated. The growth of Europe will increase total savings and also its imports from the rest of the world. This will balance out the negative effects of the single market. Indeed, Neven shows that the consequences of the single market might be negative for the world, since the terms of trade will be affected and world exports reduced through trade diversion. A growing Europe will increase its imports and induce output growth to the rest of the world through an increase in demand.[5]

Two major consequences of EMU will be the phenomenon of concentration and the change in the rate of technological innovation. Let us turn now to the effects of these on the rest of the world.

Technology and Productivity

We have considered the implications of EMU for technology. On the one hand, more competition could lead to smaller monopoly power, so that firms would invest less in R&D and the rate of innovation might decline. On the other, greater spillover effects between firms could lead to technological improvements and to a higher total factor productivity.

As for EMU's effects on the rest of the world, a greater diffusion of knowledge in the European Community will, through transfers of technology and imitation, increase the productivity of other countries.

Specialization and Localization

In the preceding section it was shown that the removal of exchange rate risks will induce a process of specialization between countries inside EMU. This process will enhance growth, especially in the sectors of goods exhibiting economies of scale and based on human capital. How will this process affect countries outside of Europe? Here we shall focus on countries that have the human capital required to develop and to produce goods exhibiting spillover effects; among countries surrounding the European Union, Israel will serve as a good example. Compared to other countries, especially those in the Mediterranean area, it has a high level of human capital (see Table 1).Moreover, the costs of producing high-tech goods are lower than in Europe because wages of skilled workers are lower. On the other hand, an industrial center for high-tech goods already exists in Israel.

For a country such as Israel, the process of specialization due to the monetary union could mean that if the barriers of trade with Europe, and more specifically exchange rate risks, are not too high, then Israel could become one of the poles of specialization.

A numerical example will illustrate this point. In Table 3 we begin with our previous example, and add data on Israel. As noted, Israel already has an industrial center for high-tech goods in general, and for computer software in particular. It is assumed that production costs in Israel are lower than in Europe since wages are lower (though the technical spillover is not less than in Europe).

Table 3
Industrial Location due to EMU (2nd case)

Localization of production	Production costs Ceramic	Chemicals	Computers	Transaction cost (including exchange rate exposure) Before EMU	After EMU
Italy only	6	10	5	10	3
Germany only	10	6	5	10	3
In both countries	12	12	8	0	0
Israel					
Producing for a small market	4	20	5		
Producing for a large market	3	20	5		

Before the process of unification, both countries, Germany and Italy, produce computer software. Because of the monetary union, exchange rate risk disappears, and the barriers to trade are reduced. Thus both countries could go on producing after EMU, or only one of them, since the gains from specialization are not high enough.[6] Israel, however, has lower costs of production that can be reduced even further, while widening its market. A possible outcome is that Israel specializes in producing computer software for Europe.

For this equilibrium to be sustained, the barriers to trade with Europe have to be low. This means that the Israeli currency should be closely pegged to the ECU; and that Israel should follow closely the European standards. It also means that government policies should not render imports and exports of services difficult. Israel might then enter the European area with its high-tech goods and services. Table 4 shows that exports of high-tech goods to Europe have already been increasing more than to the United States.

Table 4
Israeli Exports of High-Tech Industries
(index, 1985 = 100)

	1985	1986	1987	1988	1989	1990	1991
EU	100	102.5	136.3	188.8	222.3	282.4	366.1
U.S.	100	101.6	136.9	167.5	171.2	207.3	243.7

The main point of this example is that if Israel reduces its barriers costs, by linking itself to Europe, it could specialize in high-tech goods that require high levels of human capital, since in this sector it has a comparative advantage. The other point that needs clarification concerns timing. If the process of concentration is completed, and we assume that a European country (in our example Germany or Italy) is already producing computers, then the concentration benefits have already been gained. There is already an equilibrium and there is no reason for Israel to enter the market. The dynamics, then, are important. Countries such as Israel should now reduce their barriers with Europe before the process of concentration begins. Later it will be too late; even lower wages are not enough to compensate for the creation of large centers in Europe.

The Maastricht treaty involved not only a monetary union, but also some political decisions. The section that follows notes an important consequence of a political union: the technology race.

Political Union and Growth

The Maastricht treaty also carries a political message: the choice of a unified Europe. The monetary union was the easiest instrument to adopt in order to signal that political union is in fact the European goal. However, this political unification will affect the economics of the rest of the world even more than the monetary union.

The creation of a single European political entity means that there will be three blocs: NAFTA, Europe, and Japan with its Asian satellites. All sectors of the economy may be affected. Here, however, we shall focus only on the influence of this situation on the development of technologies. Nowadays, developed nations no longer struggle for power through war, but in the economic arena, and technology is the instrument of strength.

Competition could lead to duplication of research and hence to waste of resources. World cooperation in pure science and fundamental research would benefit everyone. Cooperation between blocs is particularly needed for projects that require huge fixed costs of research and development. If, for reasons of prestige and power, the three blocs were to fail to coordinate their R&D policy, the waste of resources could be tremendous. One could imagine, for instance, that both Europe and the United States would develop a superplane and, for purposes of industrial strategy or prestige, each would finance separate projects!

The three blocs, and particularly Europe, should realize that the balance of power does not lead to control of R&D as a crucial variable in the struggle for power. R&D policies should not become the pursuit of political aims by other means. Europe, as a political power, should weigh its policy carefully, since the economic consequences can go far beyond the monetary union itself.

Conclusion

This chapter has looked at some of the implications of a monetary union for the development of countries. For now EMU seems far away, but the process of unification of Europe seems inevitable, whatever form it will take. During the time needed to achieve unification and reallocation of resources, outside countries should strive to make the right moves. When Europe completes its process of restructuration, it will be more difficult for countries to overcome the new sectorization and productivity of Europe. To use a metaphor, it is possible to become a satellite of Europe when the mass of Europe is not yet in high density; this equilibrium is stable. However, if Europe already has a huge mass, then satellites are not viable as such.

Notes

1. M. Abramovitz, "Resource and Output Trends in the United States Since 1870," *American Economic Review* 46 (1956): 5-23; R. Solow, "A Contribution to the Theory of Economic Growth," *Quarterly Journal of Economics* (1956): 65-94.

2. M. Porter, *The Competitive Advantage of Nations* (New York: Free Press, 1990), p. 117.

3. These three principles were already emphasized in A. Marshall, *Principles of Economics* (London: Macmillan, 1920).

4. P. Krugman, *Geography and Trade* (Cambridge: MIT Press, 1991), p. 75.

5. D. Neven, "EEC Integration Towards 1992: Some Distributional Aspects," *Economic Policy* 10 (1990).

6. We have a case of multiple equilibria. Three equilibria are possible: (1) only Italy produces computer softwares; (2) only Germany produces them; (3) both countries produce them. Since the two centers already exist, it is quite natural that they will continue to exist after EMU.

Chapter 10

Should Israel Enter the EMS?[1]

LEORA RUBIN MERIDOR

European Monetary Union (EMU) has not yet been achieved, although it seems probable that it will be finalized at some point in the future. The 1992 events have cast their shadow, and even the monetary arrangement that had prevailed for quite some time, the EMS, is now at a critical stage (particularly with respect to Italy and the United Kingdom). I will therefore not restrict this note to a specific regime, be it the current one or the future united one, but will instead focus on the major elements that already exist and will continue to exist, and touch only lightly on those elements that are specific to EMU. The purpose of this note is to try and draw conclusions, based on recent experience, regarding the monetary policy Israel should implement in view of the fact that it is so close geographically and economically to Europe.

Europe is undergoing an intense process of integration. New EC regulations have been adopted and the Community will probably be enlarged by the admission of additional countries. European unity did not begin in Maastricht; it goes back many years. Israel observed this process as an outsider but by no means ignored it. Policies in Israel were advocated and implemented that reflected the desire to be part of the process as much as possible. Trade agreements that were signed were characteristic of this approach, and in the last few years Israel has adopted a strategy of accepting many of the guidelines of the EC. For example, the reform of Israel's capital markets, and in particular the liberalization of capital flows, is consistent with the policy of the EC.[2] Such a strategy is based on the realization that although a small economy cannot play an independent role, it can adopt a policy similar to that of its large neighbor, or major trading partner. Sweden, for example, has chosen this course, and though it is not an EC member or part of the EMS its policies and its exchange rate regime in particular until recently resembled those of EMS members. When plans for greater European unity (Europe 1992) were announced, Sweden accepted the major directives even before some of the members themselves. However, as will be shown later, Sweden did not keep its fiscal fundamentals in order and was thus unable to maintain the stability of its exchange rate and its monetary policy.

Israel's approach to government debt in recent years can be regarded as consistent with the Maastricht guidelines: the debt-GDP ratio declined gradually and consistently for three years (1990-1993) and, according to the fiscal policy announced for the next three years (1993-1996), will continue on track, approaching the 60% target though not yet reaching it. There are other examples, though they will not be touched upon here since our focus is the monetary issue.

Monetary policy in a small, open economy such as Israel is closely linked to the exchange rate regime. There are two extreme options: on the one hand, an independent monetary policy with a floating exchange rate, and on the other, an exchange rate that is fixed to that of a major trading partner, automatically tying monetary policy to that of the large country; the more liberalized the capital markets the stronger this tie. Such options are of course relevant only for the short run, since in the longer run fiscal policy has to be consistent with monetary policy; otherwise the country runs into trouble such as loss of foreign reserves as in the case of Sweden. After the stabilization program of 1985 Israel tried to keep inflation low, using the exchange rate as the nominal anchor. At first the restrictions on capital flows enabled Israel to have an independent monetary policy, namely, a very tight one, but with the progress of liberalization this freedom was reduced. It was not easy to bring inflation down from the 20% level where it had hovered after the stabilization, and only recently has there been some success (in 1992 the CPI rose by only 9.4%). I would suggest, however, that had Israel been a European country and part of the EMS, it could have reached a lower inflation rate earlier. The data for such countries as Italy, the United Kingdom, or France (see Figure 1) clearly show the convergence of these countries' inflation rates with that of Germany, which is the major trading partner of each of them. The EMS, which enabled inflation in these countries to decrease, tied their monetary policy to Germany's. They could not have implemented that policy without the agreement implicit in the EMS, since they and their exchange rates lacked the requisite credibility. By tying themselves to Germany and its policy they surrendered some independence and indirectly gained credibility, which made it possible for the exchange rate to serve as a leading anchor for the price level. They also, by linking themselves to Germany, automatically accepted Germany's preferences regarding the trade-off between inflation and growth, namely, a low inflation rate, if possible zero, at the expense of low growth and even high unemployment. When things are going well

Figure 1
EMS: Consumer Prices

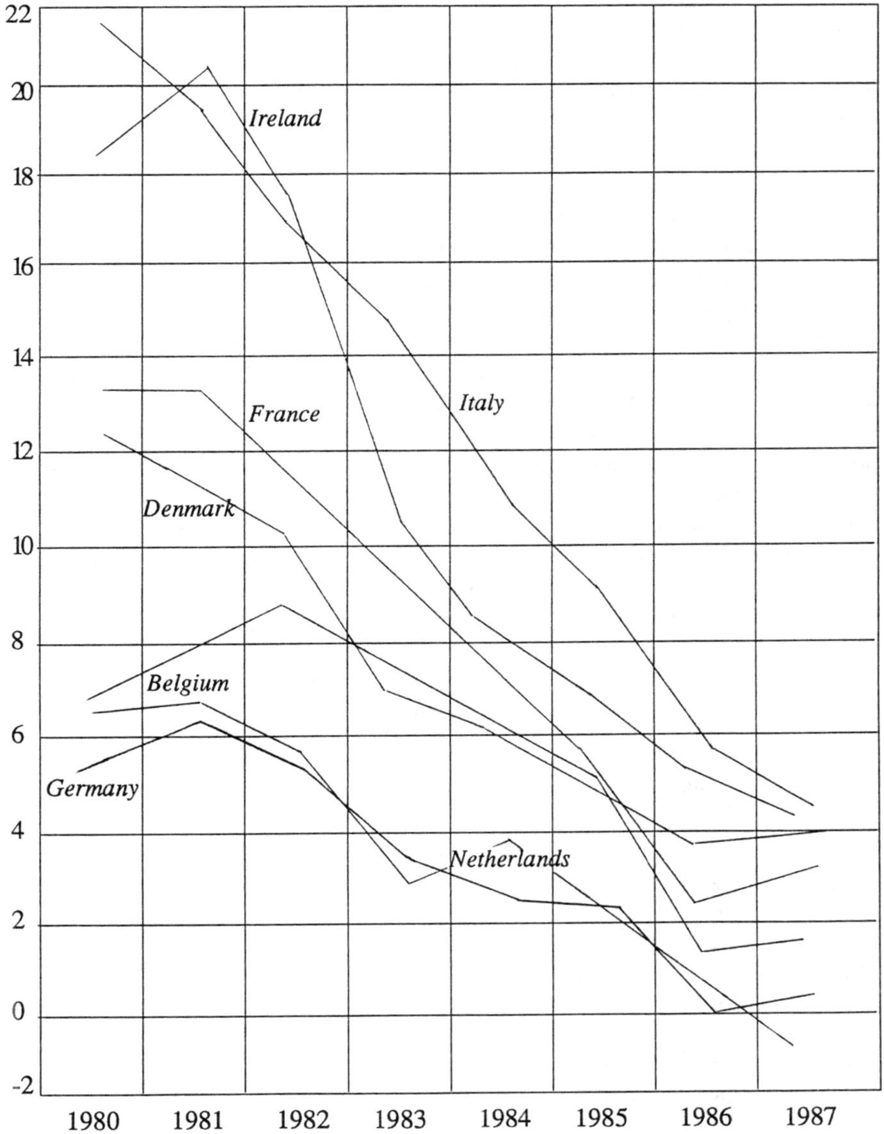

Sources: International Monetary Fund, *International Financial Statistics*, various issues.

and there are no real shocks, such a regime gives small countries many advantages. One of these is that the country is forced to carry out a proper fiscal policy. During the late 1980s, in fact, Israel sought to enact such a policy as far as possible, namely, by restricting the freedom of the monetary authorities in order to gain credibility for the exchange rate. This would have enabled the more intensive use of the exchange rate as an anchor. However, this was not feasible without joining the EMS. On the other hand, as we shall see, not being a member also had some advantages.

When there are shocks, in either the leading country or the small one, difficulties arise. The monetary policy that, after the unification of East and West Germany, was implemented as a result of the increase in government expenditures is a good example of such a shock and its implications. The increase in interest rates in Germany has pushed up interest rates in all the EC countries, thus threatening their growth and in particular hampering countries with high unemployment such as Italy and the United Kingdom. However, under the current exchange rate regime arrangement these countries have some freedom to carry out measures for reducing the damage. In the past currencies were realigned, making different inflation rates possible. In the most recent episode these countries left the exchange rate regime temporarily, enabling the exchange rate to float and the interest rate to decline. This solution would not have been possible with EMU. The underlying premise is, of course, that EMU will lead interest and inflation rates to converge with those indicated by the leader of the Union. It is still an open question whether EMU will help to strengthen Germany's lead or not.[3]

Table 1
Sweden: Some Economic Indicators

	Gov. deficit/ GNP rate	Unemployment rate	Growth rate	Interest[1] rate	Inflation rate	Exchange rate-change
1985	-3.8	2.8	2.2	13.1		4.0
1986	-1.3	2.2	2.2	10.3	4.2	8.5
1987	4.3	1.9	2.8	11.7	4.2	7.6
1988	3.5	1.6	2.3	11.4	5.8	-1.1
1989	5.6	1.4	2.3	11.2	6.4	-1.8
1990	3.9	1.5	0.4	13.1	10.5	6.8
1991	-1.5	2.7	-1.4	10.7	9.4	-0.5
1992	-7.9	4.5	-1.2	10.0	2.2	
1993*	-9.9	6.5	-1.4		3.6	
1994*	-9.8	6.8	1.3		2.2	

* Estimates.

[1]Long-term bond yield.

One possible development is that EC members would try to implement a fiscal policy different from the one prevailing in the EC on average, or, more precisely, in Germany. Table 1 presents some of Sweden's main economic variables, showing its different fiscal policy as represented by the large budget deficit. This policy could not last for long, and the huge capital outflows and the loss of reserves have forced the authorities to abandon the exchange rate regime and let it float until the fundamentals are restored.

With this in mind, let us consider a hypothetical situation in which Israel had joined the EMS in the past, thereby benefiting from some of the associated advantages, and in particular reducing inflation to European levels. Yet, with the shock of the massive immigration of Jews from the former Soviet Union, this position would have endangered Israel's ability to absorb the immigrants into its economy. To understand why this is so, some basic facts are helpful:

1. About half a million immigrants had arrived in the country by the end of 1992 (increasing Israel's population by about 10%), and another half a million may come in the near future.

2. In order to absorb the new job seekers, a massive volume of investment is needed. If no such investment occurs unemployment will soar, unless the number of jobs increases substantially. But jobs will increase only if real wages in the business sector decline drastically in the short run—something that is not feasible given the structure of Israel's labor market (namely, the strong bargaining power of the unions). Nor is this advisable, since it would reduce the welfare of the established population and harm the economy. To facilitate the desired investment process, low interest rates are needed. Moreover, the lower the interest rates in the short run, the higher potential employment and the lower the reduction in real wages.[4] Had there been a binding agreement linking Israel's monetary policy to Germany's, the reduction of interest rates would not have been possible, and the consequences would have been reflected in higher unemployment and possibly even in the failure of the absorption process itself. Israel has adhered to a monetary policy that has kept interest rates lower than the high rates in the West, thereby encouraging economic activity and investment. The result has been a 70% increase in investment during the years 1990-1992 and a 10% rise in employment. As a result, the unemployment rate has risen by only two percentage points.

To conclude, it is instructive to note the difference in the policies adopted by Germany and Israel in facing a similar shock. In both cases it was necessary to absorb additional population with insufficient productive capital.[5] Israel has not been fully successful, but by international standards it has done quite well. Table 2 shows the difference between the employment situations in the two countries and in particular the different unemployment rates. On the basis of this experience it seems reasonable to conclude that in view of the shocks a country such as Israel may undergo in the future, it is more appropriate for it to retain an independent monetary policy. It seems, then, that Israel's not being part of the EMS, let alone of EMU, has turned out to be advantageous.

Table 2
Israel and Germany: Some Comparisons

	Unemployment rate		Growth rate		Real interest rate		Inflation rate	
	I	G	I	G	I	G	I	G
1989	8.9	7.9	1.7	4.1	2.5	4.3	20.7	2.8
1990	9.6	7.2	5.4	4.9	1.9	6.2	17.6	2.7
1991	10.6	8.7	5.9	3.6	2.9	5.1	18.0	3.5
1992	11.2	9.6	6.5	1.4	2.6	5.5	9.4	4.1
1993*	10.7	10.3	3.6	1.2				
1994*	10.0	10.1	6.1	2.9				

*Estimates.

Table 3
Main Economic Indicators for Selected Countries

		1985	1986	1987	1988	1989	1990	1991
	U.K.	10.6	9.9	9.5	9.4	9.6	11.1	9.9
Interest	France	10.9	8.6	9.4	9.1	8.8	10.0	9.1
rate*	Germany	6.9	5.9	5.8	6.1	7.1	8.9	8.6
	Italy	13.0	10.5	9.7	10.2	10.7	11.5	10.1
	Spain	13.4	11.4	12.8	11.7	13.7	14.7	12.4
	Sweden	13.1	10.3	11.7	11.4	11.2	13.1	10.7
	U.K.		3.4	4.2	4.9	7.8	9.5	5.8
Inflation	France		2.5	3.3	2.7	3.5	3.4	3.1
rate	Germany		-0.1	0.2	1.3	2.8	2.7	3.5
	Italy		5.8	4.7	5.1	6.3	6.4	6.4
	Spain		8.8	5.2	4.8	6.8	6.7	5.9
	Sweden		4.2	4.2	5.8	6.4	10.5	9.4

Table 3 (cont'd.)

	U.K.	2.9	2.3	0.7	-1.2	-1.2	-0.8	0.0
Gov.	France	2.7	3.4	1.2	2.3	1.9	2.1	1.4
deficit/	Germany	1.1	0.9	1.1	1.7	0.2	1.6	2.5
GNP	Italy	15.2	12.4	11.7	11.6	11.4	11.2	10.9
rate	Spain	7.0	4.6	3.9	3.6			
	Sweden	-3.8	-1.3	4.3	3.5	5.6	3.9	-1.5
	U.K.	3.7	4.1	4.8	4.4	2.1	0.6	-2.2
Real GDP	France	1.9	2.5	2.2	4.5	4.1	2.3	1.2
rate of	Germany	2.1	2.2	1.4	3.5	4.1	4.9	3.6
change	Italy	2.7	2.8	3.1	4.1	3.1	2.0	1.6
	Spain	2.3	3.3	5.6	5.2	4.8	3.6	2.4
	Sweden	2.2	2.2	2.8	2.3	2.3	0.4	-1.4
	U.K.	11.8	11.8	10.3	8.5	7.1	6.8	8.7
Unemploy-	France	10.2	10.4	10.5	10.0	9.4	9.0	9.5
ment	Germany	9.3	9.0	8.9	8.7	7.9	7.2	
rate	Italy	9.3	10.1	10.9	11.0	10.8	10.3	9.9
	Spain	19.5	20.0	20.1	19.1	16.9	15.9	16.0
	Sweden	2.8	2.2	1.9	1.6	1.4	1.5	2.7
	U.K.	0.3	0.2	0.4	0.2	0.3	0.3	-0.1
Population	France	0.4	0.4	0.4	0.4	0.5	1.0	0.6
rate of	Germany	-0.3	0.1	0.1	0.5	0.9	2.0	1.4
change	Italy	0.2	0.2	0.2	0.2	0.1	0.2	-1.1
	Spain	0.4	0.3	0.3	0.2	0.2	0.2	0.2
	Sweden	0.1	0.1	0.5	0.5	0.6	0.8	0.9

*Long-term bond yield.

Notes

1. This chapter was written in March 1993.

2. Article 73b of the Maastricht treaty states: "all restrictions on the movements of capital between Member States and between Member States and third countries shall be prohibited."

3. It has been argued that the opposite will occur, namely, that Germany will lose some of its relative strength; but this subject will not be dealt with here.

4. One should note, however, that interest rates have to be above a critical value to ensure investment.

5. Although in Germany there was only a shortage of productive capital whereas in Israel there was also insufficient housing, the immigrants continued to arrive in Israel.

Chapter 11

The Mediterranean, Israel, and the Futures of Europe

EMILIO FONTELA

Introduction

Israel and Europe have a common future: the Mediterranean. The issues in this domain offer scope for common interest and joint actions. In the Mediterranean basin, exploring cooperation scenarios is a necessary condition for constructing a zone of prosperity. This chapter concentrates on the futures of Europe, but it also raises some Mediterranean issues and suggests some ideas for European-Israeli cooperation.

The future issues in the Mediterranean basin were studied in the Blue Plan (UNEP), in a project directed by Jacques Lesourne in 1986-1988.[1] More recently, in 1992, the French Datar has developed new scenarios that take account of developments in Eastern Europe and concentrate on the western Mediterranean.[2]

The main issues are relatively clear:

Demography: Population is growing fast in the Arab world (the Maghreb today has 56 million inhabitants, and projections are for 80 million in 2000 and 150 million in 2025). Local employment possibilities are low, and emigration is contemplated by a growing proportion of the population (Lesourne expected 25-60 million immigrants in the EC by 2025).

Food: The Arab countries of the Mediterranean have lost the possibility of food self-sufficiency, and their deficit is rapidly increasing; under the existing financial conditions (high level of indebtedness), the food deficit creates a constraint on imports of machinery and intermediate products and thus limits the possibilities of industrialization.

Environment: Population is increasingly concentrating in coastal areas, creating a growing pressure on environmental resources and in particular on the Mediterranean Sea.
Technology and capital: Because of the growing sociopolitical risks in the Arab Mediterranean countries, private transfers of technology and capital from Europe, the United States, and Japan have practically disappeared.

The implications of these situations are fairly clear: trend scenarios are conflictive and incorporate many basic problems (fundamentalism, local wars, sudden famines, etc.) in an area that is vital for Europe, and for Israel.

To understand the future of Israel and Europe in this area, one must first consider the possible future evolution of the European Union.

The Futures of Europe

The EC Toward Economic Unification

The EC is, in the context of world history, an innovation: a case in which a set of democratic countries decided to progressively adapt their institutions in order to create a harmonious system of structural relations of the type that exists within a federal state. All of the countries shared a belief in market economics, and the final element of the process is an economic good: a single common currency.

The political meaning of unification is debatable and debated, and Europe is far from consensus about it. But the economic meaning of unification is absolutely clear: a territorial entity with a single currency is economically united (and the new independent states emerging from the Soviet Union have clearly understood this fact in insisting on creating new currencies of their own). The European Economic and Monetary Union (EMU) constitutes, therefore, the final step of economic integration.

The evolution of the EC (now EU) can be characterized by three stages:

1. The Common Market, basically a customs union, an area of free trade with an external common tariff.
2. The Single Market, including some improvements on the previous stage (suppression of nontariff barriers) and some extensions (free movement of services, freedom of establishment), as well as opening of public sector practices (procurement, monopolies) and the fundamental freedom of movement of primary factors (capital, labor).

3. The Economic and Monetary Union, including some improvements on the previous stage (further mobility of primary factors, stronger competition policies), ceilings for public deficits, fixed exchange rates, followed by a single currency and a common monetary policy. In a way, EMU means a Single Economic Policy.

As shown in a previous analysis of the future of the EC,[3] EMU, the European economic unification, cannot be dissociated from a deepening of the integration process requiring also a "social Europe" (a generalization regarding all countries of welfare state attainments) and a new institutional architecture (which requires rethinking the role of the European Parliament, the Council, and the Commission and establishing some "federal" rules of the game for the political and fiscal system).

After Maastricht (i.e., the decision to move from Stage 2 to Stage 3 of the unification process), the political debate has been stimulated in all EC member countries; the idea that the path to EMU involves substantial losses of national sovereignty is spreading among the citizenships. The renewed interest in the concept of "subsidiarity" (of determining the "true" level for appropriate institutional development: what is "really" European, national, regional, or local?) is part of this evolution toward the "new architecture." The search for the right course will undoubtedly be a difficult one involving conceptual debates, national votes, changes in political balances, and so on; none of the institutional agents involved in the process will easily relinquish its current power. Furthermore, although the advantages to all parties involved in Stage 2 have been clearly proved and no doubts have been raised about them at any point in the recent past, it is also becoming increasingly clear that in Stage 3 there are both advantages and disadvantages, and that their distribution is unequal among European nations and regions.

The EC has decided to move into Stage 3 of its unification process at a period of establishment of a new international economic structure, deepening of interdependence, and economic friction: the North-South gap has widened, the socialist sphere has collapsed, and there is a need for further promotion of a free-trade structure at the world level as protectionist temptations increase everywhere. In this context, a key question for the future concerns Europe: will the unification process be a "closed" one, a process of internal deepening, or will it be "open" and involve some form of broadening or widening?

Two fundamentally different approaches to the future are possible: the normative approach, which begins with value judgments about a desirable future and works backward to focus on policy issues of the present that are clearly related to this presumably desirable course; and the exploratory approach, which begins with present trends and policy decisions and identifies their possible (or most probable) outcomes.

An analysis of the future of Europe in the normative mode clearly should begin with a desirable grand design for a sustainable world growth process, in which the role of Europe would be essential (of the three leading economic entities, the U.S., Japan, and the EC, it is the one with the strongest trade, investment, and cultural links with the South). It is evident, however, that at present European priorities are internally rather than externally oriented: a process of unification is necessarily inward looking (this does not imply protectionism, as a "fortress" is by no means a required step for unification; it simply means that world issues are usually relegated to secondary status: Rio or the Uruguay Round are certainly considered important, but less so than Maastricht).

Nevertheless, a grand design for Europe in the world is indeed required, but probably it would be best developed in the light of limitations, constraints, and unacceptable situations revealed by the exploration of existing trends and policies. Hence, this chapter relies on an exploratory approach, using two lines of reasoning that are not necessarily opposed and may indeed be complementary. The initial trends and issues are the same in both lines of exploratory thinking: a population getting older and subject to strong immigration pressures; a technology that has lost many battles with the United States and Japan in the new context of the information society. In both scenarios the EC has to find ways to reduce immigration flows and to recover technological competitiveness; at the same time it has to move toward full employment (the key social issue of the future). The initial "institutional" frameworks, however, are different: the closed process is developed in a scenario of deepening that is essentially based on the Maastricht decisions to move into Stage 3 of economic unification; the open process is developed in a scenario of broadening that takes as its main starting point the demands for further enlargement coming from EFTA and other surrounding countries.

The EC as a Closed Process: The Scenario of Deepening

Historical context. The Treaty of Rome was signed in 1958, and although it aimed at creating an Economic Union, its first practical focus was on the idea of creating a common market. There was already experience of a common market in Europe: three of the six founding members of the EC, Belgium, the Netherlands, and Luxembourg, had agreed on a customs union in 1944 and brought it into force in 1948 (the 1958 treaty establishing the Benelux Economic Union was largely a codification of agreements and protocols worked out since 1944). The theoretical economics of a customs union had also been explored considerably in practice, with generally favorable welfare results for the countries involved.

Beyond these obvious (and realistic) economic interests, however, the Six had a clear political aim: to put an end to European wars between Germany and France (there had been three in less than a century) by strengthening to an indestructible level the economic links between these nations. This political aim was progressively eroded by time, by success itself of the integration process, and by the first and the second enlargements. The unity of destiny of the Six, as perceived in the 1960s, may have justified at a certain point their final economic and political integration. This unity of destiny was less evident during the 1970s, after the entry of Great Britain, and still less during the 1980s after the entry of some countries that had largely remained outside of the Franco-German military conflicts.

Thus, by 1985, when the EC started a renewed accelerated process of integration "toward 1992," the European leaders had to find new motivations, and these were essentially economic: the welfare gains of greater integration and the expected gains in competitiveness vis-à-vis the United States and Japan. Economies of scale at all levels, including political power itself, justified an acceleration of integration. The prospect of economic gains was attractive to all economic agents—consumers expecting higher incomes, producers expecting higher profits, governments expecting more support from satisfied voters. This was, most probably, the basis for the sudden turn from "Europessimism" to "Euro-optimism." The Cecchini Report provided analytical support for the idea of economic integration.

The competitiveness argument needs competitors; these competitors were to be found in the United States and in Japan. The Fortress Europe concept (unrealistic as it is, with the EC being largely more import-intensive than either the U.S. or Japan) was an obvious outcome of this new trend.

However, the sudden, generally unexpected end of the Cold War created a new situation in the immediate context of the EC. German reunification became another factor augmenting the need for an acceleration of the integration process. Although, by the end of the 1980s, no clear timetable existed, it was natural to expect that not all the objectives of a Single Market would have been attained by 1993, and that an extension of the period of implementation as well as some consolidation (in areas such as fiscal taxation or competition regulations) could be planned for a few years to come, before tackling the final EMU project.

Maastricht, therefore, appears to be a combination of completing the Single Market *and* starting toward EMU with a set of "convergence" economic policy objectives. Time will tell whether this move was premature, but it definitely has the advantage of indicating clearly and openly, at a very early stage, the issues of Europe's long-term future. The events since September 1992 (the French vote, monetary conflicts, devaluations, diverging views on interest rates, etc.) show that the steps that lie ahead will be more difficult than expected.

Characteristics of the deepening process. The decision to speed up the European integration process, and to move already toward a common monetary policy before the end of the century, has made it necessary to define a process of "convergence" of monetary and fiscal policies with some quantitative objectives. In order to reach EMU, countries should by 1996 have: a maximum inflation rate of 1.5% above the average of the three EC countries with the lowest rate; interest rates lower than the average of the three countries with the lowest rates, plus 2%; a public deficit of less than 3% of GDP; a public debt of less than 60% of GDP; and no devaluation of currency in 1994 and 1995, while remaining in a ±2.25% minor band of the EMS. These quantitative objectives are simply an expression of the need for a diminution of obvious disparities in economic policy parameters.

Because EMU is also, however, an "economic" union, it is clear that convergence should not be only "monetary"; it also has to be "real," in other words, economic disparities between nations should decrease and low-income countries should grow faster than average. It is quite probable that the convergence criteria will be subject to renegotiation and in 1996 other factors will be taken into consideration; but it is also evident that the convergence concept has stimulated policy changes, in particular in those countries that for the moment are far from meeting some of the monetary convergence criteria.

The majority of these convergence plans adopted in all countries are restrictive in terms of fiscal policy (reducing current public spending, increasing taxes), and most of them are also restrictive in terms of monetary policies. As was anticipated, "converging macro-economic policies is easily identified with common restrictive (anti-inflationary) policies."[3] These restrictive policies are certainly part of the explanation for the sudden decline in expectations of European growth. In studies done in late 1990, the GDP growth rate in 1992 was expected to be 3.5%; this forecast was later lowered to 2.25%-2.5% per year; the most recent estimates are around 1.7%-1.8%, perhaps even less.

From 1960 to 1973, the EC achieved an average annual growth rate of 5.0%; for the 1990s, Euro-optimism envisaged a progressive return to this growth process. In a study of the EC published at the end of 1990, projections were made for a 3.0%-3.5% rate for 1991-1995 and 3.5%-4.0% for 1995-2000 since "the end of the integration process (EMU) should free all member countries of external or budgetary constraints and should stimulate growth."[4] But after Maastricht Europessimism is again rising; most probably the agreements on monetary convergence have been ill-timed.

Deepening of the integration process requires both economic and monetary convergence. Although it is obvious that the Maastricht negotiators had this simple fact in mind, it also seems, in hindsight, that the monetary point of view was overemphasized.

Economic convergence is related to two aspects of the integration process. One is "institutional" convergence, involving movement toward a more similar institutional framework; in this direction the EC is advancing rapidly and well. The principle of *mutual recognition*, coupled with minimum basic requirements, allows for a strong convergence process mixing negotiated directives with simple market processes (e.g., tax-rates competition). The second is income and wealth "real" convergence, involving movement toward a reduction of economic disparities (the average income in the poorer European region is four times smaller than in the richest region). Often this reduction of disparities is associated with the notion of increasing social and economic cohesion.

Even before Maastricht, some studies had clearly shown that moving toward monetary and institutional convergence was detrimental to "real" convergence: indeed, it was likely to increase disparities between the center and the periphery of the EC.[5] To attempt to avoid this problem, a Cohesion Fund was established in Maastricht in order to increase income transfers from the richest to the poorer countries of the Community. But this form of redistribution, while useful (e.g., to help develop linkage infrastructures in transportation or telecommunications), is of little ultimate effect if macro-economic policies end up being overrestrictive for the poorer regions (which was to be expected from monetary convergence and is actually taking place).

The greatest actual constraint affecting the deepening process is competitiveness: in principle, all "convergences" should help the EC to increase its competitive position vis-à-vis the United States and Japan; after all, this has been an explicit objective of EC integration since 1985. Competitiveness in a modern economy is closely linked to technological efficiency, to the capacity for technological diffusion and innovation. Studies on the spatial pattern of new technologies (i.e., the technologies of the new paradigm of the Information Society) show that in Europe they are concentrated in a few areas, practically all them within the old European "Center" (the industrial regions distributed from southern England, Paris, the Rhine Valley, up to northern Italy).[6] A technology policy oriented toward stimulating competitiveness is likely to increase the concentration in the center. Thus both the need for monetary convergence and the requirements of international competitiveness are likely to increase the gap between center and periphery, and in general all the dualisms that characterized the unbalanced socioeconomic structure of the EC.

This analysis of the EC's future development as a "closed" process shows that new policies, beyond those agreed in Maastricht, are required in order to diffuse technological development over the totality of the European territory, avoiding the center-periphery model. If not, "deepening" may foster a progressive disaggregation of the EC on the model of what is called a variable geometry (i.e., some regions of the Center moving to create a supra-nation; others lagging far behind). Alternative closed scenarios exist, but are difficult to develop; they are based on the concept of diversity (a multicentered European territory and a multicultural society),[7] and require a rapid move toward political and fiscal federalism. All in all, the road ahead is steep and full of obstacles.

The EC as an Open Process: The Scenario of Broadening

Toward the future. An essential element of the closed process of EC deepening was, implicitly, a certain continuation of the existing world environment of the 1980s. But the world has changed. The EC now has a new frontier, a set of countries entering the market system and wanting to establish close ties with the Community. Furthermore, globalization has now emerged as a strong economic trend. Globalization of firms is challenging the whole idea of "nationally based" competitiveness; and some problems are becoming global (e.g., the environment). For the first time it has become possible to envisage a future world with a single economic ideology (market economics), world enterprises, and world institutions dealing with world problems. In the framework of subsidiarity conceptually developed at Brussels, there is now a new dimension for decisionmaking: the world. Hence we must begin thinking about the possibility of the EC as an "open" process, involving a progressive broadening of its institutions and mechanisms.

Some lessons can be learned from the EC experience and may be useful for developing the open process:

1. Of the total production of any country, only a small part is subject to foreign competition; the share of nontraded activities is larger than the share of traded activities, mainly because economic structures are moving toward the tertiary sector, and in this sector most outputs cannot be traded (e.g., public services). Free trade is important, but it is not the key issue for competitiveness. Bringing competitiveness into the nontraded area is quantitatively more important.

2. For increasing competition in nontraded activities, freedom of capital movement, advanced technology, highly skilled human resources, freedom for starting activities, freedom of access to markets for public services, and so on are essential. In other words, the Single Market is an experience about how to open the nontraded sector to competition.

3. Even for the theoretically tradable sector, often there is no trade possible due to nontariff barriers (particularly local market regulations). The EC experience is demonstrating that the mutual-recognition principle may be as important for stimulating trade in this area as is the most-favored-nation principle in the more traditional area of trade restricted by tariffs and quotas.

If the world of the future will be ideologically a market-driven one, in which competition is essential for welfare, then the EC experience in removing barriers to competition is useful for the world. Therein lies the fundamental basis of the open EC process.

Characteristics of the broadening process. A number of surrounding countries are following with increasing interest the evolution of the EC. The EFTA countries have first negotiated an agreement for a European Economic Area (for 1995), broadly accepting the Single Market concept, and after that have applied for full membership (implicitly accepting Stage 3, the EMU). From Turkey to Morocco, some Mediterranean countries have also officially or unofficially indicated their interest in joining the EC, and have thus raised the question of the geographical limits of a "European" Community (is Northern Africa European?). East European countries, for their part, have several times expressed interest in joining the EC at some point. Another interested country is, of course, Israel. All these developments bear out a simple fact: the EC has started a process that is attractive and intriguing to other countries.

Returning to the evolutionary concept of the three stages of EC development—Common Market, Single Market, and EMU—it appears that, to begin with, a trade-based Common Market is the idea for the world that stands behind GATT and the Most Favored Nation clause. Free trade is important and interesting for the world as a whole; regional common markets are only a transient type of organization on the way to a global free market.

A Single Market is also essential for the world, and the EC is showing how to achieve it. The concept of the EEA (European Economic Area) could easily be extended to the world; mutual recognition is a universal concept. The EFTA countries have opened the way to a type of agreement that could easily be accepted by any country, developed or developing, neighbor or distant. Although in the present context of "trade friction" the following proposal may seem dubious, what is the "technical" (in terms of maximization of economic welfare) reason that could hinder an application by Japan to the EEA?

Stage 3, EMU, however, raises other sorts of problems because of the needed transfer of economic policy responsibilities to a higher, supra-national decisionmaking body. This evolution does not entail economic problems in the case of highly developed countries (EFTA), but, as noted earlier, is not necessarily efficient for the periphery countries. Thus, in the present geopolitical context, the scenario of broadening should initially include a new EC enlargement for some EFTA countries, and creation of an expanding EEA (including Israel) with a Development Belt made up of Mediterranean as well as East European countries (thus establishing a regional North-South cooperative relationship).

In its path toward economic unification, the EC is following a closed process, with some obvious defensive consequences: regional welfare and competitiveness are guiding considerations. Changes in the world environment, however, suggest that the EC should adopt in the future an open process, integrating new countries and propounding to the rest of the world the idea of an expanding Single Market. Should the EC come to realize the great significance for world welfare of its open process, then most probably the timing of EMU, the third and final stage of European integration, should be reconsidered. Furthermore, the generalization of Stage 2 by enlarging the EEA has wider implications for the world as cohesion acquires a new dimension, this time between North and South. For developing countries entering a Single Market, with all its implications regarding free functioning of markets, a change in production structures will be necessary, and this will require an EC development policy involving active capital and technology transfers (as has already been modestly begun with Eastern Europe).

If the EC open process ends up proposing new forms of reciprocal development processes for North-South relations, then it will be a process of great import for world economic integration.

EC-Israel Cooperation

The set of problems raised by the trends observed in the Arab Mediterranean countries are common to the EC and Israel. Furthermore, the issue of a Development Belt that the EC will face in the future also directly affects the EC-Israel relationship.

It is clear that in economic terms, Israel could enter into an association agreement with the EC along the lines of those covering the EEA, without major economic problems. Such an eventuality, however, could not be dissociated from a broader framework such as that of a Development Belt that would involve extensive cooperation with all Mediterranean countries. The Development Belt implies a strong commitment by the EC (and possibly by Israel) to the local development of technology infrastructures and productive activities in the southern Mediterranean. Some lines of possible cooperation include: (1) infrastructure; town planning; transportation, water, and energy systems; control of environmental pollution; and in general all technologies required to solve the many problems of rapid urbanization; (2) agricultural technology, water resources management, and industrial process technologies; and (3) all technologies and investments related to welfare services including education, health, security, and housing.

Practically all human activities in the Development Belt would require technological stimuli and capital inputs from the EC (and possibly Israel), and as public programs are clearly insufficient, the promotion of mixed public-private partnerships would be essential (e.g., Eureka-type projects for the Mediterranean). If European-Israeli cooperation is ever to be solidly established in the Mediterranean, it must deal with the challenges of the new North-South codevelopment path.

Notes

1. For the current activities and publications of the Blue Plan, contact Michel Batisse, Blue Plan UNEP, Place Sophie Laffitte, Sophie Antipolis, 06560 Valbonne, F.

2. For the Datar Scenarios on the Mediterranean, contact Xavier Girard, Quaternaire, 34, rue de Liege, 75008 Paris.

3. E. Fontela, "European Economic Integration in a Long Term Perspective," in OECD, *Long Term Prospects for the World Economy* (Paris, 1992).

4. EC-DG-II, "The Outlook and Potential for Growth in the Community at the Beginning of the 1990's," *European Economy* 46 (December 1990).

5. CADMOS, "European Scenarios on Technological Change and Social and Economic Cohesion," EC-FAST-MONITOR, FOP 240, Brussels, June 1991, and the Appendix to this chapter.

6. U. Hilpert and D. Hickie, "Archipelago Europe: Synthesis Report," EC-FAST-MONITOR, FOP 242, Brussels, November 1991.

7. E. Fontela, "Europe: Cohesion, Diversity and Quality," *The Quality*, September-December 1991, and the Appendix to this chapter.

Appendix: Four Scenarios About the Future of the EC Cohesion

(Summary of CADMOS [S. Boeckhout, E. Fontela, E. Morand], "European Scenarios and Technological Change and Social and Economic Cohesion," see note 4 above)

In 1985 the EC began a rapid process of institutional change toward unification (the Economic and Monetary Union). This process will have internal geostrategic consequences (in terms of relations between the European center and its own periphery) and will require certain policies in relation to the rest of the world, and in particular to the surrounding areas.

In the CADMOS study, we analyzed scenarios and their possible consequences.

In order to elaborate the scenarios for this study, two basic dimensions (European institutions and regional development) have been combined taking into account the following alternatives:

Dimensions for factors of change:

E. European institutions	B. Regional Development
E1. Conventional wisdom	B1 Core-periphery
E2. Deepening	B2. New South
E3. Widening	B3. Diversity

Of the nine possible combinations of these alternatives, only four have been retained:

Scenario T1:	E1-B2:	TREND
Scenario T2	E2-B1	STRONG CORE
Scenario A1:	E3-B2:	DEVELOPMENT BELT
Scenario A2:	E2-B3:	DIVERSITY

All of these scenarios started from a situation characterized by a European core-periphery process, with the "core" evolving from the initial triangle Paris-London-Ruhr basin, to a region covering as well the English Midlands, the Benelux countries, the German Rhineland, the north of Italy, and extending progressively to Hamburg, Copenhagen, southern France, and northern Spain.

Scenario T1: Trend.

The trend scenario combines the positive growth effects of the single market, with a slow development of the core-periphery model and the progressive geographical extension of the core. In this scenario, EC regional and technological policies evolve along the current lines; expected changes have been carefully studied, and future development is clearly "under control" of the economic and social agents. The future is an (improved) image of the recent past (late 1980s).

Scenario T2: Strong Core.

In the second trend scenario, EMU and a social Europe are dealt with. It is a "deepening" scenario enhanced by the basic need for "competitivity." Market forces facilitate the deepening process, and under these circumstances the core-periphery development process is stimulated even more than in scenario T1.

In this scenario, the core of the more advanced EC regions keeps its current advantages in the field of science and technology; it competes in excellence with the other OECD countries, and massively diffuses new knowledge and new technologies through its new products and processes.

Within the EC, specialization takes place on the basis of the traditional division of labor, the "periphery" attracts new investments to take advantage of lower labor costs, and R&D systems in less developed regions are essentially concentrated on technological transfer issues, receiving "best technological practices" from the core and adapting them to local needs.

Scenario A1: Development Belt.

The institutional development of the EC (assuming some form of association with the countries of the second periphery, from Eastern Europe and the Mediterranean) is coupled in this scenario with a growth process in the Mediterranean regions of the EC, as well as in the border regions with the east of Europe. This scenario examines the possibility of some of the less developed regions of the EC acquiring a specific dynamic model out of their role as promoters of new activities in the development belt.

Scenario A2: Diversity.

As the process of deepening is likely to promote a strong competitive core (scenario T2), it is important to explore as an alternative a scenario in which diversity is used as an asset for European development.

T1: TREND

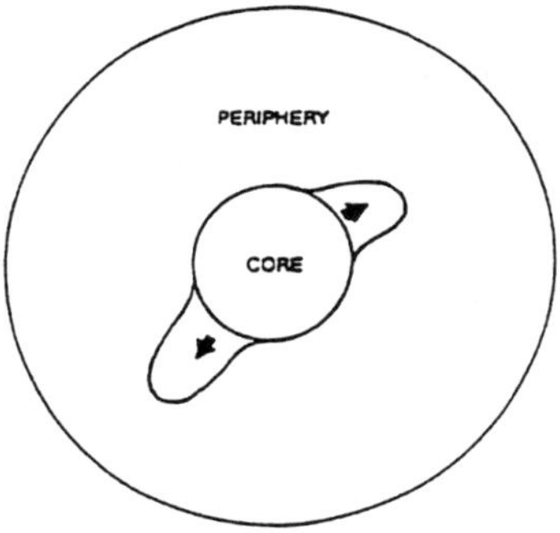

T2: STRONG EC CORE

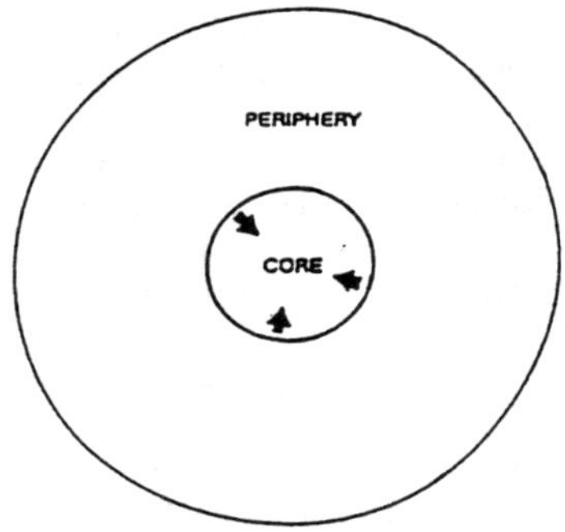

A1: DEVELOPMENT BELT

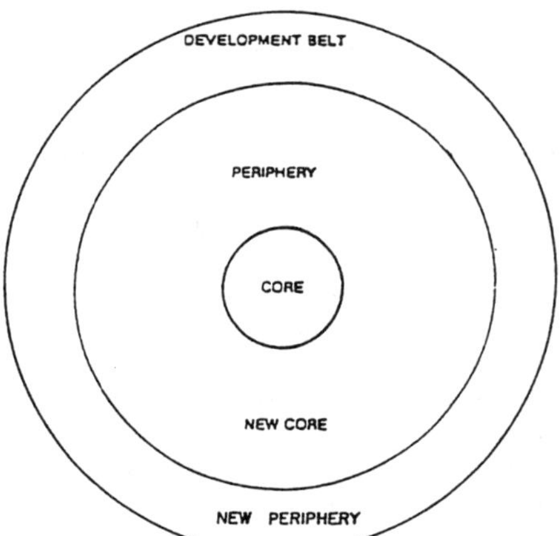

A2: ENHANCED DIVERSITY

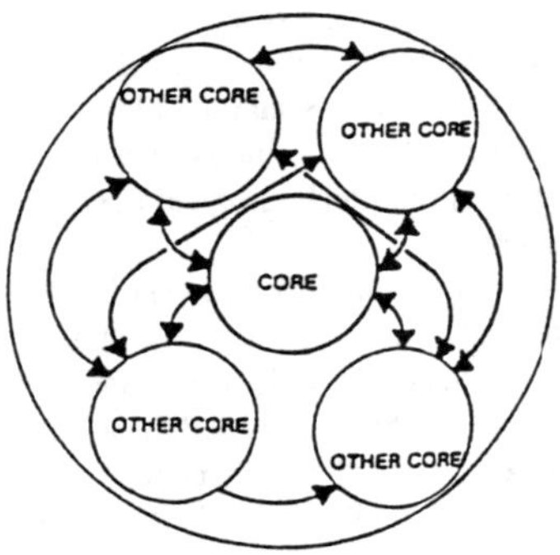

In the scenario of Diversity, the plurality of cultures, lifestyles, institutions, and so on that are historically integral to Europe are expected to become an asset not only for regional development but also for strengthening Europe's competitive situation vis-à-vis the United States and Japan, for answering world needs and addressing world problems by means of institutions, cooperation, and codevelopment based on multicultural values.

Using data on 29 socioeconomic indicators for 142 European regions and a multicriteria analytical method, it has been possible to compute a single "cohesion" index measuring the level of disparities among the regions measured by the indicators.

The four scenarios have been translated into evolution of the indicators and the corresponding cohesion indices measured for each scenarios. The results obtained were the following:

Index of cohesion

Initial situation (1990)	1.00
Scenario T1 (Trend)	0.88
Scenario T2 (Strong Core)	1.27
Scenario A1 (Development Belt)	0.83
Scenario A2 (Diversity)	0.73

The results of these indices can be interpreted as follows:

An index above 1 implies an increase in the dispersion in relation to the present situation, in other words, a potential loss of cohesion.

An index below 1, on the contrary, is to be associated with higher cohesion.

The Trend Scenario (T1) confirms the observations available for the recent past (late 1980s). As a result of the integration process stimulated by the single market, and of the policies for regional and technological development already in place, disparities have and are expected to decrease.

The Strong Core Scenario (Scenario T2) also quantifies the fears raised by economic and monetary unification, with emphasis on competitivity; a strong core process is likely to increase disparities (the early 1990s are confirming these negative expectations).

The Development Belt Scenario (Scenario A1) is contributing to a decrease in disparities as a number of periphery regions will show higher growth prospects.

Finally, the Diversity Scenario (Scenario A2) was designed as providing original solutions to the cohesion issues, and the quantitative results confirm these expectations.

PART III

CULTURAL ASPECTS

Chapter 12

Europe and the Jews: Symbiosis, Misrepresentation, Pitfalls

ABRAHAM ASHKENASI

What Is Culture?

Culture is an amorphous term. Does it refer to the official pretensions of officious institutions, or to earthy, particularist manifestations of society at large? Was there ever such a thing as "European culture," or even the "national culture," bruited among intellectuals and especially historians, that is ostensibly tied to a certain language or organized geographic space?

These are difficult questions; what is clear, however, is that within the nation-states of Europe in the late eighteenth and early nineteenth centuries, the various dynasties, national or other, fostered and promoted artistic development. It is also clear that the technological, including communication, advances of the nineteenth and twentieth centuries made music, art, literature, and so on readily available to a much broader public. This public was indeed universal because of Europe's political and linguistic global expansion, and yet this "art," this "culture," touched only a minority everywhere and may or may not have influenced other areas of "cultural" development. Civic and political culture, for example, as well as religious beliefs and institutions, developed asymmetrically in Europe; whereas music, art, and literature, as well as technological aspirations if not capabilities, developed symmetrically. Nationalism, together with its invidious nineteenth-century handmaiden chauvinism as well as vulgar racism, developed everywhere in Europe. At any rate, "national" cultures were widely spoken and written about and still are.

Whatever Elgar may have had in common with Mahler, or Verdi with Tchaikovsky, Tolstoy with Hugo, and so on, Europe was a hodgepodge of competing societies, politics, and cultures. Of the many fault lines involved here, the deepest ran through Germany: North-South, Protestant-Catholic, East-West, autocratic-agricultural/capitalist-parliamentary, broadly crisscrossed it. The German language united all of Central Europe, but Czernowitz on the Galician-Ukrainian border had little in common with Lübeck or Bozen. These "cultural," indeed ethnic, fault lines augmented the various developments in Germany. Its cultural dynamism in the nineteenth century—its internal divisions, ideological excesses, technological advances, emancipatory theories and sciences, impressive sociopolitical establishments, incomplete civic culture, and competitive social groups—were like "Europe" itself writ large.

This meant a great deal in terms of ideological—and, always conjointly, psychological—developments in Germany. Personal identification with the diffuse idea of "nation" was enhanced by the tenuous nature of the structure itself: the more uncertain things are, and are becoming, the more one grasps at shibboleths that are supposed to connote strength. Personal self-definition becomes entwined with "larger" things that impart a specious but pervasive aura. One may not really understand the thing one ostensibly belongs to, but it matters little. German nationalism was ethnocentristic where no ethnic group existed. It posited a German past where there had been none. It was aggressive, but eminently successful. Germany was Europe's most powerful nation—economically, militarily, demographically, and of course culturally; but what was this culture? Germans regard it as having been special. Its undeniable vibrancy seems to me, however, to have been a function of the meeting of the East-West and North-South fault lines of Europe. The "cultural" borders were open, and nineteenth- and twentieth-century European romanticism—much of which, to be sure, was German—lent emotional vitality to the individual seeking psychic security.

Along these fault lines, and in close contact with the Germans, lived the largest non-"national" people in Europe—the Jews, themselves experiencing powerful and wrenching cultural asymmetries.

The Jews and European Culture

Personal insecurity was by no means limited to Germans. The mighty social waves of capitalism, industrialism, political nationalism, liberalism, and reaction crashed against the rabbinical walls that Jewish Orthodoxy had built around itself to keep the flocks within the holy Covenant. In Western Europe, beginning in the eighteenth century and especially after the Napoleonic Wars, Jews were becoming "emancipated," i.e., they were embracing the most amenable part of the Western social structure, namely, the "culture." This seemed a perfect compromise for them; it implied retention of their birthright, such as it was, but allowed, along with participation in the capitalist economy, integration and, yes, assimilation into Europe.

Perhaps this process began in reformist Holland. Is there a bridge between Erasmus and Spinoza, or was the questioning spirit of Enlightenment already there, guiding the perplexed, from Moses to Moses to Moses (i.e., Moses, Maimonides, Mendelssohn)? In any event, *Kultur* was transmitted, in German, through the German provinces in Poland to Lithuania, and by way of Austria-Hungary over Lvov through Galicia into the great Pale of Russian Jewry, in their poor but effervescent villages. In this culture lay the path to the new, away from the fetters of the past. Capitalism was attractive to some, socialism to many others. But "European"—predominantly German—culture was, for Jews from Offenbach eastward, the panacea, the bridge to the emancipated intellect.

Was there a symbiosis, then, between European and Jewish thought and values, between public European "culture" and that significant portion of European Jewry fleeing the rabbinical restraints of an older wisdom, as well as the small-town dynamics of the ghetto and the *shtetl*? The answer is undoubtedly affirmative. Mendelssohn was to Kant what Freud was to psychology, Einstein to physics, Marx to various revolutionaries; and, in the other direction, Fichte to Moses Hess, Wagner to Mahler, Matisse to Chagall, Hegel to Pinsker. Large numbers of bright young Jews jumped aboard the train of European emancipatory "Enlightenment," which sped on promising terrestrial messianic deliverance—young Jews such as Heine, Trotsky, Rathenau, for a time Ben-Gurion. Kafka rode it but brooded about the fading promise, and fled in his mind's eye toward "Amerika" as the train sped on toward its awful destiny. Its last stop was Auschwitz.

Today's Israel and Its Misrepresentation

Somehow the idea has been fostered that Israel was still part of the European culture after 1945. This notion suited both European apologists and Israeli sentimentalists. True, the social democracy of Ben-Gurion and Arlozorov was in place. British notions of justice survived the Mandate. The shaky civic culture and political legitimacies of Western Europe seemed similar to those of Israel. People tried to compose like Schönberg and paint like Chagall; and yet in the works of Agnon we discern a difference, and we confront it on the oriental streets, in the militant mystique of the new generation. Israel is only partly still Jewish, in the way Jews were only partly European. Israel's European trappings are all there, especially European-style nationalism, political and social organization, and official culture, but the country has a different nature, and is misrepresented abroad.

For one thing, Israel is of course a great conglomerate of peoples, most of whom are not European in origin. Even those who are but were born in Israel have undergone a completely different socialization process from their European counterparts. In the postwar years, the kibbutz movement, the Israel Philharmonic, the Haifa Theater, and such grand old Europeans as composer-philosopher Josef Tal or President Chaim Herzog came to symbolize Israel in Europe; cultural affinity grew, yet was based on misrepresentation.

This appealed to those with guilty consciences (especially the Germans), and particularly in Germany this gross misrepresentation of Israeli culture has prevailed. More than anywhere else, this development was abetted by "interpreters" of Israel in the German vernacular such as Kishon, Wolfsohn, Zimmerman, Broder, and Uri Avneri. The net result is, despite some differences of interpretation, an enhanced Eurocentric conception of what Israeli "culture" is. But in actuality Israel is an aggressive and contentious place; the international and regional confrontation is accompanied by an ongoing and often nasty internal struggle. Israel is not an intellectual center with mellifluous classical tones and hues. It also harbors within it a revived religiosity that is older than the European "Enlightenment" and indeed stands opposed to it in almost every way. Between this religiosity, constant existential pressures, and interethnic tensions, the European civic culture is also threatened.

If "culture" is the last refuge of the perplexed or unsure, then the question arises as to what "Europe" has to offer an Israeli. For some it is an attractive escape from the cacophony of Israel's daily life; for some, especially the elderly, it is a nostalgic return to a past that never existed; for many others it is an opportunity for conspicuous consumption; for yet others, especially the many Russian immigrants, it still, atavistically or not, represents all that it did in the nineteenth century. But the overall situation is paradoxical: large sums can be found privately for symphony halls and opera houses, but all of this—vibrant as it is—is grafted onto a society that, with its religious and/or oriental overtones, has little connection to this kind of culture and even less understanding of it.

To be sure, cultural dislocation is today a widespread phenomenon. It is readily apparent in the United States, whose influence on today's Israel is probably paramount. American pop culture is both ephemeral and socially explosive, ripping at the seams of society; much of Israel's pop culture is the same. When the fabric of life is strained and unraveling, it is not surprising that "established" artists, novelists, orchestras, dancers, and so on become internationalized and seek to strengthen their links to the "stable" past.

In fact, much of the same is true for Western Europe as well; the processes are also evident in Eastern Europe. Thus, the official interpretation of culture and the management of exchanges often involve painful misrepresentation.

Pitfalls and Possibilities

Israel is regarded as some sort of European cultural bastion in its region. To a degree it is, but it has been inaccurately portrayed as being mostly that. Actually it has deeper similarities to much of the older, oriental culture in the area. The similar thought patterns of a Semitic language are at work, as well as the oriental antecedents of much of the society. In addition, the flight into religiosity and away from civic and emancipatory culture is seen among both Jews and Muslims and reflects their common disillusionment with the sociocultural realities of the post-Napoleonic European world. To concentrate exclusively, in European-Israeli relations, on the supposed similarities (orchestra, theater, university exchanges, etc.) is a serious distortion.

Between Europe and the Third World there are differences in the demographics of society and in the role of the family. In this respect, Israel with its blend of peoples constitutes an interesting social bridge. The painful social compromises and the tensions are perhaps more important to Europe than the neo-Chagallian painters. What is involved here is the visceral Judeo-Muslim need, rooted in the old Middle Eastern patterns, for familial warmth and generational continuity. The fear of modernity, the search for primordial social bondedness, the rejection of the emancipatory "truths" of Europe and of the cultural ramifications of total European penetration, are, to be sure, much stronger elsewhere in the Middle East than in Israel. But the understanding of these tendencies can be enhanced through acceptance of Israeli difference, which would entail a change in the emphasis of cultural relations.

Emancipated intellectuals and artists of all sorts jet back and forth between Israel and Europe, but what do they really contribute to cultural understanding? Generally little, for they tend to emphasize superficial similarities, presumably linked to their own identity, and not the differences, wherein the real creative potential lies. Indeed, paradoxically, it is just the cultural variety of Israel—its seeming difference from Europe—that makes it all the more significant, and perhaps ultimately, in many ways, similar.

For one thing, Israel has coped well with multiculturalism. Kurds, Moroccans, Germans, Hungarians, Russians, Americans, Romanians, and now Ethiopians have been integrated at least into the civic culture; and perhaps, beyond that, something truly indigenous and Israeli is germinating, though it has not yet taken shape. At any rate, the success of integration, even if still on a relatively superficial level, is impressive. This is something that warrants the attention of today's Europe, through cultural and intellectual exchange and analysis.

Furthermore, the aspect of religious revival, including the intellectually stringent Lithuanian as well as the ebullient Hasidic and oriental Judaism, makes Israel interesting for Europe. Perhaps these kinds of religiosity are easier to contemplate and understand than their Muslim Sufi and fundamentalist counterparts. In any case, if one wants to understand this part of the world one must pay sufficient attention to these elements in society. Eventually, perhaps, the interest can be made mutual.

Similarly, let us not neglect a youth culture that is more violent with every passing war-torn year. Indeed, Europe needs no lessons here; much of European youth (especially lower-income males) is slipping away into nihilistic adventurism—in which European antisemitism finds fertile ground. And yet alienation is similar in both places, and perhaps we need fewer contacts between fresh-faced kibbutz youngsters and their systematically organized European counterparts. Instead, perhaps we should look more deeply into those places in both societies where most of us never look until it is too late. Strenuous new initiatives for cultural exchange and mutual understanding are needed if we are to avoid the pitfalls of complacency and intellectual and emotional aggrandisement on both sides. Undoubtedly, the basic framework has to be the common acceptance of the civic cultural values of social tolerance and political legitimacy. Beyond that, however, new paths must be taken to confront differences in both development and socialization; and we may be unpleasantly surprised, as has occurred before in this century, at what is festering beneath our level of vision.

Cultural complacency is the handmaiden of intellectual obduracy and political failure. In some way the echo of Judaism in Europe should reverberate through the Israeli experience, but it should address the important questions of today's Israel, and offer some answers for a multinational, multilingual, multireligious, and multicultural Europe. Perhaps it can also help teach Europe that identity and expression are better sought through the rich plurarity of real life.

Chapter 13

The Cultural Dimension of a Unified Europe: Implications for Israel

ANKE MARTINY

The Identity of Europe

This chapter must begin with the question: what do we mean by Europe? Do we mean the European subcontinent? Do we refer to the new historical structure that emerged after the fall of the Roman Empire and the large migrations, and, following the reign of Charlemagne, entered history as the Holy Roman German Empire? Or do we mean the European Community?

From the 1950s up to 1990, Central Europeans had a clear conception of what Europe meant: it referred to the part of Europe west of the Iron Curtain, or simply to the European Community. The Iron Curtain severed Central Europeans from the historical experience of a single Europe: this belonged to the past. Moreover, the division of Europe into two parts took place in the middle of Germany. Berlin was a small, Western island within the eastern sphere of power and was itself divided by a wall; West Berlin was linked to West Germany by narrow corridors—on land by freeways and railway lines, in the air by fixed air corridors; with the help of yearly currency payments the Western Allies ensured the maintenance of those links, which had been negotiated for a price. Europe consisted of two economic zones and two defense zones. More essentially, two opposing ideologies—the "free West" and the "totalitarian East" in Western terminology, the "bourgeois capitalistic West" and "real socialism" in the language of the East—produced a propagandistic barrier, across which two cultures maintained a mutual antagonism.

At present the term Europe mostly connotes what we might call "the West as seen by the West," which is attributable to the fact that in 1989-1990 the West, without waging war, won a victory over the East. The communist ideology has collapsed, and the entire economy of the East is in a shambles. It is the unexpectedly and unpreparedly victorious Western world that now sets the tone, materially as well as culturally. For Israel and its neighboring Arab countries, this development represents a totally new foundation for relations with Continental Europe. As seen from the Middle East, this Europe, until recently, was divided and politically polarized, and depending on one's political affiliation one was oriented toward either the western or the eastern half. The void that has newly emerged has hardly any clear contours.

Emergence of the European Community

To give a better perspective on the current situation, it will be helpful to review briefly the development of the European Community. In Luxembourg on September 13, 1952, the European Coal and Steel Community, which was founded immediately after World War II, decided to appoint a special assembly to elaborate a common constitution for the planned unification of the six member countries: the Federal Republic of Germany, Belgium, France, Italy, Luxembourg, and the Netherlands. An agreement on a European Defence Community was also signed in Paris. Both agreements aimed at close cooperation not only in the fields of economy and defense in the heart of Europe, but also in matters of security and foreign policy. Both projects, however, were abortive, since the agreements were not ratified.

In 1955, however, the Federal Republic of Germany, a Central European state, became a member of the West European Union and of NATO. In 1956 the Atlantic Council, considering an expansion of NATO to the political and economic fields, founded the so-called Council of the Three Sages. In 1957, the Common Market of the members of the Coal and Steel Community was founded and the European Parliament was created. In addition, the Council of Ministers, the European Court, and the Economic and Social Council were established.

In 1970, what was by then known as the European Economic Community began negotiations with Great Britain, Ireland, Denmark, and Norway concerning their joining the EEC; of these only Norway declined. At that time it was still optimistically assumed that a full political and currency community could be achieved by 1980. Although that did not transpire, during the 1980s other countries such as Greece, Spain, and Portugal became members of the EEC. The energetic President Jacques Delors designated January 1, 1993, as D-day for complete economic unification of the Europe of the Twelve, and indeed, with the Maastricht treaty of December 1991, concrete steps were taken that will lead to a Union in the areas of currency, taxes, and so on.

At present it does not appear that the Maastricht treaty will be adopted in all its details by all twelve countries. On the other hand, the EFTA states—Switzerland, Austria, Norway, Sweden, and Finland—are strongly considering joining the EC; the rejection of Switzerland's membership has caused a deep political crisis in that country. The East European states—Hungary, Poland, Chesko, and Slovakia—have expressed their wish to join in the future. Turkey and Israel are clearly considering a closer association. Alternative scenarios arise of a Europe unified either "in width" or "in depth." Neither alternative, however, refers to culture.

The EC Experience and Its Import for Israel

This brief overview of the emergence of the European Community reveals that the concept was purely functional. The plan was to bring about better economic opportunities through a harmonized market. This, to a certain degree, necessitated a common financial policy. In order to implement the plan, a parliament and a court were needed. In this manner, the founding fathers sought to initiate the evolution of the political union of a European Democracy. The construction of this union—except for the Economic and Social Council—had no social components. Certainly nothing was said about a cultural union, nor were there any deliberations about the cultural dimension of such a Europe. In a recently published manifesto entitled "Since the Country Must Change," former German chancellor Helmut Schmidt and his coauthors state: "The new Europe also runs the danger of concentrating solely on growth rates, national product and foreign trade balance. We should not forget that our old continent was primarily characterized by spiritual values, that historically, Europe used to be a spiritually unified area."[1] That has no doubt been forgotten during the first 40 years of the European unifying process.

From an Israeli perspective, what is of interest here is that economic problems were regarded as primary. It was believed that by finding solutions to these problems, processes of peace and unification could be set in motion. History indeed shows that addressing the key economic problems of that time—those involving coal and steel—was the starting point. With respect to the present situation of Israel and its neighbors, the question is what key problems should be dealt with first in order to begin moving toward peace and unification.

If we ask about the contribution to political culture made by this Europe, the following facts are indicative. The bureaucracy was located in an immense three-winged building in Brussels until recently, when because of the asbestos in the concrete it was completely evacuated and the offices were dispersed throughout the city. The European Parliament convenes alternately in three cities—Brussels, Strasbourg, and Luxembourg—like an opulent circus. The European institutions are also divided among those three cities. The European Court is located in The Hague, the European Patent Office in Munich, the European Central Bank will be established in Frankfurt. Nowhere, however, is there a cultural homeland. The Parliament deliberates in nine languages: English, French, German, Italian, Spanish, Portuguese, Dutch, Danish, and Greek; the members of the European Parliament are elected according to nationality: Germans elect Germans, Irishmen elect Irishmen, and so on. There is no common list of European parties: Italians working in Germany can vote only from the Italian list; Germans working in Brussels vote from the German list. Although there are common parliamentary groupings, over 40 years no new parliamentary culture has developed. Common lists are, however, expected for the European elections in 1994, when citizens of the EC will be able to vote wherever they are residing at the time.

Meanwhile European law has gained precedence over national law, so that the national parliaments must change national laws according to European laws. However, in the making of European laws it is often the far-removed "Eurobureaucracy" that is involved. Parliamentary control of legislative procedures is insufficient.

With respect to the degree of legal harmonization within the Community, the economic laws, including those pertaining to the technical security of appliances and to financial services, as well as to the whole area of health and consumer protection, have mostly been harmonized. Laws in the field of finance have been only partially harmonized. Tax laws have not yet been harmonized, but this will be promoted by elements in the Maastricht treaty pertaining to this subject. What has so far not been subjected to any harmonization at all are the social laws: health insurance, old age pensions, family benefits, encouragement of studies—each of the 12 member states of the EC deals with these areas independently. Since overall the social condition of the West European democracies is impressive, it is astonishing that a higher degree of unity has not yet been achieved in this regard.

Constitutions and legislations are, of course, components of political culture. In this regard, it is interesting that in Israel little thought has been given to which European elements are part of Israel's legislative culture. For instance, it is clear that the idea of the social state, which has been prevalent in Israel since the Histadrut was founded, is a European heritage. Over the years, however, modifications have been made in the character of the social state, and their possible application to Israel's legislative development should be examined.

European harmonizations in the field of culture are only beginning—specifically, in the domains of cinema and the media. In the case of the media this is simply attributable to economic causes, and the same, essentially, holds with respect to cinema, since here the American competition practically controls the European market insofar as production, distribution, and theaters are concerned.

French, Italian, German, and English movies lose more market shares every year; everywhere the same American movies are shown, sometimes synchronized, sometimes subtitled.

Yet no one has seriously tried to take the measure of the cultural dimension of this old continent with its rich heritage. Although several European summit conferences have had the subject of culture on their agenda, nothing has come of this, not even European debates with wide resonance.

The situation being as it is, it is not surprising that Europe's cultural dimension has not become visible or even influential. As far as Israel is concerned, it is certain that the cultural traditions of various European countries have penetrated by way of immigration from these countries. It cannot be said, however, that within Israeli society there is any substantial tendency to seek roots for Israel's culture in Europe. The links, to be sure, are intensive and diversified; but the identity of Israeli culture, if it has one yet, is certainly not derived primarily from European culture, but more from American influences.

Europe's Cultural Federalism

Even before the German reunification, German president Richard von Weizsacker convoked in Bonn a conference of the ministers of culture of the Federal Republic, that is, those responsible for cultural affairs of each of the eleven federal states, in order to discuss with them the challenges posed by a united Europe. In Germany, as opposed to France or England, the field of culture is constituted in a federalistic manner and there is no national minister of culture. Without being indiscreet, since the meeting was not public, I would like to note one thing about what transpired: the president was quite disappointed. He learned nothing about common European cultural values that could finally be realized; nobody offered him even the elements of a vision of how a culturally unified Europe might look. Instead, the ministers of culture complained about noncomparable degrees, disparities in teachers' pay, and the questionableness of certain curriculum contents in the various federal states. In Germany, such a situation still prevails.

Among European politicians dealing with culture there have been several outstanding personalities, such as the Frenchman Jack Lang, the Spaniard Jorge Semprun, and the Greek Melina Mercouri. But no notion of an overall cultural framework has emerged from England, the Netherlands, Italy, or Denmark. There is, indeed, no common European culture; what characterizes culture in Europe is its diversity. And yet, if confronted with someone from the United States or the Third World, any culture-conscious Frenchman, Dutchman, Italian, or German will stress that besides his nationality, culturally he is European.

Europeans, particularly West Europeans, claim that by uniting in the European Community, they have overcome the evils of the national state and have established a new, free, democratic order in which all participate, though from their own national standpoints. The values of the French Revolution and of the Age of Enlightenment have to a large extent been implemented in their countries, and they feel that their culture has also nourished the culture of the United States, although one of the essential achievements of the European tradition—the social welfare state—has not been realized there. Indeed, the European free, democratic states governed by law and order, with their strong social underpinnings, constitute a cultural achievement that was realized relatively easily during 40 years of peace.

European culture, then, is federalistic and reflects the unmistakable national characteristics of the states according to their respective histories. The uniqueness of this culture lies in its variety and its democratic character. These two features have the potential to provide a model for other regions of the world. Pluralism and democracy go together, and in their cultural expression counteract fundamentalism and claims of ultimate, exclusive truth. This could potentially offer much to a region such as the Middle East.

The New Europe, Nationalism, and Pluralism

With the fall of communism in Eastern Europe, West Europeans have become aware of the fundamentally questionable nature of the European Community from the cultural point of view. After all, Prague is as much a part of Europe as Rome, Warsaw as much as Paris, Budapest as much as Madrid. Will the Community of the Twelve remain viable, not to mention expanding, without first taking account of the cultural question? Europe has become larger, since Western Europe can no longer be conceived as separate from the East. The relatively clear-cut, though dangerous, world of the East-West conflict no longer exists; East Europeans have become citizens of the world as all other people.

At the same time, the resurgence of virulent East European nationalisms poses a serious danger, as seen in the alarming case of Yugoslavia. Indeed, all the countries in Eastern and southeastern Europe are multinational states, although this is less true of Hungary and Poland than of Romania and former Yugoslavia. In these ethnically mixed polities, it is difficult to establish a national identity based only on whose ancestors were the first to settle. This leads to extreme nationalism up to horrific phenomena of "ethnic cleansing," as is now occurring in the Bosnian imbroglio. It is painful to see that from a cultural standpoint some of the Eastern and southeastern European states seem to have learned nothing better from the fall of the communistic ideology than the revival of nationalistic ideologies.

Western Europe's essential cultural contribution should be to make it clear that multinationality in one state is normal, viable, and can be culturally enrichening. The West European countries have been managing, in various ways, the presence of national, religious, and cultural minorities. They have not always, or at least not completely, succeeded—and in this regard serious problems have recently arisen, of course, in Germany—but in principle, the West European democracies have laid the groundwork of multicultural harmony. This experience is the cultural message that West Europeans should be transmitting to their troubled counterparts in the East.

The consequences of the collapse of the communist ideology for Israel and the other Middle Eastern countries are not yet clear. The region has been so preoccupied with promoting and managing a peace process that any spiritual developments not directly connected to that process are presently in the background. This situation, however, will change, and Israel will certainly take an interest in Europe's cultural contribution to reconciliation in the Middle East. The present generation of West Europeans, however, have been pampered by 45 years of peace and welfare; those younger than 45 have no direct experience of war and destruction in Western Europe. They know, of course, about differences in values, about international tensions and conflicts, and about terrorism. But they know little of such problems, characteristic of the Middle East, as insurrection or fundamentalism.

In this regard Germany is in a key position. Although it is not the only country in Europe and the Free World suffering from rising right-wing extremism and violence, Germans are aware that simplistic "solutions" can lead to horrible consequences. With this background, it is reassuring that Germany is indeed firmly integrated in the European Community. Above all, this demonstrates—and not only so far as Germany is concerned—the importance of the Community's social and cultural dimensions.

Note

1. M. Donhoff, M. Miegel, W. Nolling, E. Reuter, H. Schmidt, R. Schroder, and W. Thierse, *Ein Manifest: Weil das Land sich andern muss* (Reinbek bei Hamburg: Rowohlt, 1992), p. 18.

PART IV

SCIENTIFIC COOPERATION

Chapter 14

How Can EC-Israeli Research Cooperation Be Expanded?

M. MACIOTI

Israel is a recognized scientific power. As measured by the indicator of volume of scientific publishing, Israel's output, in recent years, has been higher than that of Czechoslovakia or Hungary.[1] Jerusalem's output of scientific publications (1981-1985) equals that of Bombay, a city 16 times larger. Haifa's publications equal those of Rotterdam, and Rehovot's those of Seoul. In fact, in terms of scientific output per capita Israel ranks first in the world.[2]

Israel is an impressive technological power as well. Using the indicator of patenting, we find that 1090 patent applications were filed in 1991 by residents of Israel—equivalent to the number of applications filed by residents of Belgium or Norway, or slightly less than in the case of Italy (a country with a population 13 times larger than Israel's). Applications for registration of industrial designs by residents of Israel in 1991 numbered 1440—higher than India and almost equal to the applications filed by residents of Finland, Denmark, and Norway combined. Sixty applications for registration of varieties of plants were filed by residents of Israel in 1991, equal to the number filed in Sweden.[3]

The number of patents Israel takes in the United States is increasing (304 in 1991, 377 in 1992), and is on a par with those taken on the American market by Belgium, a country twice Israel's size.[4] Israel is also active on the European patent scene; in 1992 Israeli inventors filed more patent applications in Munich than the Republic of Korea.[5]

These indicators show that there is a sound basis for cooperation in science and technology between Israel and Europe. It should be noted that the European Community has limited means (equivalent to about 4% of the public research budgets of the Twelve) and, according to the principle of subsidiarity, will only step in when the scope for multilateral relations is clearly advantageous. Furthermore, it is worth mentioning that, beyond its relations with the EC and its member states, Israel is an associate member of CERN (European Council for Nuclear Research) and a full member of EMBO (European Organization for Molecular Biology).

Traditionally, R&D cooperation between Israel and the EC has been conducted under three programs: ISC (International Cooperation in Science), STD (Science and Technology for Development) (until 1991), and Avicenne (since 1992). Under ICS (1984-1992), the EC's contribution to joint research has been about 6m.ECU (the EC finances 60%, Israel 40%). The priority themes have covered such areas as advanced structural and functional materials, biotechnology, optoelectronics, nanoelectronics, and desertification. Under Avicenne (5m.ECU in 1992), 18 Mediterranean projects have been financed by the EC, 10 of which have Israeli participation. A new call for proposals was issued by the EC in 1993.[6]

Beyond R&D, several other Mediterranean programs link Israel and the EC in valuable technical cooperation. Cases in point are the programs MEDSPA (protection of environment) and ACNAT (protection of natural habitats), which, since 1992, have become part of the new program LIFE (400m.ECU for 1992-1995). LIFE deals with technical assistance, transfer of technology, and ecological emergency action, in the broad area of the environment. MED-URBS is a program of cooperation between local collectivities on both sides of the Mediterranean; it has a budget of 5m.ECU. MED-CAMPUS deals with the development of human resources and has a budget of 6.5m.ECU. MEDINVEST is a scheme to help small and medium-size enterprises (SME) with training, improved access to technology, pilot projects, and the like; its budget is 10m.ECU.[7] Two Israeli banks participate in the ECIP (European Community Investment Partners) initiative, aiming at the creation of joint ventures in the Mediterranean. For its part, the European Investment Bank is currently making available two loans totaling 40m.ECU to the Industrial Development Bank of Israel (30m.ECU for industry and tourism and 10m.ECU for environmental protection).

Broadly speaking, EC-Israeli cooperation has been based on the 1975 agreement. Since December 1992 a new agreement has been under negotiation; moreover, the EC and Israel are thinking of concluding a new specific agreement defining Israeli participation in EC R&D programs.

In view of these developments, it might be interesting to consider the scientific areas where it would appear that an expansion of cooperation between the EC and Israel would be mutually beneficial. One way of doing this is to refer again to scientific publishing.[8] Israel's research profile, based on 1981-1985 scientific publications in international journals (high activity, high attractivity), presents differences as well as commonalities with the corresponding profile of European countries. For example, aerospace engineering and technology or horticulture are strong points in Israel but not particularly well represented in Europe. The Appendix summarizes the situation.

An analysis of international scientific publishing reveals several commonalities between Israel and greater Europe (the EC, the European Free Trade Area, as well as Turkey), as summarized in Table 1.

Table 1

International Scientific Publishing

Atomic molecular and chemical physics (IL) (GR, F, SP, NL, I, D) (A, CH)
Biochemistry and molecular biology (IL) (F, SP, NL, B) (N, S, CH)
Biophysics (IL) (F, NL, SP, B, D) (S, N)
Botany (IL) (GR, UK, SP, NL, D) (TR)
Computer applications and cybernetics (IL) (GR, SP, NL, B)
Dentistry and odontology (IL) (GR, DK, UK, NL) (N, SF, S)
Genetics and heredity (IL) (DK, SP, NL, B) (S, SF)
Materials science (IL) (UK, F, SP, I)
Nuclear physics (IL) (DK, F, NL, B, I, D) (SF)
Obstetrics and gynaecology (IL) (DK, UK, IRL) (S, SF, A, N)
Optics (IL) (F, SP, I, D)
Physics of condensed matter (IL) (GR, F, SP, B, D) (CH)
Urology and nephrology (IL) (GR, DK, SP, IRL, B, I) (S, SF, A)

Key: A=Austria, B=Belgium, CH=Switzerland, D=Germany, DK=Denmark, F=France, GR=Greece, I=Italy, IL=Israel, IRL=Ireland, N=Norway, NL=Netherlands, SF=Finland, SP=Spain, TR=Turkey, UK=United Kingdom

Source: *Scientometrics* (June 1989).

It emerges that physics (atomic physics, molecular and chemical physics, nuclear physics, condensed matter), life sciences (biochemistry and molecular biology, biophysics, botany, genetics and heredity), and medical sciences (dentistry and odontology, obstetrics and gynecology, urology and nephrology) are areas where prima facie an expansion of European-Israeli scientific cooperation would be valuable. Life and medical sciences take a large share in the scientific publishing of both Europe (from Greece's 40% to Denmark's almost 75%) and Israel (almost 60% of total scientific output). Note that molecular biology and genetics as well as urology are particularly fast-growing fields of science; this is also true of physics of condensed matter.

As suggested by EC Commission President Jacques Delors in his presentation to the European Parliament (February 1993), important areas for international cooperation are cultural exchanges as well as management of the resources of the sea. On that same occasion, President Delors broached the idea of a Water and Energy Community in the Middle East, on the lines of the European Coal and Steel Community (ECSC). In Strasbourg in March 1993, Israeli Foreign Minister Peres mentioned water and tourism as possible areas for future cooperation in the Middle East.

The EC has, indeed, been fostering cooperation on water issues with several of Israel's neighbors. Thus, with Egypt, the EC finances a Channel Maintenance Project (weed control, irrigation), at a cost of 40m.ECU; with Jordan, it has a ground water investigation project around the Hammad and Sirhan basins, worth 4m.ECU; with Syria, it is conducting a water supply project in the Bseira and Hama rural regions, budgeted at 7.5m.ECU. Equally, MED-URBS includes water management among its priority themes.

EC-Israeli scientific cooperation could be of great benefit to the Mediterranean and the Middle East. It could, indeed, benefit the world. A triangular cooperation linking Israel, the EC, and the Muslim republics of the CIS could, by way of example, directly benefit Central Asia (as well as the EC's own societies). There are at present a significant number of scientists from the Central Asian republics of the CIS in Israel, and there are Israeli scientists helping those republics in agricultural research, irrigation, environmental management, and so on. The EC, for its part, has its own TACIS program (Technical Assistance to the Commonwealth of Independent States), which currently focuses on food, human resources, infrastructure, and enterprise support. The EC has launched its own foundation for cooperation with the scientists of the FSU.[9]

One of the great assets of Central Asia is its wealth in bioresources. According to the famous Russian geneticist N. Vavilov, Central Asia is the region of domestication of some 40 important plants, among which are three species of wheat (*Triticum*), two of onion (*Allium*), five of pear (*Pyrus*), and three of almond (*Amygdalus*).[10] On the other hand, five countries of the EC, two of EFTA, as well as Israel rank among the 15 most cited publishers in the area of botany.[11] Seemingly, a program of EC-Israeli-Central Asian cooperation in gene collecting and storage for plants of economic importance (a program to which other countries of the Mediterranean region, such as Turkey, might wish to contribute) could bring great benefits to the whole of humanity.

Notes

1. ISI, *Current Contents Address Directory* (Science and Technology), vol. 1 (Philadelphia, 1987).

2. MOST, *Scientific Research in Israel* (Jerusalem, 1992).

3. WIPO, *Industrial Property Statistics*, Publication A, February (Geneva, 1993).

4. Commissioner of Patents and Trademarks, "Annual Report," F.Y. 1992, May (Washington, D.C., 1993).

5. EPO, *Annual Report 1992* (Munich, 1993).

6. A call for proposals in the Mediterranean region for joint research on health problems was launched by the EC with a deadline of September 15, 1993.

7. The first Euro-info Centre in the Middle East (assisting Israeli companies' participation in the European market) was inaugurated in Tel Aviv in November 1993. There are plans to organize a Med-Partnership in Israel in 1994 in the framework of the MEDINVEST program.

8. *Scientometrics* 16, 1-6 (1989).

9. The International Association for the Promotion of Cooperation With Scientists From the Independent States of the Former Soviet Union (INTAS) was established under Belgian law in summer 1993.

10. N. I. Vavilov, *Izbrannye Trudy*, vol. 2 (Moscow: Akademiya Nauk SSSR, 1960).

11. *Scientometrics* 16, 1-6 (1989).

Appendix: Scientific Publications: Areas of High Activity and High Attractivity

BELGIUM
Allergy
Analytical Chemistry
Biochemistry and Molecular Biology
Biophysics
Cardiovascular System
Computer Applications and Cybernetics
Dermatology and Venereal Diseases
Endocrinology and Metabolism
Genetics and Heredity
Hematology
Mathematical Physics
Microbiology
Mineralogy
Nuclear Physics
Nuclear Science and Technology
Pharmacology and Pharmacy
Physical Chemistry
Physics of Condensed Matter

Physiology
Research and Experimental Medicine
Respiratory System
Rheumatology
Spectroscopy
Toxicology
Tropical Medicine
Urology and Nephrology
Veterinary Medicine

DENMARK
Allergy
Anatomy and Morphology
Anesthesiology
Cytology and Histology
Dentistry and Odontology
Dermatology and Venereal Diseases
Ecology
Endocrinology and Metabolism
Gastroenterology
General and Internal Medicine
Genetics and Heredity
Hematology
Marine and Freshwater Biology
Neurosciences
Nuclear Physics
Obstetrics and Gynecology
Ophthalmology
Orthopedics
Otorhinolaryngology
Pathology
Pediatrics
Pharmacology and Pharmacy
Physiology
Psychiatry
Research and Experimental Medicine
Rheumatology
Statistics and Probability
Surgery
Urology and Nephrology
Veterinary Medicine

FRANCE
Applied Physics
Atomic Molecular and Chemical Physics

Biochemistry and Molecular Biology
Biophysics
Crystallography
Cytology and Histology
Dermatology and Venereal Diseases
Electrochemistry
Embryology
Endocrinology and Metabolism
Gastroenterology
Materials Science
Mathematical Physics
Microscopy
Mineralogy
Nuclear Physics
Optics
Organic Chemistry
Physical Chemistry
Physics of Condensed Matter
Polymer Science
Rheumatology
Spectroscopy

GERMANY
Anatomy and Morphology
Andrology
Applied Chemistry
Astronomy and Astrophysics
Atomic Molecular and Chemical Physics
Biophysics
Botany
Chemical Engineering
Crystallography
Cytology and Histology
Embryology
Food Science and Technology
Gastroenterology
Inorganic and Nuclear Chemistry
Instruments and Instrumentation
Metallurgy and Mining
Microbiology
Microscopy
Nuclear Physics
Nuclear Science and Technology
Optics
Organic Chemistry

Paper and Pulp Technology
Parasitology
Physical Chemistry
Physics of Condensed Matter
Physics of Particles and Fields
Veterinary Medicine
Virology

GREECE
Analytical Chemistry
Applied Mathematics
Astronomy and Astrophysics
Atomic Molecular and Chemical Physics
Botany
Civil Engineering
Computer Applications and Cybernetics
Dentistry and Odontology
Electrical and Electronic Engineering
Geosciences
Inorganic and Nuclear Chemistry
Mechanics
Nuclear Science and Technology
Pathology
Pediatrics
Physics of Condensed Matter
Physics of Particles and Fields
Polymer Science
Urology and Nephrology

IRELAND
Agriculture
Food Science and Technology
General and Internal Medicine
Inorganic and Nuclear Chemistry
Microbiology
Obstetrics and Gynecology
Organic Chemistry
Pharmacology and Pharmacy
Psychiatry
Urology and Nephrology
Veterinary Medicine

ITALY
Analytical Chemistry
Andrology

Applied Chemistry
Applied Mathematics
Astronomy and Astrophysics
Atomic Molecular and Chemical Physics
Biomedical Engineering
Cancer
Cardiovascular System
Crystallography
Cytology and Histology
Endocrinology and Metabolism
Gastroenterology
Hematology
Inorganic and Nuclear Chemistry
Instruments and Instrumentation
Materials Science
Mathematical Physics
Mineralogy
Neurosciences
Nuclear Physics
Nuclear Science and Technology
Optics
Organic Chemistry
Pharmacology and Pharmacy
Physical Chemistry
Physics of Particles and Fields
Polymer Science
Research and Experimental Medicine
Spectroscopy
Urology and Nephrology

NETHERLANDS
Acoustics
Allergy
Analytical Chemistry
Anatomy and Morphology
Applied Mathematics
Astronomy and Astrophyics
Atomic Molecular and Chemical Physics
Biochemistry and Molecular Biology
Biomedical Engineering
Biophysics
Botany
Cardiovascular System
Computer Applications and Cybernetics
Crystallography

Cytology and Histology
Dentistry and Odontology
Dermatology and Venereal Diseases
Endocrinology and Metabolism
Genetics and Heredity
Hematology
Immunology
Mathematical Physics
Microbiology
Microscopy
Neurosciences
Nuclear Physics
Ophthalmology
Ornithology
Paleontology
Pathology
Pharmacology and Pharmacy
Physical Chemistry
Research and Experimental Medicine
Soil Science
Spectroscopy
Veterinary Medicine
Virology
Water Resources

PORTUGAL
Cytology and Histology
Microbiology
Physical Chemistry

SPAIN
Allergy
Analytical Chemistry
Anatomy and Morphology
Atomic Molecular and Chemical Physics
Biochemistry and Molecular Biology
Biophysics
Botany
Chemical Engineering
Computer Applications and Cybernetics
Crystallography
Electrochemistry
Energy and Fuels
Food Science and Technology
Genetics and Heredity

Inorganic and Nuclear Chemistry
Materials Science
Mathematical Physics
Microbiology
Mineralogy
Mycology
Optics
Organic Chemistry
Physical Chemistry
Physics of Condensed Matter
Physics of Particles and Fields
Polymer Science
Urology and Nephrology

UNITED KINGDOM
Allergy
Anatomy and Morphology
Anesthesiology
Applied Chemistry
Botany
Construction and Building Technology
Dentistry and Odontology
Dermatology and Venereal Diseases
Ecology
Embryology
Endocrinology and Metabolism
Gastroenterology
General and Internal Medicine
Hygiene and Public Health
Inorganic and Nuclear Chemistry
Marine and Freshwater Biology
Materials Science
Mechanics
Medical Laboratory Technology
Microscopy
Mineralogy
Mycology
Nutrition and Dietetics
Obstetrics and Gynecology
Operations Resources and Management Sciences
Ornithology
Orthopedics
Parasitology
Pathology
Pharmacology and Pharmacy

Psychiatry
Respiratory System
Rheumatology
Statistics and Probability
Surgery
Tropical Medicine
Veterinary Medicine

AUSTRIA
Analytical Chemistry
Anatomy and Morphology
Anesthesiology
Applied Mathematics
Atomic Molecular and Chemical Physics
Biomedical Engineering
Cardiovascular System
Dermatology and Venereal Diseases
Endocrinology and Metabolism
Food Science and Technology
Gastroenterology
General and Internal Medicine
Hematology
Metallurgy and Mining
Microscopy
Mineralogy
Nuclear Science and Technology
Obstetrics and Gynecology
Ophthalmology
Otorhinolaryngology
Pediatrics
Pharmacology and Pharmacy
Urology and Nephrology

FINLAND
Allergy
Analytical Chemistry
Anesthesiology
Cytology and Histology
Dentistry and Odontology
Dermatology and Venereal Diseases
Endocrinology and Metabolism
Gastroenterology
General and Internal Medicine
Genetics and Heredity
Hygiene and Public Health

Immunology
Microbiology
Nuclear Physics
Obstetrics and Gynecology
Ophthalmology
Orthopedics
Otorhinolaryngology
Paper and Pulp Technology
Pathology
Pediatrics
Pharmacology and Pharmacy
Research and Experimental Medicine
Rheumatology
Surgery
Toxicology
Urology and Nephrology
Zoology

NORWAY
Allergy
Anesthesiology
Biochemistry and Molecular Biology
Biomedical Engineering
Biophysics
Cancer
Cardiovascular System
Cytology and Histology
Dentistry and Odontology
Dermatology and Venereal Diseases
Ecology
Environmental Sciences
Fisheries
Gastroenterology
Geology
Hematology
Immunology
Inorganic and Nuclear Chemistry
Marine and Freshwater Biology
Microbiology
Neurosciences
Obstetrics and Gynecology
Operations Resources and Management Sciences
Ornithology
Orthopedics
Otorhinolaryngology

Pathology
Pharmacology and Pharmacy
Physiology
Radiology and Nuclear Medicine
Research and Experimental Medicine
Rheumatology
Toxicology
Urology and Nephrology
Veterinary Medicine
Zoology

SWEDEN
Allergy
Analytical Chemistry
Andrology
Anesthesiology
Biochemistry and Molecular Biology
Biophysics
Cancer
Cytology and Histology
Dentistry and Odontology
Dermatology and Venereal Diseases
Ecology
Endocrinology and Metabolism
Environmental Sciences
Gastroenterology
Genetics and Heredity
Hematology
Hygiene and Public Health
Immunology
Marine and Freshwater Biology
Microscopy
Neurosciences
Obstetrics and Gynecology
Ornithology
Orthopedics
Otorhinolaryngology
Paper and Pulp Technology
Pediatrics
Pharmacology and Pharmacy
Physiology
Psychiatry
Research and Experimental Medicine
Rheumatology
Surgery

Toxicology
Urology and Nephrology

SWITZERLAND
Atomic Molecular and Chemical Physics
Biochemistry and Molecular Biology
Crystallography
Cytology and Histology
Embryology
Immunology
Instruments and Instrumentation
Mathematical Physics
Mechanical Engineering
Microscopy
Nuclear Physics
Nuclear Science and Technology
Pharmacology and Pharmacy
Physics of Condensed Matter
Physics of Particles and Fields
Tropical Medicine

ISRAEL
Aerospace Engineering and Technology
Andrology
Applied Mathematics
Atomic Molecular and Chemical Physics
Biochemistry and Molecular Biology
Biomedical Engineering
Biophysics
Botany
Cancer
Civil Engineering
Computer Applications and Cybernetics
Dentistry and Odontology
Energy and Fuels
Genetics and Heredity
Horticulture
Immunology
Limnology
Materials Science
Mechanics
Nuclear Physics
Obstetrics and Gynecology
Operations Resources and Management Sciences
Optics

Orthopedics
Otorhinolaryngology
Pediatrics
Physics of Condensed Matter
Soil Science
Statistics and Probability
Urology and Nephrology
Virology
Water Resources

Source: *Scientometrics* (June 1989).

Chapter 15

International and European Cooperation in Scientific Research: A German Point of View

BEATE KOHLER-KOCH

Scientific Research and International Scientific Cooperation: A Growing Concern for Public Policy

Throughout Europe the advancement of science is regarded as a public good and the support of scientific research as a legitimate object of public policy. Especially in the area of basic scientific research, it is the state that provides the financial means and determines the institutional framework. Thus under the auspices of the state a highly differentiated university system has developed in Europe, supplemented by an equally diversified system of highly specialized public research institutions.

Although there is considerable national variation, certain common features and trends in Europe include: (1) a striving for more efficiency to bring into line the demand for expanding research efforts with limited public funds, (2) a more intensive cooperation between public and private research in order to bridge the gap between basic and applied research and make better economic use of scientific research; and (3) a growing willingness to promote international cooperation and transfer regulatory competences in the field of science and research to the European Community.

Governments support international cooperation in scientific research because they consider it to be the most promising strategy to meet three major contemporary challenges. First, science and technology are regarded as the decisive productive factor in the global race for economic competitiveness. Although there is a broad consensus all over Europe that it is primarily private business that must cope with this challenge, public authorities provide support in different ways: public engagement in research on high-technology products, financial and administrative support for international cooperation in "precompetitive" research, as well as incentives for the international mobility of researchers and the internationalization of higher education.

Second, environmental risks and demographic imbalances form a category of global challenge that requires international concerted action and joint efforts in scientific research. Scientific cooperation has assumed a prominent place in the international political agenda in terms of improving our understanding of the problems we face and our capacity to cope with present risks and avoid future ones. Public authorities engage in and promote a broad range of activities from joint research to providing the infrastructure for better communication of scientific findings, more effective exploitation of science for technological innovation, and more efficient dissemination of technologies.

Third, apart from trying to cope with the challenges of international interdependence, supranational cooperation in scientific research is accorded importance in Europe because it is part of the process of political integration. From the very inception of the EC, scientific cooperation was promoted within its framework not only for economic or technical reasons; it has always been part of a political strategy. This explains why in many cases governments support Community programs in scientific cooperation even though the net benefits are less promising than they would be if the cooperation included non-European partners.

The Internationalization of Scientific Communities

Despite the fact that European governments consider it a foremost task to ensure the optimal development of scientific research, this is a policy area that easily evades political regulation. The same holds true for international scientific cooperation. Scientific communities are international by nature. Since they easily exceed national frontiers, they can hardly be directed by politically devised strategies or contained in politically defined regional settings. Although governmental policies aim at influencing the formation of the international scientific communities, like all other communities they follow their own logic of community building. Patterns evolve over time and vary according to discipline. Nevertheless, these communities have some characteristics in common that give some indications about basic rules and driving forces. When surveying the present state of international scientific cooperation, some of what one finds is surprising and some is what one might expect.

To begin with, very little is known about the structure or scope of international cooperation in scientific research.[1] There is no systematic information at hand about the number of countries participating in international projects, the relative importance of international research activities compared to national ones, the intensity of international cooperation in different disciplines, the relevance of multilateral compared to bilateral cooperation, and the like. The main reason for our patchy knowledge about scientific cooperation is that it mainly depends on the individual initiative of researchers and the decentralized activities of particular research institutes or university departments.

For at least a rough picture of international scientific activities, one may turn to the *Science Citation Index.*[2] Analysis of this empirical data set yields the conclusions[3] that:

1. Scientific research is to an overwhelming extent a national affair.
2. International cooperation has grown rapidly in recent years, but because of a low starting point annual growth rates of 7%-8% increased the share of international joint publications to only about 10% of the total amount of scientific publications in the early 1990s.
3. Some disciplines are more international than others; as is traditional, mathematics is taking the lead, followed by geology and space research and physics.
4. Regional distribution is heavily imbalanced; international scientific cooperation mainly takes place between the member states of the OECD.
5. Although the larger OECD countries such as the United States, United Kingdom, Germany, France, and Canada take the largest share, it is the small countries such as Switzerland, Belgium, Austria, and Ireland that in relation to their national scientific activities are well represented in the international field.
6. Among OECD countries cooperation is most intensive in the field of "big science" with its costly equipment requirements, and growth rates have been most spectacular in engineering and technology.

From these findings one may conclude that the propensity to cooperate reflects (1) the very nature of the science involved (equipment requirements, economic applications, etc.); (2) the scientific capacity and therefore attractiveness of the potential cooperation partners; (3) the competitive nature of the national scientific environment in question; and (4) the increase in internationalization of industrial research.

The Multifaceted Nature of European Scientific Cooperation

Cooperation in scientific research is much more developed in Europe than in other parts of the world. There is a whole network of intergovernmental and nongovernmental organizations, of multilateral and bilateral programs and activities.

A number of European institutions of joint research are dedicated to special areas of scientific activities and have overlapping memberships. The following are only the most prominent:

CERN	(European Organization for Nuclear Research)
	(Conseil Européen pour la Recherche Nucléaire)
EMBL	(European Molecular Biology Laboratory)
ESA	(European Space Agency)
ESO	(European Southern Observatory)
ESF	(European Science Foundation)
EUI	(European University Institute, Florence)
ILL	(Institute Max von Laue-Paul Langevin)
ESRF	(Europäische Synchrotronstrahlungsanlage, Grenoble)

Since the 1950s, the European Community has played an important role in European scientific cooperation. Over the past decade it considerably increased the number and size of its programs. By opening Community programs to the EFTA countries and associated East European countries, it extended its geographical scope. More important, however, the Community gained political weight. In the 1980s it was able to launch some successful high-technology programs (in particular the well-known ESPRIT program), and with the amendment of the Community treaties through the Single European Act and recently the Treaty of Maastricht it was endowed with additional legal powers. In this way the EC became a political actor, and the EC Commission assumed the role of a political entrepreneur forging coalitions between business and governments to promote its idea of a European Science and Technology Community.

Although EC-governed scientific cooperation gained considerable momentum over the past two decades, it is neither a closed shop nor without external competition. Apart from the various specialist organizations mentioned above, since the early 1970s COST (European Cooperation in the Field of Scientific and Technical Research), and since 1986 EUREKA (European Research Coordination Agency), have developed as successful frameworks for launching a series of scientific cooperations between members and nonmembers of the EC, with the EC taking an active part.

Since (West) European cooperation in science and technology is well documented in recent publications,[4] there is no need to go into further detail here. Instead

I shall focus in the next section on recent trends and some interesting controversies surrounding the Fourth Framework Programme for Community Research and Technological Development.

Less visible than the EC-inspired and -monitored research cooperation is the dense network of cooperative activities outside the official frameworks. There are numerous cooperative agreements among universities (German universities alone have concluded about 1500 cooperation agreements with other universities all over the world)[5] and research institutions that certainly contribute much to scientific cooperation, but it is difficult to measure their impact. Most of them only provide the necessary organizational framework for an exchange of students and teaching staff. More promising are transnational regional cooperations such as the recently established European Confederation of Universities at the Rhine (EUCOR) including Freiburg (Germany), Basel (Switzerland), and Strasbourg (France). Their aims are quite ambitious and go beyond the regular exchange of students and teaching staff, and include establishment of joint curricula and integrated studies, setting up of integrated institutions, engagement in joint research projects, and developing a common research infrastructure. Other existing agreements such as the Saar-Lor-Lux-West-Palatine Cooperation, the French-German University Institute for Technology and Economics (DFHI), the Conference of Baltic Universities, or the university cooperation between the "four motor regions" (Baden-Württemberg, Catalonia, Lombardy, and Rhône-Alpes) have concentrated up to now on joint teaching programs but are starting to expand into scientific research as well.

Recent Trends in EC Cooperation in Scientific Research

The influence of the EC policies in science and technology on the process of the internationalization of scientific research in Europe is marginal and yet important. This paradox may be explained by taking a closer look at the nature and financial scope of the EC programs and their political and economic setting. The total amount involved in community programs represents only some 4% of government expenditure by the member states (the German government generously supported the Commission's plea to increase its amount to 6%).[6] The programs focus, however, on a small area of science and technology and therefore they account in some highly relevant fields such as information technology for about 30% of the member states' expenditures. EC programs in general support applied though "precompetitive" research (two-thirds of the projects in the Second Framework Programme were of direct industrial applicability according to the Commission's own estimation)[7] and therefore are considered to be "of only marginal relevance to basic research."[8] This judgment may be true for the research activities within the framework of EUREKA.

In EUREKA it is up to the business world to initiate and decide about joint research programs. Enterprises cooperate in order to achieve technological progress and strengthen their competitive position on the market. The science and technology programs of the EC are of a different nature; they are part of an evolving field of EC policymaking, and this process in itself is part of the whole process of "community building." To look at it as a conglomeration of single programs would be to underestimate the Community's impact, and neglect the political dimension and the dynamics inherent in recent developments:

1. EC activities in the field of science and technology are part of a broader economic and political strategy of completing the Internal Market, preserving Europe's international competitiveness, and deepening the process of political integration. Therefore, the agreement to expand the Community's competence in this field was not only based on considerations about the benefits of scientific cooperation. It was, rather, part of a compromise between competing interests that have as much to do with cost sharing and pooling of resources as with expectations of profitable technology transfer and rent-seeking behavior. All of the EC-framework programs have been package deals that struck a balance between these competing interests. Besides, some countries only accepted them because they were part of the bargain to go ahead with the internal market program and political integration. Therefore, it is difficult to say in which direction the Community's science policy will move in the future. In the past the EC Commission played an important role, acting as a "political entrepreneur" that brought together interested parties and influential political actors in order to establish a consensus regarding expansion of Community activities in science and technology. The success story of ESPRIT (European Strategic Programme of Research and Development in Information Technology) makes worthwhile reading[9] because it shows how a dynamic commissioner managed to forge a "winning coalition" with the dominant enterprises that was able to promote a joint program in information technology despite divergent national interests and the hesitation of some governments to engage in a European science and technology project. Whether or not the role of scientific cooperation will be strengthened and what sorts of priorities will be established in the future depend on the overall development of the integration process and the ability of different political actors to channel their interests into EC decisionmaking. At present there is a rising demand for a steady growth in EC allocation for science and technology and a broadening of its scope to include basic research and areas not related to the objective of increasing EC competitiveness.

2. The policy process in EC science and technology affairs provokes some expansive logic of its own. Apart from the EC Commission CREST (Scientific and Technical Research Committee of the EC) and the whole apparatus of program management, committees are vital for the agenda setting and for formulation,

implementation, and reformulation of EC science and technology policy. These committees not only bring together representatives of the European scientific and technological communities but provide a strong incentive for the formation of transnational networks of the different communities. They attract and strengthen those sectors that favor the upgrading of the European component in scientific research. They are not only a place for bargaining but a forum of communication and a platform for the propagation of a more intensive European cooperation in scientific research.

So far, industrially oriented programs have dominated the Community's research activities. It is therefore no surprise that enterprises most active in the technological sectors are, along with their particular interests, best represented. In the meantime, however, the European Parliament has gained additional political competences and seeks to use them effectively. It is the European Parliament that calls for enlarging the scope of EC scientific research to cover social and political aspects such as the quality of life and the future of European integration.

3. EC funds for joint research are limited, but in times of scarce resources they are very attractive. And as governments are eager to achieve a *"juste retour"* they give support to their national clientele that find it difficult to gain access. Information on Community programs, selection criteria, application procedures, and even assistance in organizational matters such as contacting foreign partners are offered to universities as well as small and medium-size enterprises that find it difficult to cope with the technicalities of the Community procedures. Governments thereby highlight the importance of international scientific cooperation and encourage their own national science communities to "go European."

The provision entailed in all EC programs that partners from different EC countries have to take part in a project provides additional incentives for European cooperation. Transnational research networks are expanding, beyond the actual needs of meeting the requirements of the EC. Empirical analyses reveal the paradoxical situation that whereas transnational research cooperation initiated in EC projects is often considered to be of marginal effect and has a short duration, the willingness to cooperate on a European level is rising. A "new thinking" has emerged that attaches great importance to joint research, exchange, networking, and mobility. There is a common belief, which gives rise to self-fulfilling prophecies, that the Single European Market will demand a European dimension in research and training.

At present the EC is working on the next framework program for the years 1994-1998.[10] It follows existing trends but puts more emphasis on environment, transportation, the life sciences, and cooperation with third countries. Although the Maastricht treaty has not yet been ratified, the Fourth Framework Programme takes into account the new options it offers, especially with respect to including all the research activities covered by the treaty "whatever their form and under whichever common policy they fall"[11] and the potential for coordination of national research policies.

The proposal of the Commission pursues two main objectives: strengthening of the competitive position of European industry at the international level and improvement of the quality of life. Although the majority of the proposed research topics still are related specifically to the needs of industry, the Commission interpreted the new wording of article 130f in the Maastricht treaty as encouragement to take up broader issues contributing to the satisfaction of society's needs. Core themes suggested are sciences and technology for: a new urban habitat; the preservation of European cultural heritage; the struggle against social exclusion; the understanding of global environmental change; and addressing Europe's major health problems. In addition, many of the core thematic areas advanced for making Europe's industry more competitive take into account the human factor. Nevertheless, the number of actions, their characteristics, and the distribution of funds constitute a clear indication that the main objective still is to improve Europe's competitiveness in advanced technologies in the fields of information and communication, industrial manufacturing, genetics, and energy.

New to the program is an enhanced role for the social sciences. The contribution from the social sciences (in a broad sense, including economics, law, political science, sociology, etc.) is, however, still marginal and for the most part subsumed under the program on "Industrial Technologies." During the negotiation of the Fourth Framework Programme several social science institutions and individual scientists took the initiative to revise the program in this regard. The EC Commission itself (i.e., DG-XII, the department in charge) commissioned a study on the "Social Sciences in the Context of the European Communities" and in addition presented a memorandum of an internal interservice group.[12] The external report was presented by prominent scientists who at the time were chairing the U.K. Economic and Social Research Council and the Staning Committee for the Social Sciences of the European Science Foundation, respectively. Its thrust was to assign a higher value to social science research with respect to the management of technological change and science policy. Even in that limited context, the report demonstrates in a very convincing way that the Community could better make use of the potential benefits from European social science. The authors distinguished five barriers to the effective mobilization of European social science: (1) the still predominant orientation of social science research to the nation-state (including outdated application of "subsidiarity"; (2) the current gap between the quality of most national data and what is available on a European level; (3) the weakness of links between research institutions; (4) the need to develop and improve human resources; and (5) correction of false images of the social sciences. Their recommendations focused on ways of promoting the effective mobilization of European social sciences, such as developing networks, improving data resources, and supporting a modest social science research program.

The proposal of the Interservices Group was bolder: it advocated a social science research program that would go beyond questions of technological change or operational studies undertaken within the respective policy areas of the Community, and should instead contribute to "a better understanding of the similarities and diversities between the national social systems, of the impacts of Community policies in the framework of different cultural contexts, and . . . of culturally bound attitudes."[13] Under the heading of "Integration and Diversity: The Dynamics of European Societies," three main initiatives are suggested:

1. Cross-cultural and cross-national comparative and cooperative research on European integration, the transformation of European societies, and international relations.
2. Equivalent research activities on the European economy.
3. Concerted action to build a European infrastructure in the social sciences.

Contributions of the social sciences to "science, technology, and society" and "strengthening competitivity" should be dealt with separately.

The idea of strengthening the contribution of the social sciences and even adding a separate social science program to the Fourth Framework Programme of the EC received support from the European science community and national political actors. In a resolution unanimously accepted by representatives of ten European Science Research councils and science ministries,[14] an "identifiable, separate programme on the social sciences" is called for. This was already recommended by different national delegations in meetings of CREST in 1992. Finally CREST decided, in its meeting of December 18, 1992, to set up an ad hoc group on social and economic sciences that met in March 1993 and agreed on a common recommendation much in line with the British position:

1. The Fourth Framework Programme should seek to strike a balance between (a) identifying the specific social science contribution to the programs in the physical and biological sciences, and (b) bringing together research with a social science focus under a separate category.
2. Joint European research should concentrate on topics of "European integration and diversity, economic competitiveness and the quality of life."
3. The social science research program should support the research infrastructure, for example, by harmonizing and promoting standards in data production and collection, documentation and archiving.

In October 1993, on the invitation of the European Commission, the European Science Foundation made a further effort to contribute to the debate on the importance of social science research to Community policy development. Three broad themes were suggested for systematic study: globalization and fragmentation; science, technology, and society; and European integration and social exclusion.[15]

The European Commission accepted part of these suggestions and included a chapter on "socioeconomic targeted research" in its proposal, concentrating on three broad themes: evaluation of Europe's science and technology options; research on education and vocational training; and research on social integration and exclusion in Europe.[16]

The Council, meeting in January 1994, signaled that it will support such a target through a very limited social research program that will be concerned with problems of technological innovation, economic competitiveness, and unemployment.

Another novelty of the Fourth Framework Programme is that it puts particular emphasis on the promotion of cooperation with third countries and international organizations. This has a strong regional, i.e., European, bias. On the one hand, it is intended to strengthen relations with the highly industrialized countries of Western Europe. The agreement creating the European Economic Area already provides for full participation of the EFTA countries in EC research activities. On the other hand, the Community wants to contribute to the development of the scientific and technological potential of the Central and East European countries. Emphasis is placed on the mobility of scientists, the development of "paneuropean" scientific networks, and joint research projects that are particularly well suited to contribute to the rehabilitation of these countries' productive systems and to the improvement of the quality of life in their societies.

Another objective is to strengthen synergies with other science and technology cooperation frameworks in Europe. The already close relationship between the Community and EUREKA is intended to be reinforced. The idea is that projects that at the same time contribute to the development of key generic technologies and have a strong element of applied, close-to-the-market research activity will get the support of both the Community and EUREKA: projects presented to the EC Commission will by way of concertation and common agreement be transformed into EUREKA projects, of which the activities concerning the development of generic technologies could be financed by the Community whereas the applied-research aspects would have to find other sources of finance.

In addition, the Community wants to strengthen its role in COST. It supports the expansion of COST both in scope, including new fields of research and the participation of additional disciplines such as the social sciences and chemistry, and in the number of participating countries. Already in 1991 Czechoslovakia, Poland, and Hungary were accepted as new members.

The development of COST, the even closer cooperation between the Community and EUREKA, and the extension of the Fourth Framework Programme to the EFTA countries and the Central and East European countries have two characteristics in common: (1) a greater role of the Community in the cooperation in scientific research, and (2) a concentration on Europe as the most relevant region.

In those cases where cooperation is extended beyond the European framework, the selection criterion is the scientific and technological capacity of the partner that promises the access to advanced knowledge. Cooperation takes place on a bilateral basis with highly industrialized countries, notably the United States and Japan, and in the framework of multilateral agreements such as those on Intelligent Manufacturing Systems, New Information Processing Technology, Human Frontier Science, and so on. Compared with these core activities, science and technology cooperation with developing countries is of minor importance.

A German View on International and European Science Cooperation

In May 1992 the German Science Council, an advisory body representing the academic world as well as both the national government and the state governments, presented a memorandum on the "internationalisation of scientific relations"[17] that strongly advocates strengthening international cooperation. Although the sciences have already reached a high level of international interconnectedness, the Wissenschaftsrat asked for strong political support to intensify this further. From its point of view, such political activities will have to take into account the changing context in which international scientific cooperation will take place.

Thus, with respect to the process of political integration and association in Europe, political aspirations within the EC to establish a European Science and Technology Community imply a reorientation of German international scientific relations, which since the end of the Second World War have mainly been oriented toward the United States. With the breakdown of the communist regimes in Central and Eastern Europe, closer political relations with those countries have been established. From a German standpoint, it is a challenge and a political duty to support the transition to democracy and efficient market economies in Germany's immediate neighborhood. This includes strengthening scientific relations and cooperation with the East.

Furthermore, the globalization of markets for high-technology products requires higher research investments. Public support for the advancement of science and technology is more and more regarded as a prerequisite for international competitiveness. In addition, the scientific aspects of advanced manufacturing technologies require a highly educated labor force. As markets become international, such a labor force requires international experience and knowledge of languages in addition to its scientific training.

Another consideration is that global environmental risks and a growing vulnerability due to international environmental interdependence call for international political as well as scientific cooperation. There is a consensus on the need for augmented international research efforts aimed at assessing the nature and magnitude of environmental change, the functioning of the ecosystem, the effects of human activities on key processes that govern climate, biogeochemical cycles, and so on, and at increasing our scientific and technological abilities to cope with growing risks.

Last but not least, there is growing concern about a deepening technological gap between the highly industrialized and the developing countries. Because of the high level of international interdependence, growing ecological risks that call for a change of policies in the developing world, as well as a lingering alienation between the two worlds, it is considered of utmost importance that existing scientific-technological cooperations be critically evaluated in view of new priorities. One of those priorities is to achieve better intercultural understanding.

In its recommendations, the Wissenschaftsrat placed just as much emphasis on the internationalization of academic teaching and research. Student mobility is still very low and should be increased by a number of administrative and financial improvements. Public incentives for the international exchange of academic teaching staff and researchers are considered to be working well but in need of enhancement. There is agreement regarding the strengthening of European activities in science and technology but not as an exclusive strategy and with some reservations concerning priorities and organizational framing. Several critical points have been raised with respect to EC policies.

First, access is felt to be difficult, procedures are cumbersome and time-consuming, and the acceptance rate in comparison to national funds is relatively low. In addition, the objectives of the EC research programs, with their priorities placed on applied research and on direct economic and technological benefits to be realized in a short time, are not compatible with the objectives of research carried out by universities or by other public research institutions such as, for example, those of the Max Planck Gesellschaft. Because of structural differences and difficult procedures, the German participation in EC programs is below average.

Second, even with respect to the European support of research in key technologies of major industrial interest there are several reservations. From a neoliberal point of view, which is still prevalent in elite political and economic circles, the German government should resist the temptations of increasing Community involvement in industrial research and oppose the trend of using research and technology policies as instruments of a European industrial policy.[18]

Third, although the EC Commission tries hard to sell the message that "there is no contradiction between the specific nature of RTP policy, notably with regard to the excellence which must characterise it, and the objective of cohesion,"[19] it did not manage to convince the German partners. The German delegation complained already in the evaluation of the Second Framework Programme that scientific relevance, innovativeness of contents, and hence the contribution of an activity to strengthening competitiveness are accorded minor importance.[20] The Wissenschaftsrat, for its part, asked that it be guaranteed that the objective of cohesion will not dominate the EC research policy based on article 130f but rather will be pursued through actions undertaken by the Community via the structural funds.[21]

Another point of concern is the application of the principle of subsidiarity in Community action. The German interpretation is far more restricted than that of the Community, according to which subsidiarity is "intrinsic" not only to "big science" activities but also to technological activities that benefit a larger number of industrial sectors and entail long-term investments.[22] From a German point of view, Community activities in the field of research and technological development should concentrate on those items where the European "added value" is obvious and no comparable effects could be attained by national or bilateral transnational efforts.[23]

Especially when it comes to basic research, the German partners are very hesitant to give the Community a greater say. The Länder are afraid that this might impinge on their political competence, and the scientific community and the universities are concerned that they might lose part of their autonomy. This is the main reason why the Wissenschaftsrat proposed a strengthening of international scientific cooperation, not by transferring even more power and money to the EC but by introducing the principle of academic self-government into the field of European research policy. The suggestion is either to build up a new European institution or to transform the existing European Science Foundation in a way compatible with the principles of autonomy, self-regulation, and peer review to ensure scientific excellence.[24]

Israel and Germany in International Science Cooperation

In the field of science policy as well, it is the political change in Europe and all the problems entailed in the German unification process that attract public attention. As long as they are not directly involved, political actors as well as the scientific community take little notice of bilateral cooperation in scientific research, even if it enjoys a long tradition and is of considerable volume. This is particularly true in the case of Israeli-German cooperation. There is an intense network of scientific exchange and joint research activities between the two countries; cooperation is well institutionalized, and if measured in terms of funds raised in relation to GNP per capita, Israel ranks first among Germany's cooperation partners. The German side supports the bilateral cooperation in scientific research with an annual contribution of about DM 30 million. There are special programs jointly coordinated by the German and Israeli ministries of science and technology on ecology, biotechnology, water technology, agriculture, medicine, energy, and new engineering materials. The German-Israeli Foundation for Scientific Research extends support to joint research projects. In addition, the Minerva Foundation, a subsidiary of the Max Planck Society, provides financial support to research, especially in the natural sciences.

Apart from the promotion of research cooperation, a scholarship program gives young scientists the opportunity to spend a year or two in the other country engaged in scientific research. This program is well established and has created long-lasting relations between individual scientists as well as between research institutions. One of the reasons is that scholarships are not offered merely on a short-term basis and that the institutes the young researchers visit are distinguished ones. On average over the years, more than twice as many scientists apply as can be accepted. In general, more Germans have taken an interest in going to Israel than vice versa (approximately 60% to 40%). About 70 scholarships are offered each year, ensuring a steady flow of scientific communication between the two countries.

The present discussion about a European Science and Technology Community gives the impression that in this area, too, a "fortress Europe" might emerge. There are strong integrative tendencies that should not be underestimated. The EC Commission as well as the European Parliament are in favor of a European trend in any policy area because this will strengthen their own institutional role. Member states support such transfer of competences whenever it gives them access to additional funds. Even a country such as Germany, though it is a net contributor to the EC household, has an ambiguous attitude: shifting competences to the EC level means that governments may escape being held responsible for reducing financial support and rejecting demands of politically influential pressure groups. Nevertheless, the Europeanization of scientific research has so far played more of a role in political rhetoric than in political reality. Bilateral political agreements such as that between Israel and Germany, and the association with research excellence in the partner country, will retain their value in the future. This judgment should not, however, deter anyone from involvement in the burgeoning multilateral activities of joint research among scientifically advanced countries.

Notes

1. OECD, *Choosing Priorities in Science and Technology* (Paris, 1991) .

2. M. P. Carpenter and F. Narin, "The Adequacy of the Science Citation Index (SCI) as an Indicator of International Scientific Activity," *Journal of American Society for Information Science,* November 1991.

3. OECD, *Wissenschafts- und Technologiepolitik: Bilanz und Ausblick 1991* (Paris, 1992).

4. J. Starbatty and U. Vetterlein, *Die Technologiepolitik der Europäischen Gemeinschaft: Entstehung, Praxis und Ordnungspolitische Konformitat* (Baden-Baden, 1990); M. Felder,"Forschungs- und Technologiepolitik zwischen Internationalisierung und Regionalisierung," FEG Studium no. 1,Marburg, 1992; Grewlich, *Europa im globalen Technologiewettlauf: der Weltmarkt wird zum Binnenmarkt* (Gutersloh, 1992) .

5. Westdeutsche Rektorenkonferenz, *Kooperationsvereinbarungen (Partnerschaften) zwischen deutschen und auslandischen Hochschulen* (Bonn, 1987) .

6. "Deutsches Memorandum zur Europäischen Forschungspolitik," Bonn, 1992.

7. Commission of the European Communities: CREST, "Scientific Research and Technological Development in the Community: The Facts in Figures," Luxembourg, 1988.

8. OECD, *Choosing Priorities,* p. 67.

9. M. Sharp and C. Shearman, *European Technological Collaboration* (London/New York, 1987); W. Sandholtz, *High-Tech Europe: The Politics of International Cooperation* (Berkeley, 1992) .

10. Commission of the European Communities, "Working Document of the Commission Concerning the Fourth Framework Programme of Community Activities in the Field of Research and Technological Development (1994-1998)," Brussels, 1992.

11. Ibid.

12. Commission of the European Communities, "Integration and Diversity: The Dynamics of European Societies—Advocating Research in Social Sciences and the Humanities for the 4th Framework Programme," report of the Interservices Group "Interface: Social Sciences/Technology," Brussels, 1992.

13. Ibid., p. 2.

14. Norwegian Research Council for Science and Humanities, "Resolution on the Fourth Framework Programme for Community Research and Technological Development From Ten European Social Science Research Councils," Oslo, December 1992.

15. European Science Foundation, "Social Science Frontiers in European Research," report of a Workshop on Social Science in the Fourth EG Framework Programme on Research and Technological Development (1994-1998), Brussels, October 1993, p. 3.

16. Commission Européenne, "Proposition de Decision du Conseil (arretant un programme specifique de recherche dans le domaine de la recherche socio-economique finalisee)," Brussels, January 1994 (conf.), p. 7.

17. Wissenschaftsrat, "Empfehlungen zur Internationalisierung der Wissenschaftsbeziehungen," Koln, 1992.

18. Starbatty and Vetterlein, *Die Technologiepolitik*; M. E. Streit, "Industriepolitik: eine ordnungspolitische Herausforderung," in G. Fels and O. Vogel, eds., *Brauchen wir eine neue Industriepolitik* (Koln, 1987), pp. 131-151.

19. Commission of the European Communities, "Working Document," p. 3.

20. Commission of the European Communities: CREST, "Bewertung des zweiten FTE Rahmenprogrammes," Bericht des CREST an den Rat, CREST/1212/1/92, Brussels, 1992, p. 32.

21. Wissenschaftsrat, "Empfehlungen," p. 72.

22. Commission of the European Communities, "Working Document," p. 2.

23. Wissenschaftsrat, "Empfehlungen," p. 71.

24. Ibid., pp. 74-76, 80.

Chapter 16

The State of Cooperation in Scientific Research: Israel and the EC

ALEX KEYNAN

Introduction

To begin with, it is important to clarify that international *scientific cooperation* is very different from other kinds of international cooperation. For example, political or economic international cooperation is cooperation between nation-states. Such cooperation is usually based on *formal, well-defined agreements*. The results of such agreements affect society directly and are controlled by it.

However, although international scientific cooperation can be carried out at various levels, it is basically cooperation between individual scientists, or groups of scientists. Such cooperation is *informal* in most cases and its objective is to facilitate the advancement of knowledge, usually knowledge that is available to the public. Furthermore, whereas cooperation between nation-states is optional in most cases, and changes continuously in its content and structure, cooperation between scientists is a vital necessity of science and an intrinsic part of the sociology of science, as we shall see later; science cannot flourish without it.

International scientific cooperation occurs on a wide spectrum of organizational levels. On its most basic level, it is an informal, noninstitutionalized cooperation between individuals living in different countries. On its most elaborate levels, international scientific cooperation might be based on an agreement between governments to support cooperative scientific projects considered to be of benefit to the cooperating countries. On such elaborate levels, these agreements do clearly resemble other kinds of international cooperation.

Before dealing with some of the basic concepts on which international scientific cooperation is based, it will help to clarify what is meant here by science. In common usage, science can mean two different things: basic research, which tries to understand nature and its basic rules; or applied research or technology. The ultimate objective of basic research is the acquisition of new knowledge. Applied research or the development of technologies are activities that aim to use existing knowledge to solve practical problems and to create new products or processes.

There are also sociological differences between applied scientists and technologists on the one hand and the basic research community on the other. These differences are most evident in the way that the two communities handle information. Scientists are usually partners in a large international network of individuals with common interests, in which information more often than not flows freely. They usually know by word of mouth, or through frequent meetings, what is happening in their field, and do not have to read much to get the information they need although, to be sure, their reputations depend on their publications. Technologists, on the other hand, are more secretive about their work; they obtain any written material relevant to their projects, and if they publish at all they do so in patent. Indeed, as de Solla Price pointed out: "The scientist wants to write but not read. The technologist wants to read, but not write."[1]

In this chapter I shall focus primarily on international cooperation between scientists as opposed to technologists, in the context of European-Israeli relations.

Basic Concepts of International Scientific Cooperation

The Universality of Science

Scientific knowledge is the creation of the individual. Society may support or inhibit the creative individual, but there is nothing to replace him. Hence, though society can regulate some aspects of the activities of science, especially in its interface with society (e.g., tests on humans and animals, rules of safety and confinement), democratic societies, at least, have learned that they cannot "regulate" science. It is the scientific community that judges what constitutes scientific truth. The results of scientific inquiry are published in international journals and are only valid when confirmed and accepted by peers, wherever they might be. Therefore, universalism is part and parcel of the normative, everyday structure of science.

According to Merton,

> scientific truth claims, whatever their source, are to be subject to pre-established impersonal criteria, consonant with observation and with previously confirmed knowledge. The acceptance or rejection of claims entering the list of science is not to depend on the personal or social attitudes of their protagonist. . . . The Haber Process cannot

> be validated by a Nuremberg Decree, nor can an anglophobe repeal the law of gravitation. . . . The imperative of universalism is rooted deep in the impersonal character of science.[2]

By its nature, science is universal knowledge, shared by all mankind; it does not belong to any nation-state. In contributing to science, one is part of an international "invisible college," not limited by borders, ethnicity, or even linguistics. International cooperation is therefore not a marginal activity of the scientific community, but part and parcel of it. All this is not meant to imply that scientists do not compete with each other—they do, and it is a positive factor in the advancement of science if restrained by certain rules; they may even conceal information so as to ensure priority, and exhibit every other kind of human weakness. But all of their "political behavior" is tactical; strategically, a scientist has to prove the validity of his or her claims to peers on the international plane. Scientists have also long realized that progress in science is stimulated by ongoing interaction among creative individuals or teams often at great geographical distance from each other. The scientific community, therefore, looks for mechanisms that facilitate such cooperation.

Science and National Interests

It is now commonly believed that the achievements of science and their translation into technology have profoundly influenced the direction of modern society. Therefore, a country's ability to create and use science determines to a large extent its place in the family of nations.

As we have seen, science is international, but scientists are members of nation-states. Their ability to pursue their work and conduct their lives is dependent on the social and political structures of the society in which they live. Their funding is national, and very often reflects national priorities of the public that finances their activity. The international aspect of science is not generally evident, but its contribution to society tends to make the headlines.

As basic research approaches technology, governments also desire to control its applied results. The complex relationship between science and government involves elements both of support and control. It is gradually being realized that governments have to support not only technology but basic research as well. Indeed, the governments of most industrialized Western countries do support basic research on a significant scale, but at the same time try to control the direction and results of that research by selecting fields to support what they perceive to be of national interest. Public control of the results of basic research is limited, however, because open publication is part of the basic research process. Thus, governments try to control the dissemination of the results of applied research and technology, especially those of military or economic importance. The main objectives of such control include shielding useful innovative information in defense technology from adversary countries, and industrially useful information from competing countries.

International cooperation in basic science is, then, quite different from cooperation in applied science and technology. International cooperation in basic research occurs continuously between scientists. Governments are approached only if funds are needed, but they do not generally dominate or regulate such relations with the exception of financial control, which makes government a "silent" partner. In contrast, international cooperation in the development of new technologies, whether initiated by scientists or by governments, is usually government dominated, especially in the field of military technology. Such technology is, of course, subject to secrecy, and scientists and engineers dealing with "classified information" or "military secrets" are restricted in their international contacts by stringent laws.

In summary, it may be said that though scientists engaged in fundamental research usually experience no conflict of loyalty between the universality of science and their commitment to their country, the principle of universality prevails. The principle of serving one's country (or company) prevails, however, in the field of applied science and technology where the international flow of information is either self-controlled by commercial considerations or controlled by government regulation.

Whereas scientists tend to cooperate with other scientists worldwide if this serves their own research purposes and the progress of science, governments have both positive and negative considerations in undertaking scientific cooperation with other governments. Governments' positive considerations are based on the fact that by sharing resources and knowledge, each government can achieve its research goals at lower cost and in less time. Negative considerations have to do with the concern that by publicizing a commercially valuable invention a nation might lose its competitive edge in certain fields. In any case, the success of international cooperation depends not only on cooperation between the governments but also on the cooperation of the scientific or engineering community in question.

Motives, Levels, and Modes of International Cooperation

The concept of international scientific cooperation includes many different kinds of cooperation performed on a variety of levels, from interpersonal to intergovernmental and multinational.

In basic research, international cooperation between individuals is very common. Thousands of such links exist, and they involve anything from exchanges of information to exchanges of graduate students. Such agreements are informal, based on an exchange of letters and mutual trust. If joint funding is needed in the case of large-scale science, applications to the government are made and agreements become more formal.

Motivations for cooperation are different for scientists and governments, respectively. Merton's imperative of universalism sheds light on why individual scientists initiate international cooperation. Scientific, rather than political, considerations are most often what motivate scientists to initiate international scientific cooperation, though they sometimes use their strong influence in their respective governments to facilitate this. For example, European scientists were able to convince their governments that each of their countries alone could not support the large institutes and expensive equipment, including large accelerators, that they needed for nuclear and particle physics. They therefore cooperated and established CERN (the European Laboratory for Nuclear Research), which is financed by governments but administered by scientists.

Governments, however, initiate cooperation for different reasons. Often governments perceive a need for a particular "know-how" base with economic potential, which cannot be achieved by their own scientific community in a reasonable time. Scientific cooperation agreements with other countries are intended to gain time and increase the volume of research, without necessarily increasing their own scientific infrastructure in an unwarranted way. Sometimes, governments are limited by financial constraints in certain research efforts and hence seek partnership with other governments. In some cases, governments initiate cooperation with other countries for reasons of foreign policy and security. For example, the United States made a great effort to cooperate with the USSR during certain periods of the Cold War, and also with China as part of the normalization of their relationship. Still another objective is cooperation in science and technology for international development. The U.S. assists many Third World countries with a view to promoting their economic development and stabilization. Israel's relationship with many Third World countries is also based on aiding in their social and economic development.

Governments of small countries, or countries not large enough to compete with the industrial superpowers, cooperate in science and technology in order to survive in today's very competitive market. The best example of such cooperation can be found today in the framework of the European Community. The guiding philosophy is that no one European country is large enough to compete in the modern market, but a consortium of European countries could achieve this goal. The complicated cultural and political relationships between the various European countries, their more or less independent industries, and the bureaucracy in Brussels make scientific-technological cooperation in the EC a formidable challenge as well as an interesting subject for study.

International science cooperation is thus a multifaceted activity based on a diversity of motivations. The one common denominator of this activity is that, whatever its mode or scope, success requires devoted scientists, technologists, and engineers who are motivated to cooperate with each in achieving the agreed-on goals.

Trends in Israel's Scientific Cooperation: The Shifting Balance Between Europe and the U.S.

The beginnings of Israeli science can be traced to discussions within the Zionist movement at the beginning of this century on the nature of the future state, reflecting different and conflicting ideologies.

In 1924, individuals in the Zionist movement who believed that the Jewish state should not only be a sovereign political entity but also or primarily a kind of spiritual center for the Jewish world established The Hebrew University of Jerusalem (the first research university in the Middle East). Among its founding members were major intellectual and public figures of the Western world such as Albert Einstein, Sigmund Freud, Chaim Weizmann, and Paul Ehrlich, to name just a few. The university was not intended to be a local teaching institution, but a focus for the intellectual and scientific creativity of the Jewish people; hence its orientation was international. Ever since, a critical factor in the development of Israeli science has been its international orientation. Israel has always been very aware of its small size and believed that links to the international scientific community could help overcome some of the disadvantages of its smallness and geographical isolation from the large centers of science.

The first academic appointments of the university were professors from European universities, mostly from Germany, England, and Hungary as well as a few from the United States. The Hebrew University was originally an academic institution, patterned on the European university system. Although The Hebrew University decided that Hebrew should be the language of instruction, the Technion, established at the same time as an engineering school and based in Haifa, began to teach in German, indicating the link with the mostly German origins of both institutions. The strong links with European science were maintained until 1933 when the Hitler era began in Europe.

Some academic links between Israel and the American scientific community existed from the beginning of scientific activity in Palestine, especially in agriculture and medicine (California is the alma mater of some of Israel's agricultural scientists, and the Rockefeller University in New York of some its researchers in preventive medicine). Academic links with the United States were strengthened during the postwar era, when many young Israeli scientists did their postdoctoral research there. To the present day, most Israeli scientists have spent postdoctoral and sabbatical periods in the U.S. and only very few in Continental Europe.

There are several reasons for this strong American orientation of Israeli science. There is a wide choice of science labs in the United States, and a great likelihood of obtaining funding for doctoral and postdoctoral training there. Israelis' scientific connections are considerably assisted by Israeli scientists who have emigrated to the U.S. and other countries and hold high academic or managerial positions. Most important, however, is the excellence of American science, which, stimulated both by the large numbers of outstanding immigrant scientists who fled from Europe in the 1930s and by increased research funding from the federal government, underwent tremendous development in the postwar years.

In the 1950s, Public Law 480 of the U.S. Congress enabled the United States to obtain payment in local currencies for food surpluses delivered to foreign countries, including Israel. The funds were partly spent in Israel for research sponsored by the U.S. Department of Agriculture. Private U.S. foundations and the National Institute of Health also contributed much toward joint U.S.-Israel research cooperation. "Friends of" organizations in the United States that are affiliated to various Israeli universities contribute, as well, to training and research funds. Hence, overall, to some extent Israel became more a part of the American research system than of the European one, with the exception of England, which, since the Mandate period, held a special attraction for Israeli scientists. Some British scientists indeed settled in Israel, and over the years the Royal Society has maintained a small exchange program for senior and junior scientists with the Israel Academy of Sciences and Humanities. Still, only a small percentage of Israel's scientists choose England over the U.S. for postdoctoral work or sabbaticals.

The establishment of the U.S.-Israel Binational Science Foundation in the early 1970s created a permanent framework for cooperation between U.S. and Israeli scientists. This was followed a few years later by the establishment of the U.S.-Israel Binational Agricultural Research Foundation, and a similar foundation for cooperation in industrial research. These measures also helped propel the whole Israeli research system toward the U.S.

None of these developments, however, interfered with the ongoing contacts of Israeli scientists with their European colleagues. Israelis were participants in European congresses, workshops, and seminars, and European scientists regularly attended Israeli scientific meetings. Still, long research periods in the U.S. and a U.S.-oriented funding mechanism kept Israel more closely connected to the U.S. than to its European neighbors.

Although links between American and Israeli scientists are still stronger than European-Israeli links, over the past 20 years Israel's connections with European science have gradually increased. The first country in Europe that adopted a de facto policy of establishing scientific cooperation with Israel was West Germany. For obvious reasons, during the postwar years German science was almost completely boycotted by Israelis. This was never an "official boycott"; but on an individual level, to this day there are still Israeli scientists who are unwilling to cooperate with German scientists. The reparations agreement with Germany did not automatically create diplomatic relations between the two countries; nor did it automatically lead to increased scientific cooperation.

The origins of Israel's cooperation with Germany can be traced to a chance meeting in 1958 between Professor Amos de Shalit of the Weizmann Institute and Wolfgang Gentner, then director of the Max Planck Society for Nuclear Physics in Heidelberg. Both of them later approached the Volkswagen Foundation for a grant to encourage exchange visits between their two countries as well as joint research projects between German scientists and scientists at the Weizmann Institute. In 1961 the Max Planck Institute sent its own delegation to Israel, headed by Professor Otto Han. These contacts led to the establishment in 1963 of a permanent framework managed by the Minerva Foundation for cooperation between the Weizmann Institute and the Max Planck Society, which is still active today. The heads of the Weizmann Institute supported these cooperative agreements with the Max Planck Society not only for pragmatic reasons but also because they believed that scientists should always be pioneers in bringing about normalization between nations. At a later stage, the Volkswagen Foundation became active in financing research in Israel. Although other European countries have formalized agreements with Israel, mostly between the Israel Academy of Science and European national academies (providing for exchange agreements of both senior and junior scientists), no other European country has initiated such an extensive framework as exists with Germany.

The European academies that have exchange agreements with the Israel Academy include the Royal Society, the British Academy, the Dutch Royal Academy, the Swedish Academy, the Institute de France, and, more recently, some East European academies as well. The various national agreements do not, however, reflect the close informal relations that most Israeli researchers have with one or more European laboratories. There is no good documentation on the extent of these contacts, but England, France, and Germany are the countries that have the most individual scientific cooperation with Israel, followed by Italy, the Netherlands, and Sweden. Having said all this, however, it remains the case that the strongest international connections of Israeli science are with the United States.

Israeli scientists see no reason that a small state should not have a creative scientific community. Individual excellence and originality are not limited to empires or superpowers; they may occur in any country that gives its citizens appropriate educational opportunities, appreciates the importance of science, and maintains the infrastructure to conduct it. Israeli scientists and their government are also, however, ever mindful of the fundamental importance of the international dimension of scientific endeavor. Israel maintains a consistent policy of encouraging the international mobility of Israeli scientists and any other means of creating strong links with the international scientific community. It is very doubtful, considering Israel's size, that it would have been able to create such an elaborate infrastructure for research and teaching without sizable help from abroad. It is in this context that Israel views international cooperation in science.

Israeli Scientific Cooperation With the Individual European Countries

Although, as noted, Israel's largest volume of international scientific cooperation (measured by the number of joint research projects, exchange visits, or joint publications) is with the United States, Israeli scientific authorities have strong motives for encouraging cooperation with European countries.

For one thing, U.S.-Israeli scientific cooperation has its intrinsic limitations. Although individual American scientists are often interested in cooperation with Israeli scientists, the U.S. as a country has regarded itself, at least until lately, as self-contained in science and not greatly in need of cooperation with other countries. It certainly has no definite policy to encourage such cooperation.

Hence, although the continued cooperation with U.S. science is essential, it does not prevent Israel from seeking greater involvement in European science. Leaders of European science are aware that most of the European countries do not have the entire spectrum of scientific activity, nor the financial ability to organize a "critical mass" in many important fields of science. Therefore, they are more aware of the need for international scientific cooperation to achieve their goals.

There should, thus, be an objective motivation for the leaders of European science to cooperate with Israel, provided Israel has the ability to be creative in science. Europe, in light of its limitations, has, as we will see, a tendency to pool its efforts in an international way, and this includes efforts in science and technology. This tendency is manifested in the organizational structure of the EC, which includes science and technology.

There are at least three levels of Israeli-European cooperation in science: cooperation between individual scientists, which is extensive but difficult to document; cooperation with the various European nations; and cooperation with regional West European scientific organizations. Since the mid-1960s, the Israel National Council of Research and Development, and more recently the Ministry of Science and Technology as well as the Israel Academy of Science and Humanities, have sought to participate in these various West European organizations.

Cooperation With Germany

As noted, Germany has the most organized framework for scientific cooperation with Israel among all European countries. The German-Israel Science Foundation (GIF) was established by agreement between the two countries in 1986 and began operating in 1988, and has an annual endowment of DM150 million that will increase substantially in the coming years. In 1992 the GIF, which is managed by a joint German-Israeli committee of scientists and persons representing the public, funded 175 joint German-Israeli projects (out of 1400 submitted proposals). With an annual budget of DM12 million, it provides a stable framework for continuous research cooperation of scientists from both countries. This binational foundation's pattern of organization emulates that of the U.S.-Israel science foundations, which have existed for over 20 years and have proved an excellent framework for cooperation. These foundations are managed by scientists, and their decisions are based on peer review; they pursue those scientific objectives that are important to the cooperating countries and experience a minimum of political interference.

The GIF is not the only framework for joint German-Israeli research projects. Both the German and Israeli Ministries of Science and Technology also have a standing framework for cooperation between individual scientists of both countries. Their cooperation is based on this interministerial framework, which provides for about 90 annual joint research projects, financed by an annual budget of DM7.5 million that is provided by the German Ministry of Science and Technology. The areas in which cooperation occurs are determined by a joint Israeli-German committee.

Since 1973 over 500 joint Israeli-German research projects, totaling over DM100 million and involving more than 1500 research scientists, have been conducted in this framework; and over 1000 exchange visits as well as numerous German-Israeli publications have resulted from the relationship. This year programs are being funded in the following fields: biotechnology, medical research on cancer and cardiology, research on nonconventional energy sources, water technology, environmental research and ecology, aquaculture, material science, and laser research.

Relations between German and Israeli scientists in the framework of this program are changing. In the past the German scientists acted mostly as "referees," but the present trend is for them to be active participants in the projects. There is also a trend of financing large projects, such as in ecology and in water technologies. Two programs on energy studies are concerned with the development of novel solar cells and with a pilot plant for chemical storage of solar energy. During the 1991 visit to Israel of German Minister of Science Riesenhoffer, another DM1 million was allocated for the absorption of Russian immigrants in the framework of joint German-Israeli cooperation.

The German-Israeli relationship is unique in continuously looking for new and imaginative ways of increasing cooperation. One such new mechanism is the Minerva centers, each of which is established by a one-time grant to one of Israel's universities for establishing an endowment for a specific center of cooperative scientific activity. The endowment usually comes to DM1.5-3 million, and its income is matched by the university. At present there are some 20 Minerva centers operating in various Israeli universities, 15 of them at The Hebrew University. This is another way of institutionalizing the cooperative scientific relationship.

Israeli scientists can also apply for research funding to various private German foundations, some of whom have supported innovative and original research by Israeli scientists.

Cooperation With France

Close relations on an informal level developed in the postwar years between Israeli and French scientists. Some Israelis spent time in French laboratories, and some French scientists visited Israel on a regular basis. In the late 1950s, France opened some of its national physics and chemistry laboratories to visiting scientists from Israel. One of the obstacles to formalizing an exchange program of scientists between Israel and France has been language. In the past the French government insisted that in the framework of government-financed visits the French scientists should lecture in French, and that Israeli scientists should use French during their visits to France. However, the Israeli scientific community never included enough French-speaking scientists to warrant this arrangement. This language constraint was abolished after the de Gaulle government. Nevertheless, close collaborative relations between French and Israeli scientists were maintained during all these years, particularly in mathematics and physics. In addition, Israeli biologists had a strong affiliation with the Pasteur Institute, which later led to a formal agreement between that institute and the Weizmann Institute; the two hold a joint annual symposium.

For the last seven years, a Society for Israel-French Cooperation (AFIRST) has been active in initiating joint Israeli-French research seminars as well as research programs. The society was established through the cooperative initiative of Francois Gros in France and Ephraim Katzir in Israel. As a result of this activity, three years ago an agreement was concluded between the two governments to create funds supporting such cooperation. This agreement began with an annual budget of $1 million for both partners, which has increased to $2.2 million; the focus is on joint programs in computer science and biotechnology. This cooperative agreement initiated by AFIRST is now conducted by the Ministries of Science of both countries.

The Israeli Ministry of Science and Technology also has some direct agreements with French science organizations, such as the CNRS (the French National Research Center), INSERM (the French National Medical Research Center), INRIA (the French National Computer Science Research Center), and INRA (the French National Institute for Agricultural Research). Under these agreements, some 50 junior and senior researchers participate annually in a variety of exchange programs. The largest program between Israel and France is in the field of industrial research and development, having begun recently with a volume of $15 million.

Cooperation With Other European Countries

At the personal level Israel's scientific relations with England are close, but the only institutional agreements between the two countries are those between the Royal Society, the British Academy, and the Israel Academy, which have led to exchange professorships and exchanges of postdoctorate students. About 15 scientists benefit from this arrangement annually. In addition, other funding sources (EMBO, the European Molecular Biology Organization, Israeli universities' postdoctorate scholarships) will encourage the exchange of scientists with England. There is, however, no mechanism for mutual funding of joint British-Israeli research.

The Israel Academy also holds joint symposia with the Swedish Royal Academy. In addition, the Israeli Foreign Ministry's Division of International Cooperation, together with the governments of Germany and the Netherlands, promotes and monitors research projects that can benefit developing countries. These include especially adaptive research, which facilitates technology transfer in the fields of health and agriculture.

Israel's scientists cooperate with nearly every other European country, sometimes in the framework of interuniversity exchange arrangements or exchange fellowships financed by EMBO, but mostly on their own initiative and not within a specially structured organizational framework.

Israel's Scientific Cooperation With West European Regional Organizations

In the 1960s, the Israeli science policy establishment adopted the definite goal that Israeli science should participate in the integration of European science. From the protocols of Israel's National Council for Research and Development around 1965, it emerges that the integration of Israeli science into West European international scientific organizations was a policy decision of the Council and that much debate centered around how this was to be achieved. This policy was based on the realization of the benefits of Israel's participation in multinational organizations, whose pool of talent, resources, and infrastructure might enable Israel to participate in scientific projects that it could not carry out on its own. This policy was also influenced by Israeli scientists' great interest in the strong trend among European scientists to create multinational "scientific federations." Israel wanted very much to be on the "ground floor" of this newly developing structure.

One of the first joint European scientific organizations to be formed after World War II was CERN (the European Laboratory for Nuclear Research). Although Israel did not participate in its formation or financing (it became a member of CERN only in 1990), Israel's physicists had full access to CERN's facilities and maintained ongoing cooperation with this organization.

The first multinational European organization in which Israel's scientists did participate actively, even taking part in its establishment, was EMBO. This organization began when a few senior European biologists, realizing that the work in the life sciences (the study of biological mechanisms on the molecular level) being pursued in each European country in only a few laboratories presaged, overall, a revolution in this area, decided that an all-European framework would be most conducive to promoting this rapidly evolving field. This informal group of European scientists received a $1 million grant from the Volkswagen Foundation for the formation of EMBO.

The personal relationship between Professor Ephraim Katzir of the Weizmann Institute and Professor John Kendrew of Cambridge University (then chairman of the EMBO Council) played an important role in the institutionalization of Israel as a member of EMBO. Israel was a founding member and one of the first countries to contribute financially to EMBO, and although EMBO is otherwise exclusively European, Israel, as one of its founding members, is part of it. Israel also became a member of the European Molecular Biological Laboratory (EMBL) in Heidelberg when it was formed. Israel's membership in EMBO makes it automatically a member of EMBO's short-term and long-term fellowship programs, which in fact opens all European molecular biology laboratories to Israeli molecular biologists and enables European molecular biologists to spend time in Israeli laboratories and cooperate with their Israeli colleagues. Indeed, it is difficult to overestimate the importance of Israel's membership in EMBO in terms of the flourishing of molecular biology in Israel. Participation in EMBO is treasured by Israeli scientists, who consider it an excellent scientific organization that affords them ongoing interaction with some of the most creative molecular biologists in the world.

During the past 20 years, nearly all European national scientific organizations have created multinational European organizations. European federations of physicists, of biochemists, of microbiologists, and so on were established to answer a need felt by professionals in each field for international meeting grounds. Without any central initiative but expressing the wishes of the European scientific community, Israel's national scientific organizations were all invited to be part of these federations, making Israel the only country outside the European continent that fully participates in nearly all European scientific organizational frameworks. Apparently, European scientists regard Israeli scientists as belonging to an additional European country. Little, if any, political interference is evident in these relationships.

Both CERN and EMBO have councils governed by government representatives. These representatives are usually scientists, and although such organizations necessarily have bureaucracies, their scientific, nonpolitical nature and their tendency to keep bureaucracy to a minimum prevail. They are therefore much appreciated by the scientific community. All this does not mean the multinational European scientific organizations lack internal political problems; they have many. For example, the British are considering leaving CERN because British scientists believe that too much of their research budget goes to this organization. There have been endless discussions of the objectives and nature of the EMBO laboratory, with different national delegations taking different positions. What comes into play here is not national politics but science politics, with scientists representing the different viewpoints.

Israel's cooperation with the EC developed much later than with other European organizations and is more complicated. As part of the project of the unification of Europe, the EC established a special commissariat for cooperation in science, Directorate General 12. Other directorates, however, deal with higher education and specific developing technologies (e.g., telecommunications) and are therefore science oriented and relevant in terms of cooperation with the EC.

The EC has been regarded by European scientists as more supportive of applied research and technology and less so of basic research. The EC's bureaucratic structure makes it easier for industry and industry-initiated joint research projects to deal with it than for individual scientists. Therefore, the EC has not been a preferred funding source for European scientists. This image is probably changing now, especially since the EC, through DG-12, is funding some large programs connected to the European Human Genome Project.

Israel's scientific relations with the EC began in 1977 on a very small scale, with an agreement for the exchange of scientists. From the EC's point of view, Israel is not a European country and the EC statutory does not support science in Israel or other non-European countries, but it does support the cooperation of European and foreign scientists. At this stage such cooperation is not, of course, of high priority for the EC. It is in this context, however, that an agreement was signed in 1983 for joint EC-Israel research programs and the establishment of a joint EC-Israel Steering Committee to initiate and monitor such cooperation. Again, interpersonal relations were important in laying the ground here—specifically, between the late Jacob Saphir, then director-general of Israel's Research Council and later director-general of the Ministry of Science, and his European colleagues Professor Paulo Fassela, director of DG-12, and Dr. G. Valentini, former director of DG-12/G responsible for international scientific cooperation. Indeed, in recognition of his role in establishing the EC-Israel cooperation in science, the joint EC-Israel Steering Committee decided to sponsor an annual Jacob Saphir Traveling Professorship that enables an Israeli scientist to visit European laboratories, a measure much appreciated by Israel's scientists.

A request for proposals in the framework of this agreement was first issued in 1984. The areas of cooperation are agreed on between the representatives of the EC and Israel during the annual meeting of the Steering Committee and have included, so far, biotechnology, neurobiology water resources studies, electro-optics, and material science. The projects are jointly financed, about 60% by the EC and 40% by Israel. The volume of funds invested in this cooperation steadily increased from U.S. $130,000 in 1984 to an annual commitment of $2.25 million in 1989. The accumulated budget for the funding of about 50 projects was then $7 million. Altogether, from 1983 to 1992, 55 research projects, five workshops, and one international seminar were implemented within the EC-Israel scientific cooperation; at present there are 26 active projects.

As a general rule, EC-Israel research projects are supposed to involve at least two partners, one from Israel and one from the Community. Participation of additional European partners is encouraged. All proposals are forwarded to the Israeli Ministry of Science for prescreening and are granted an order of priorities. The selected proposals are then submitted to the EC (DG-12) for a second screening, and these proposals are discussed in the Steering Committee, which makes a final decision on the projects to be funded.

Other EC programs that are of interest to scientists are also open to Israelis, including postdoctoral fellowships in the framework of the EC's Mobility Program; often these are 6- to 12-month fellowships in European laboratories. The European Ph.D. fellowship program offers up to three years of support to Israeli Ph.D. students studying at European universities.

The AVICENNE Program is intended to promote scientific and technological cooperation between the EC Commission and the nonmember states of the Mediterranean Basin. The Med Campus Program supports cooperation between the university and higher educational establishments of Europe and Mediterranean nonmember countries.

Scientific cooperation between Israel and the EC is considered important by many of Israel's scientists and members of its science policy establishment who believe in the integration of Israeli science into a European framework. Still, there are some intrinsic difficulties in developing this cooperation. EC-Israel scientific cooperation is an integral part of the EC-Israel cooperative agreement and is therefore basically a political agreement, influenced by the EC's political attitudes toward Israel. Disapproval of Israel's policies by the European Parliament leads to sanctions against Israel, which sometimes takes the form of boycotting the Israeli-European scientific relationship. This does not affect Israel's standing in EMBO, CERN, or its binational relationship with Germany or France, but it automatically prevents the Commission in Brussels from signing agreements with Israel.

Like all others, Israeli scientists would like to be judged according to their scientific merits. The introduction of political considerations into questions of scientific cooperation lends the EC an image as a very unreliable partner among Israeli scientists and as meddling in academic freedom, which is a cornerstone of democracy. Since, in addition, more bureaucracy is involved in EC funding than in other international cooperative agreements, cooperation in this framework is considered very difficult.

Scientists generally believe that countries in conflict should try to keep scientific relations open. Russian and U.S. scientists cooperated during the years of the Cold War and supported the Pugwash Movement (a group of Russian, U.S., and European scientists who supported a policy of nuclear disarmament). Communication between scientists in countries in conflict is usually considered desirable by both scientists and governments. In addition to advancing science, such scientific cooperation helps foster understanding between the sides to a conflict.

On the other hand, nation-states and political organizations can use scientific cooperation, or its withdrawal, as a means of achieving foreign policy objectives. This seems to be the EC's approach to Israel, since it uses the interruption of scientific cooperation as a means of penalization. Israel's scientific policy establishment would very much like to see more cooperation in science with the EC. It would like to see the EC use science as a way of strengthening and broadening the scope of overall cooperation between Israel and Europe, rather than as a tool to achieve political objectives. But in the current situation Israeli scientists, especially the most outstanding, are reluctant to enter into an intrinsically unstable, politicized relationship. For them, cooperation with the EC is problematic.

In summary, Israel's cooperation with European scientists both at the personal level and at the level of national and regional European scientific organizations is large in scope, creative, and productive, benefiting all sides. Israel's desire that cooperation with the EC greatly expand stems both from purely scientific considerations and from aspirations to integrate into the emerging cooperative structure of European science. The future political stabilization of the Middle Eastern region might give us a better chance of reaching this goal.

Notes

1. D. K. de Solla Price, "The Structure of Publication in Science and Technology," in W. H. Gruber and D. G. Marquis, eds., *Factors in the Transfer of Technology* (Cambridge: MIT Press, 1969).

2. R. K. Merton, "Normative Structure of Science," in *The Sociology of Science* (Chicago: University of Chicago Press, 1973), pp. 267-268.

PART V

THE HUMAN RIGHTS ISSUE

Chapter 17

The Role of Human Rights in European Political Cooperation and Applications in the Middle East

GIANNI BONVICINI

One of the main objectives of the new Common Foreign and Security Policy (CFSP) provided for by the Treaty of Maastricht is "to develop and consolidate democracy and the rule of law, and respect for human rights and fundamental freedoms" throughout the world (article J-1.2.5).[1] This is the first time that a specific article of the Community refers to the protection of human rights outside of its territory, thus making it a political and legal objective of the so-called European foreign policy. In more generic terms a reference to the need for adopting democratic principles and the respect for human rights was already contained in the Solemn Stuttgart Declaration of 1983 (which had largely to do with European Political Cooperation matters) and in the Preamble of the Single European Act of 1986, but without constituting an ad hoc policy requirement for EPC (now CFSP) activities.[2]

The question of the role of the Community and particularly its political component, previously known as European Political Cooperation, in such a delicate field with such profound political implications has generated myriad positions, declarations, official statements, and, in some cases, concrete actions. Indeed, the special issue of respect for human rights within the framework of the general activity of EPC began to take on increasing importance around the end of the 1970s and especially in the 1980s. With special reference to the Middle East, the trinomial EPC-human rights-Middle East has been and continues to be one of the most characteristic (and strongly controversial) elements of Community policy toward the region. Being an area of particular concern for the Twelve and one where human rights violations are both frequent and serious, EPC has concentrated a great deal of attention and activity on this issue over the years.

Human Rights as an Emerging Issue for EPC

As noted, the importance of human rights for EPC grew during the 1980s; when the EPC was established at the Hague European Summit in 1969, however, there was little interest in the issue. No mention can be found of it in either the first (1970) or the second (1973) "Davignon" Report, which created the initial structure of EPC.

Nevertheless, in the 1970s the European Community as a whole, and not only the EPC, developed a number of political and legal instruments aimed at protecting the fundamental rights of its citizens (i.e., within the Community). In fact, the Community started to show a certain interest in human rights, at first turning its attention inward, where the lack of homogeneous national policies and the complete absence of communication instruments was a matter of concern both in terms of equal opportunity for EC citizens and of Europe's image in the world.[3] This activity culminated in the Convention on the Respect for the Fundamental Rights of EEC citizens, adopted on April 5, 1977, and soon led to the idea of introducing human rights as a regular criterion also for association agreements with third countries (i.e., outside the Community as well). The proposal fell through at the time, however (especially in the renewal of association agreements with the ACP countries), because the principle of noninterference still dominated: faced with protests from third countries, the EC soon gave in. Even the Helsinki Final Act of 1975, concluded around that same time and establishing a basket of human rights, was unable to change the situation, as realpolitik with its total control over areas of influence continued to prevail. U.S. President Jimmy Carter's attempts to defy that paralyzing logic and use the human rights clauses of the Helsinki document against the Soviet Union (an action that received scarce and skeptical support from the Europeans) apparently failed. During the 1970s, therefore, the Community and its member states adopted a low profile toward the protection of human rights outside their territory. The fear of jeopardizing the *Ostpolitik* launched by Chancellor Willy Brandt at the end of the 1960s and continued by his successor Helmut Schmidt in the latter part of the 1970s, until the time of the great challenge over the Soviet deployment of SS-20 missiles, prevented the forming of an effective EPC policy in the field of human rights. Only in the 1980s did the climate drastically change and the EPC start to address violations of individual rights in the world, the Middle East included.[4]

The Middle East on the EPC Agenda

The Middle East, as a general issue, has been a vital concern of the EPC's activity from its inception: the first declaration on the Middle East was made on November

6, 1973; the prominent Venice Declaration reflecting Europe's desire to move more autonomously with respect to the United States was made on June 12-13, 1980; more recently, in June 1992, the European Council declared its support for the Middle East peace process; and many other initiatives and declarations on the Middle East have been on the EPC agenda. Although the Venice Declaration seemed to express a European desire to become more directly involved in the Middle East even at the cost of upsetting traditional alliances, the disappointing outcomes of European-Arab dialogue in the later 1970s, which aborted because of European reluctance to deal with the more political aspects of the matter, helped Europe realize that there was little use in pursuing a secondary role in the Middle East that was only destined to fail and could even be counterproductive. The conviction grew that more complex strategies had to be adopted both at the national and Community levels.[5]

On the one hand, the EPC continued to carry out its traditional, limited function of monitoring and providing information on developments in the region. A new instrument, the Troika, combining the presidency-in-office with its predecessor and successor, was used effectively to conduct fact-finding missions and strengthen the image of more direct Community participation.

On the other hand, the members of the Community took part in direct intervention in the Middle East by dispatching peacekeeping forces to the Sinai and interposition forces to Lebanon and later the Gulf. In all cases, EPC merely provided a political "cover" and the general frame of reference for these essentially national actions. Yet the direct involvement of some European countries in managing local crises constituted an important starting point for a new European role in the Middle East. Although the mixture of Community and national action did nothing to dissipate the ambiguity around European policy in the area, Europe's increased overall activism in the region was recognized.

The Growing Importance of Human Rights in the EC's Foreign Relations

In the mid-1980s, human rights was the area in which the most important developments took place. First of all, the Helsinki process and its follow-up conferences made human rights a crucial factor in international relations, laying the foundation for the rapid evolution of the East, largely triggered by the citizens' greater awareness of their rights. Second, Western public opinion was strongly concerned with eradicating the causes of international terrorism, which to a great extent stemmed from situations in which democracy and respect for human rights were absent.

The combination of these two factors with the slow but steady worsening of the conflicts in the area and their increasingly serious international implications led to the end of a longstanding taboo: not to interfere in the internal affairs of a sovereign state. Propounded in article 2.7 of the United Nations Charter, this norm often, in fact, inhibited the protection of human rights. The 1985 G-7 Ottawa Declaration, however, marked the first step toward its elimination. This process has since continued—mainly within the framework of the Conference for Security and Cooperation in Europe (CSCE)—with the 1990 Paris Declaration and the two more recent CSCE conferences, the first on the Human Dimension held in Moscow in September-October 1991 and the second on Human Rights held in Vienna in June 1993. A report submitted by the Presidency of the Twelve to the European Parliament notes that "The Twelve have always insisted that the raising of specific human rights violations is not to be regarded as interference in the internal affairs of other states but rather as sanctioned under international law and essential for the establishment of an international political climate conducive to security and cooperation."[6]

Human rights are justly considered universal (at least in theory) and are now, as such, subject to the control and the intervention of the international authorities established to protect them. The Middle East is the arena in which this new principle of interference has most frequently been applied. Examples range from assistance to the Kurdish people in Iraq to the no-overflight rule in force against Iraqi aircraft in the area inhabited by Shiites on the basis of Resolution 688 of the UN Security Council.

The Community has taken measures in accordance with these international developments. The first step was taken by the EPC with the approval on July 21, 1986, of a Statement by the Twelve on Human Rights, which noted that:

> The Foreign Ministers affirm that in the development of their relations with non-Member States as well as in the administration of aid the European Community and its Member States will continue to promote fundamental rights so that individuals and peoples will actually enjoy to the full their economic, social and cultural rights and their civil and political rights.[7]

Thus, respect for human rights became an official part of the Community's "foreign" policy and assumed an important place among the political priorities of both EPC and the EC.

The Treaty of Rome was also revised for the first time in the same year with the ratification of the Single European Act. One of the most important changes that resulted was the inclusion of EPC, which until then had been kept formally separate, among Community activities. In particular, point 5 of article 30 introduced the principle of consistency between Community and EPC actions.[8] Its future application was to help make the link between the request for protection of human rights and the Community's external economic policies, especially association and trade agreements, more credible. Although external Community policies and other instruments such as economic sanctions[9] had been used in the past to support EPC declarations condemning the violation of human rights (such as in South Africa), the principle of consistency introduced by the Single European Act provided a legal basis and more solid political motivation for their use.

From that time onward, the policy of defense of human rights became a characteristic of EPC, and a condition for third countries seeking contact with the Community. This condition was formally included in association agreements, the most significant example of which is the renewal of the Convention for Cooperation between the EC and the APC, Lomé IV, signed on December 15, 1989. Article 5 expressly states that economic development is closely linked to the promotion of all human rights. The introduction of guarantees on human rights into the Lomé Convention does credit to the steadfastness of the Community, which had unsuccessfully proposed the same condition in earlier versions.

This strategy was further refined by the June 1991 Luxembourg European Council and officially transformed by the November 1991 European Community Council into a resolution on "human rights, democracy and development," linking economic development and democracy even more closely to fundamental human rights. This resolution required the inclusion of a declaration to that effect in all future association agreements with third countries, and in fact has helped to make the respect for democratic principles and human rights an "essential element" of EPC and EC external activities.[10]

EPC Instruments for Promoting Human Rights

The EPC also improved its instruments for monitoring the upholding of human rights. Since 1986, the presidency-in-office has been required to produce an annual report on EPC activity in the field, to be sent to the European Parliament for debate. This report provides an opportunity both for an overview of EPC interventions against human rights violations and for a general debate at the European Parliament concerning new European approaches in this domain. In October 1987 an EPC Working Group on Human Rights was established, charged principally with maintaining contacts and harmonious relations among the various regional working groups within the EPC (Middle East, Africa, etc.). This new body has brought fresh energy to the formulation of common positions by the Twelve. Finally, the heads of missions in nonmember countries and international organizations have been accorded a special role as an arm of the Community for bringing pressure, gathering information, and verifying reports of alleged rights abuses.

A decisive factor in the upgrading of the EC's role in the field of human rights has been the constant pressure of the European Parliament. In addition to debates on the EPC annual report, the Parliament has taken numerous independent initiatives regarding human rights, effectively using the instruments of hearings, motions, questions directed to the Council of Ministers, and reports on particular situations as well as its own annual reports.

Apart from debates and questions, the Parliament has been granted a small but important power by article 238 of the Single European Act: the power of consent for new association agreements. Parliamentary control has made the Community's declarations more congruent with its behavior with respect to development aid and association in certain cases of human rights violations. The Parliament's capacity to veto agreements that have not yet gone into force or to freeze ones that already have tightens the link between democracy, development, and human rights promulgated in the above-mentioned 1991 declaration and makes the exertion of political pressures on third countries even more effective. As we shall see, the use of this power, or threat to use it, can bring the European Parliament into conflict with both the Council and the Commission, as realpolitik is frequently invoked as the only feasible approach to protecting European interests.

Are EPC Instruments Effective in the Middle East?

All these instruments have been widely applied in the Middle East. We need, however, to understand what mix of these mechanisms can be effective in achieving the objective, set forth in the Treaty of Maastricht, of developing and consolidating democracy in third countries.

The problem requires consideration of the traditional EPC instruments.[11] The main ones are declarations (around 90, on the whole, in 1993 on human rights), ministerial statements, and presidency's conclusions, both at the Council of Ministers and at the European Council level.[12] Their numbers have been increasing over the years and peaked at the end of the Gulf War in connection to the rights of the Kurds and the Shiites, during the intifada, and, more recently, upon the deportation of the Hamas members from Israel and the start of the Middle East peace process. EPC declarations are traditionally felt to be of little importance. But while this may be true for general political matters, where the credibility of a declaration is largely dependent on the capability for taking action to back it up, such as the use of economic sanctions or of positive financial inducements (which was rare in the case of EPC and now, with the establishment of the CFSP, is less feasible), this is not the case in the field of human rights, where even a simple open condemnation puts a country in the position of having to justify itself toward internal public opinion (although this aspect is sometimes negligible, as in the case of Iran and Iraq), but above all toward international public opinion. Declarations of this kind, which have frequently been made against Middle Eastern countries, tend to isolate the accused country and cause it difficulties, and the nervousness with which third countries usually react to such initiatives attests to this.

To avoid, however, overly defensive reactions that could undermine mediation, the Twelve frequently use another instrument, that of *démarche* toward the diplomatic authorities of the country in question. The number of *démarches* undertaken is usually higher than the number of declarations made, averaging about 100 per year (in 1993 the number was less, around 70, even lower than the declarations). But their main distinguishing feature is that they are mostly confidential, in traditional diplomatic style. Although this makes it difficult to assess their efficacy, they seem to be a powerful instrument of political pressure in precrisis situations, above all in particularly complex situations such as the one existing in the Middle East, where excessively trenchant positions could upset the equilibria that have been so laboriously established.

Once confidential measures have been exhausted and official declarations and statements adopted, no alternative remains but to use other instruments of pressure. The next step, and probably the most important, is denial of association or trade agreements or suspension of those already in place. Indeed, EC trade policy is one of the few levers available to the Community. As a result, foreign ministers tend to keep it as a last resort and prefer first to explore other measures thoroughly. The same is true of economic sanctions, although it has long been questioned whether they were included among Community competences. Only the Maastricht treaty, at article 228-A, has finally recognized the legitimacy of their use.

As mentioned earlier, the power of consent granted the European Parliament has brought new vitality to the use of trade and association agreements and has made it more difficult for ministers to engage in delaying tactics. Two recent examples are the freezing of financial protocols with Morocco and Syria on January 15, 1992, as a result of alleged human rights violations in those countries and the request for suspension of negotiations with Israel for the upgrading of trade agreements after the deportation of the Hamas activists. In the case of Morocco and Syria the reaction of the Council, and even that of the Commission, was very sharp against the decision voted by the European Parliament, which, only six months later, after having received assurances on a continuous monitoring by the Community of human rights situations in those countries, unblocked the association agreements.[13]

Yet EPC foreign ministers often oppose pressure from the Parliament, as in the Israeli deportation incident when they claimed that suspension of the negotiations would complicate the peace process. Such stances, however, can only be temporary because it is difficult for EPC ministers to resist pressure from the Parliament for long. Overall, then, not only is the role played by the European Parliament important for the Community politically, but it fosters greater consistency between EPC and EC activity, a prerequisite for a more credible European foreign policy.

Another indirect instrument is the use of financial aid. The clearest example is that involving the case of Lebanon. Following the release of the last two German hostages in June 1992, the EC prepared to resume its aid and financial cooperation (through the European Investment Bank) with the country. The linkage between protection of human rights (in this case, of Community citizens) and EC aid policy was clearly stated in an EPC communiqué: "The Community and its member states reiterate their strong condemnation of any hostage-taking, as well as any action against freedom and human dignity, and hope that this liberation will contribute to an improvement of the situation in Lebanon and to strengthen the links between this country and the EC."[14]

The last measure that can be adopted, direct intervention, falls under neither EPC nor CFSP authority. Initiatives of this kind, such as the assistance offered the Kurdish people in Iraq, are taken on the basis of national decisions and are the responsibility of individual governments. In such cases, the EPC merely works out positions of principle and provides the necessary European political cover for multilateral initiatives decided elsewhere. This is one of the operational limits of EPC, and is dealt with in the Treaty of Maastricht by means of the concept of common action, although a clear interpretation has not yet been worked out and experiences in this field have been limited, for the time being, to humanitarian aid as in the case of Bosnia.

In conclusion, the EPC-CFSP now plays an increasingly important and previously unexpected role in the field of human rights. Despite the limits and ambiguities inherent in this mechanism for cooperation since its inception, progress in the field of human rights (unlike in other sectors, especially security) has been constant and has led to greater specificity in the use of available instruments. This recent achievement, particularly with respect to the Middle East, may be of primary importance in building an autonomous role for the Community in the region. The Multilateral Talks on Economic Development held in Brussels on May 11-12, 1992, helped to define such a role by proposing the Community as a model for overcoming situations of ongoing conflict. Such a model of regional or subregional cooperation is the only realistic instrument for peaceful coexistence once the ideological barriers that have led to, among other things, the constant violation of the rights of citizens and of entire peoples have been removed. Thus, striving for the protection of human rights means working toward greater regional integration and cooperation as experienced by Europe in its postwar history.

Notes

1. Although CFSP constitutes the correct acronym for the foreign and security policy of the Twelve, as recognized by the Maastricht treaty of 1992, I will continue to use the previous acronym EPC (European Political Cooperation), as many examples and actions still pertain to the times when it was used.

2. See N. Frangakis, *Le Role de la Cooperation Politique Européenne a la diplomatie communautaire de Droits de l'Homme apres l'Acte Unique Européen* (Athens: Centre Hellenique d' Etudes et de Recherches Européennes, 1990) .

3. See European Parliament, "Annual Report on the Prospects of Human Rights in the European Community," Rapporteur: K. De Gucht, January 27, 1993, PE 202. 357

4. See E. Regelsberger, "European Political Cooperation, Contacts With Third Countries: Past and Present," in E. Regelsberger et al. , *The External Relations of EPC and the Future of EPC*, EUI Working Papers, no. 85 (Florence, 1985).

5. D. Allen and A. Pijpers, eds., *European Foreign Policy-Making and the Arab-Israeli Conflict* (The Hague, 1984).

6. European Parliament, Political Affairs Committee, "Annual Report to Parliament on the Human Activities of the Twelve," May 8, 1989, PE 134. 013, p. 5.

7. See "Declaration on Human Rights," Brussels, July 21, 1986, EPC Council. This is the first public declaration of the Twelve on protection of human rights outside the Community.

8. Article 30, comma 5, of the SEA states that "The external policies of the European Community and the policies agreed in European Political Cooperation must be consistent. The Presidency and the Commission, each within its own sphere of competence, shall have special responsibility for ensuring that such consistency is sought and maintained."

9. See M. Holland, "Sanctions as an EPC Instrument," in M. Holland, ed., *The Future of EPC* (London: Macmillan, 1991), pp. 180-196.

10. See European Commission, "EC General Report XXVII," ch. VI, section 2, Brussels, 1993.

11. See E. Regelberger, "The Twelve's Dialogue With Third Countries: Progress Towards a Communaut d'action?," in Holland, *Future of EPC*, pp. 161-179.

12. See European Commission, "EC General Report XXVII."

13. The reaction of the Commision against the decision of the European Parliament is reported in *Middle East International*, January 24, 1992, p. 13.

14. See EPC, "Declaration of the Liberation of the Two German Hostages in Lebanon," EPC Secretariat, Brussels, June 18, 1992.

Chapter 18

The European Community and Democracy in the Eastern Mediterranean

DAVID COOMBES

Introduction

The possibility that the European Community could or should seek to influence the internal politics of neighboring states and regions was realized very gradually and is still highly controversial. That the question should be raised at all from outside the Community, especially with respect to a neighboring region of major strategic importance both for Western Europe and the wider world, is significant in itself.

The Community's political relevance has become more apparent with its gradual transition to European Union, though the change is so far more nominal than real, even now that the treaty agreed and signed at Maastricht has been fully ratified. The economic and political changes that have occurred in Central and Eastern Europe since 1989 have probably done more to heighten the political significance of European integration than developments within the Community itself over the previous 39 years, even allowing for the latter's successive enlargements of territorial jurisdiction.

From the start the Community was endowed with functions that could and did have important political, as well as economic, consequences, both internally and externally. Its member states were always committed to achieving some kind of political union, and that commitment has been reaffirmed with each successive enlargement of membership and by a series of common declarations and acts of which the Maastricht treaty is but the latest.

The internal effects of economic integration on political institutions have, nevertheless, been continually fudged; and the Community's utility and validity as an agency of political intervention in external affairs have always been disputed by one or more members at any given time, and to an extent that the issue has never been adequately resolved.

However, during the past few years the unification of geographical Europe has become imaginable in a way it was certainly not at any previous time since the Community was founded. It is this development that should be of major interest to those in the eastern Mediterranean region, and not only because it includes the prospect of further expansion in a southeasterly direction, but also insofar as the demise of the Warsaw Pact and the fall of the USSR, rightly or wrongly, encourage the states belonging to the Community to assume both new obligations and new opportunities of exterior political influence.

The question of whether the EC could or should influence democracy in the eastern Mediterranean, or elsewhere, is, nevertheless, one of political theory and institutions as much as of international relations or "geopolitics." In fact, the relevance of European integration by the Community method for political concepts such as democracy has never been obvious, even to academics, and remains obscure even to practitioners.

It is never obvious what states really intend or expect to achieve when they publicly justify their actions as furthering democracy on an international scale. Properly speaking, democracy is no more than an attribute of government, pertaining to relative not absolute values. The real effects of democracy depend on all kinds of accompanying social variables, which cannot be adequately understood outside a given historical or geographical context. Democracy is usually difficult to reconcile with other social values, such as security, justice, civil liberty, or material welfare, which are themselves only relative.

It is always wise, therefore, to ask two questions about the reasons that states want to pursue democracy outside their own jurisdictions. First, what are the domestic conditions that determine a particular state's view of democracy as a value of universal significance? Second, how do the state's actions toward others demonstrate a priority for democracy in practice over other concerns such as security and economic interest?

The first issue to be addressed here is the place of democracy in the EC itself, taking into account as far as reasonable at such an early stage the change of status to European Union envisaged by the Maastricht agreement of December 1991. Next we need to examine how far, both in theory and in practice, the Community requires democracy as a condition of membership. We shall then consider the attention the Community normally pays to democracy when conducting its own external affairs. Finally, there is the question of whether, and if so how, the decision of the Community's members to adopt a common foreign and security policy might be expected, if at all, to influence the domestic political arrangements of neighboring states.

The "Democratic Deficit" of European Integration

The European Community was founded and developed primarily as an economic organization, albeit one depending on, and resulting in, a peculiar and highly suggestive application of law in the relations between otherwise sovereign states. The likely effects on democracy of the Community's acquisition of legal powers were certainly at issue during the negotiation of the EEC treaty of 1957 and became increasingly controversial, especially in the 1970s as the EEC developed beyond its transitional period and enlarged its membership. The commitment of the nine member states in 1972 to transform their relations with each other into a European Union forced both the Community's and the states' political protagonists to address the issue of democracy more directly.

Nevertheless, the "neofunctionalist" theory that the gradual formation of a common market would necessarily lead to political unification turned out to be entirely wrong. The Community's member states have never been able to agree to political union except as a project to be realized and organized separately from economic integration.The Community's original members finally opted in 1970 to deal with political aspects of their external relations by means of European Political Cooperation (EPC). Later attempts to merge these procedures of regular consultation and cooperation between member governments (chiefly through normal diplomatic channels) with the Community's own legally founded institutions failed, including the deceptively named Single European Act (SEA) of 1986. The Treaty on European Union signed at Maastricht in February 1992 leaves the position still highly ambiguous, and a new intergovernmental conference will meet soon to reconsider it.

The member states' governments have, in fact, shown persistent and increasing determination to retain the power to make the Community's policy for both internal and external affairs and to decide how it should be executed. Unless the treaties are specific enough to provide otherwise, the governments normally decide also to retain the power of execution.

All the major decisions to implement the EEC treaty, including those amounting to a use of legislative power, were reserved for the appointed representatives of member states' governments, usually (though not always) acting as the Community's Council. The increased availability and use of majority voting in Council has reduced the power of each individual government to prevent established Community policy from being executed, to obstruct or to divert its intention. Nevertheless, it is virtually impossible to make any changes in policy, let alone to establish new powers of execution, without the prior unanimous consent of all national governments at any one time.

What the Community does or can do at any given moment, therefore, is essentially dependent on the political will of its member governments, as, no less important, is what it does not and cannot do. The institutional system was adopted in recognition of the superior power of states' governments, by the introduction in 1974 of the so-called European Council, composed of prime ministers, presidents, and other heads of government. In practice the governments use this procedure, rather than any of the established institutions, to exercise legislative power in the Community's name, as well as ultimate budgetary power, and, partly through EPC, to guide the Community's conduct of its external relations.

The European Parliament embodies one of the few but vital federalist principles on which the Community is founded: that the people of the Community's member states constitute a unity and enjoy the right to separate and direct political representation as such a unity. The EEC treaty described the Parliament as consisting "of representatives of the peoples of the States brought together (*"reunis"*) in the Community" (article 137) and provided eventually for "elections by direct universal suffrage in accordance with a uniform procedure in all Member States" (article 138).

Parliament has, in fact, been directly elected at five-year intervals since 1979, though without the required uniform procedure, which is still awaited, and in the absence of which the democratic quality of representation in the Parliament can be seriously questioned on various grounds (not least the exclusion of liberals from the U.K.).

Like the other institutions, Parliament is self-governing, with its own rules and officers. The other institutions and the member states are legally obliged to recognize Parliament's authority within its own sphere and to act accordingly. Although Parliament acting alone could never make much significant use of power, except by censuring the Commission and since 1975 by fixing appropriations for part of the small amount of public finance assigned to the Community, it does have a right to be consulted by a due procedure and that right turns out to be justiciable (the Court having ruled in 1979 that a Community act can be invalid if Parliament has not been consulted properly).

Parliament's capacity and purview have increased since 1979, mainly because there is greater scope for the ambitious to make a name for themselves and a greater willingness to show opposition to what the national governments propose. The SEA of 1986 extended the obligation on member states' governments, when acting in Council by a majority vote, to consult Parliament before implementing the treaties' provisions for an internal market and also obliged them to obtain Parliament's assent (*avis conforme*) to treaties of association or for the accession of new members. The Maastricht treaty further extends these powers of obstruction and empowers Parliament to give prior approval to the appointment of the Commission.

However, Parliament's capacity to influence action taken in the name of European Union is still far less than that of national governments, especially when the latter are unanimous or all the major states are of one mind. Moreover, its members are still essentially representatives of national parties, on which they depend for their reelection. In other words, the right, implied by the founding treaties, of the peoples of Europe to act as a body politic has not been granted in practice. Citizens within the Union are still primarily subject to and dependent on their respective national governments, even when the use of public power has been legally transferred to the Community.

Even more remarkable than the limitations on the European Parliament as a vehicle of democracy, in view of the aspirations expressed in most of the states' constitutions, is the way national governments have been permitted to arrogate powers to themselves to make irrevocable executive decisions, including those affecting relations with nonmember states, and even to preempt legislative power, without the possibility of genuine accountability to *national parliaments*. The governments have also assumed the right to act on behalf of autonomous local communities and to arbitrate among occupational and other social interest groups in Community affairs, thus greatly enhancing their own powers of patronage and public finance.

To justify this aggrandisement of the state, at the expense of civil society, it is often said that the governments concerned all depend, if only indirectly in most cases, on majority popular consent as expressed in periodic free elections. But the power assumed by governments, and frequently by permanent state officials, as a consequence of Community membership is clearly of a different degree and kind from that normally and properly assumed in the course of purely domestic affairs. The intense involvement of national authorities in the business of the Community and of EPC has lengthened the distance between them and political representatives in their own states and deprived private citizens of customary means of redressing grievances or defending special interests by organized political influence.

This deficit of democracy has been allowed to persist, and is likely to continue for four important reasons. First, the member states cannot agree to recognize the right of the Community, even in its new form as European Union, to exercise a primary legislative power, and at the same time seem to be satisfied that the delegated power they have been willing to recognize is adequately subject to judicial control. Second, however, member states have ample opportunity to act, individually and collectively, outside the Community's legal framework, justifying what they do as the free exercise of sovereignty. Third, and partly by exercising power without responsibility in these ways, member states have been able effectively to disguise their own real impotence, especially against countervailing forces of capital. Fourth, and in explanation of the first three reasons, none of the

Community's member states so far has been sufficiently committed to democracy as to give it priority over their willingness to participate in integration by the Community method.

The same states' declared objective of promoting democracy within or without the European Union must, therefore, be understood against the background of their own reluctance over a very long period to do much about the existing democratic deficit within.

Democracy as a Condition of Membership

Although the Community's founding treaties did not even refer to democracy as a condition of membership, the Treaty on European Union defines its member states as having "systems of government ... founded on the principles of democracy" (in its article F.1). The preamble to the SEA of 1986 expressed the twelve signatories' "determination to work together to promote democracy," and the new treaty's preamble confirms "their attachment to the principles of liberty, democracy and respect for human rights and fundamental freedoms and of the rule of law." The new treaty would also explicitly recognize the proposed Union's obligation to respect both the European Convention on Human Rights and Fundamental Freedoms (of 1950) and the same rights and freedoms arising from the "constitutional traditions common to the member states" (article F.2).

In fact, democracy was not normally mentioned in relation either to the Community's principles and objectives or its conditions for membership until the accession of new members. The same Paris summit meeting of nine in October 1972 that declared European Union to be a definite goal also "reaffirmed" the member states' "determination to base the development of their Community on democracy, freedom of opinion, the free movement of people and of ideas and participation by their peoples through their freely elected representatives." The only permanent condition with current legal force is that any European state may apply for membership (article 237 EEC).

The negative effects for democracy were a major ground for opposition to membership in all three of the states that eventually acceded in 1973. This first enlargement was desired primarily for economic and security reasons and also to resolve political differences between the original six members. Although it entailed the accession of neutral Ireland, it produced much greater real symmetry between the Community's membership and that of NATO. None of the new members was to champion democracy within the Community, least of all with respect to direct elections to the European Parliament, which they all resisted to the last.

The later accessions of Greece (1981), and of Portugal and Spain (1986), were also deliberately delayed by varying degrees of opposition among the existing members, mainly on economic grounds. They were eventually celebrated as significantly expanding the population and territory bound by the rules of the Common Market, but they clearly also served the strategic purpose of the Atlantic alliance.

That purpose had been made crucial by the possibility that each of the states concerned might be governed by political forces actively hostile to NATO and potentially disruptive of its aims of collective security, following the demise of authoritarian regimes during the 1970s.

Before the opening of accession negotiations, the then-nine member states sought to give the clearest warnings to the new governments of both Portugal and Spain that any economic benefits expected from association or membership would be tied to political conditions, including pluralist democracy and respect for human rights. The same conditions had not, however, prevented the Community from entering into previous agreements with those states under different governments, though the longstanding association with Greece had been effectively suspended during the period of military rule from 1967 to 1974. Special encouragement and direct support were given to political forces of moderation in all three of these countries before accession by some member states individually, especially the German Federal Republic. The process of Greek accession was noticeably speeded up as soon as it appeared that the socialist party might come to power with a neutralist policy.

The Community has, therefore, tended to define and apply its conditions for accession to membership pragmatically, in accordance with the prevailing economic and strategic interests of at least its four larger members. Concurrent membership in NATO, or active participation in its military command structure, have not been required. Indeed, membership in NATO or guaranteed neutrality have been reasons for not encouraging accession to the Community, when other conditions, especially economic, have been considered unfavorable.

On the other hand, the Community has been anxious to enlarge its jurisdiction, whenever this might be seen as a way of reducing threats to the security of the Atlantic alliance. Those of its members not too seriously affected by low-priced competition in sensitive products, or by a surplus of unskilled labor, have generally welcomed enlargement as a means of providing access to new markets for exports of capital, professional services, and manufactured goods.

Turkey is probably the only nonmember state that has so far had to be deliberately and persistently discouraged from seeking membership on overtly political grounds. Turkey's eligibility for membership was recognized as early as 1963, when it first made an association with the Community and the date of 1997 was even explicitly mentioned. Both economic and political reasons were given for repeatedly persuading Turkish governments to postpone applications, and the association between the Community and Turkey has frequently been interrupted and restricted as a direct result of complaints about violations of civic and human rights (see below). In spite of continued discouragement, Turkey officially applied for membership in June 1987.

The immediate barriers to Turkish accession are both economic and political, but in both cases could prove transitory: first, there is concern about the viability of the national economy within a fully competitive market and the related issue of labor migration, especially to Germany; second, there is Greek opposition arising mainly from the situation in Cyprus. The Commission's opinion in 1989, reflecting the views of most member governments, favored a continued association in which these and other more structural obstacles to membership could be removed and greater reassurance given on internal constitutional arrangements. However, in its report to the European Council of June 1992 in Lisbon the Commission stated that "Events have highlighted Turkey's geopolitical importance, and the role which it can play as an ally and as a pole of stability in its region; the Community should take all appropriate steps to anchor it firmly within the future architecture of Europe" (para. 29). Had Turkey's loyalty or efficacy as a military contributor to the Atlantic alliance been more questionable, considerations such as these may have obliged the Community to weigh its claims to membership with greater favor and urgency earlier.

Even if it would lead to increased security, democracy, or both in the region concerned, the accession of Turkey, and of Cyprus and Malta (which both applied in 1990), cannot be expected until more deep-seated changes have occurred, and for a very important reason. There must be a limit beyond which the Community cannot absorb a greater number of member states without first rebuilding its economic and legal foundations. The Community would find it extremely difficult to apply even the limited provisions adopted so far for an economic and monetary union to many more economically less developed regions, especially on the periphery of Continental Europe. On the other hand, a southeastern enlargement might be more conceivable, if the new members could be differentiated by receiving only restricted rights and obligations, including those of political representation.

In effect, the Maastricht treaty does provide for a differentiation of membership, both with respect to EMU and in relation to a common foreign and security policy, from both of which individual members may in effect "opt out" or be deliberately excluded. A Europe of concentric circles has already, therefore, been endorsed. But the precise status and benefits due to citizens of member states in the outer circles have not yet been made clear.

The conditions of membership have been spelled out more than ever before as a reaction to the entirely new possibility of accession by formerly communist states in Central and Eastern Europe. Those conditions, most of which are explicitly intended now for any new member, are significant as indicating what the Community currently expects in terms of democracy and with what priority in relation to other conditions. They would doubtless have to be met in full by applicants from the Balkan peninsula.

The Commission specified three basic conditions of membership in its report subsequently approved by the European Council at Lisbon and Edinburgh during 1992. The first of these, "European identity," the Commission left deliberately vague, and it failed to elaborate on the other two, "democratic status" and "respect for human rights."

Another "set of criteria" was added, however, that in the light of the Community's own evolution should be assumed to be no less relevant and possibly more instrumental as a means of influencing internal developments in the states of Central and Eastern Europe. These criteria include "a functioning and competitive market economy," and reflect the introduction into the Maastricht treaty at several points of the new injunction that the Community should operate "in accordance with the principle of an open market economy with free competition" (e.g., article 3a EC).

The Commission warned that it would be difficult to admit any state whose "constitutional status, or stance in international affairs" rendered it unable to accept and implement the proposed common foreign and security policy (see below). It also pointed out that the prospect of enlargement reinforced the need for reforms to reduce the Community's own "democratic deficit" and "strengthen the role of the European Parliament."

A supplementary report to the Edinburgh meeting set out guidelines specifically for Central and Eastern Europe and dealt mainly with security and economic aspects, though it also referred to the need for eventual political decisions regarding, among other things, "the stability of institutions in the candidate country guaranteeing democracy, the rule of law, human rights and respect for minorities."

Using Economic Relations for Political Ends

The Community has made increasing use of its commercial and economic relationships to pursue political objectives approved by its member governments. This kind of intervention is constrained both by the contractual obligations of the specific agreements with trading partners and by the general rules of the GATT. Moreover, the Community's member governments assumed the authority to define and execute any common policy in external relations primarily by means of EPC, that is, outside the legal framework provided by the founding treaties. In fact, the Community has not usually been willing or able to take alternative action of its own, without prior unanimous agreement resulting from EPC.

Although the Commission was a regular participant in EPC and the governments might decide from time to time to act with the legal authority of the Community's Council, the nonbinding decisions reached collectively by means of EPC and the Community's conduct of its own external relations, in accordance with powers transferred by the treaties, were very poorly coordinated. The situation was little improved, and was in some respects further complicated, by the SEA of 1986, which provided that the two dimensions of external policy must be "coherent," though it also provided the presidency of EPC with its own separate secretariat.

At the initiative of their Dutch presidency at the time, the foreign ministers of the Twelve, meeting as the Council on July 21, 1986, issued a statement affirming among other things that:

> in the development of their relations with non-member states as well as in the administration of aid the European Community and the Member States will continue to promote fundamental rights so that individuals and peoples will actually enjoy to the full their economic, social and cultural rights and their civil and political rights.

In fact, the Community had by this time entered into formal treaties for trade and economic cooperation with states and international organizations in most parts of the world, and such contractual arrangements with states in the Mediterranean basin had existed since the 1960s, and were extended to include Israel and most Arab states in the Middle East during the 1970s. The Community had also increasingly assumed the power, mainly on the basis of its access to "own resources" of public finance, to grant provisional forms of financial aid outside its own territorial jurisdiction.

Increasingly, economic relations have been accompanied by a procedure of "political dialogue," directed mainly on the Community's part by member states' own foreign ministries acting through EPC, but involving also representatives of the Commission, and allowing the European Parliament a limited opportunity to obtain information, make criticisms, and pass nonbinding resolutions. The ambiguity surrounding the Community's role in this process tended to confuse and disappoint the states that were party to political dialogue, as well as to detract from the utility of the process as a whole as a means of exerting political influence. The political dialogue did, however, sometimes involve a wider range of public representatives from the interlocutory states than those directly engaged in government and would sometimes extend to conferences between parliamentarians.

During the 1970s, the member governments became increasingly willing to use the powers assigned to the Community with respect to external trade and economic cooperation to threaten or impose economic sanctions of various kinds. Then and subsequently economic sanctions have been used mainly to support specific objectives of security, usually in accordance with policy already coordinated on a wider international scale, especially through the UNO. Nevertheless, the Community has also occasionally been ready to act on its own initiative, as in the case of South Africa (though American influence may have been decisive in this case) and the African, Caribbean, and Pacific states participating in the Lomé Conventions.

It is, of course, difficult to know in this kind of political intervention how far concerns regarding human and civic rights, no matter how vociferously declared, are in practice overridden by those of economic interest and military security. Only the actual participants in political dialogue could confirm whether this procedure, in its various forms, extends to issues such as the structure of political institutions, let alone whether the exchanges of view have any real effect in the countries participating.

One development of potentially special significance for democracy has been the growing readiness of the European Parliament to use its limited powers in relation to the Community's budget to influence the use of economic sanctions (especially by withholding or offering aid) in the hope of promoting human and civic rights in different parts of the world. Parliament has also since 1987 made unexpected use of its power to approve economic treaties, including financial protocols attached to them, to influence the Community's relations with both Turkey and Israel.

Following the events of 1989, the Community acquired unexpected and unprecedented responsibilities for economic and other kinds of assistance to the states of Central and Eastern Europe that had been members of CMEA. Under their Irish presidency during the first half of 1990, the member governments worked hard to define the principles and objectives that should guide their new relationship with the states concerned, as well as with the USSR, and govern the Community's performance of the new functions assigned to it both by its own members through EPC and by the OECD and CSCE. At their meeting in Dublin on April 21, 1990, the twelve heads of government announced that "The Community will work to complete association negotiations with these countries as soon as possible on the understanding that the basic conditions with regard to democratic principles and transition towards a market economy are fulfilled."

Agreements of a new and special kind were eventually reached with Hungary, Poland, and Czechoslovakia (known as "Europe agreements"), and similar ones have since been negotiated with Romania and Bulgaria. The Community's PHARE assistance in Central and Eastern Europe includes projects of cultural cooperation, and civic education as part of a "democracy program." At the Commission's initiative the Community proceeded to explore during 1993 new cooperative arrangements, some of them involving other international organizations, as a way of intensifying the political dialogue and extending it to actual participation by the associated European states in some of its own institutional procedures. It seems that the Commission itself is becoming more directly engaged than ever before in the internal affairs of neighboring states, as a result of these special agreements, extending its interest even to matters as delicate as the role of the military in politics.

"Europe agreements" are clearly intended as preparatory to eventual membership, if only in the proposed inferior category or "outer circle" established at Maastricht for some of the existing members. However, it is impossible to tell without further investigation in the field how far or in what particular ways the Community's requirements with respect to political institutions and practices have had a real impact.

Common Foreign and Security Policy

The Treaty on European Union of 1992 establishes a common foreign and security policy (article J). This policy is to be defined and implemented concurrently by the Union, using the existing institutions of the Community, and its member states, in accordance with objectives already largely approved by their governments in several previous instances through the procedures of EPC. The objectives defined by the new treaty include: "to develop and consolidate democracy and the rule of law, and respect for human rights and fundamental freedoms" (article J.1).

The Community's own legal authority would not be extended to foreign and security policy. The member states would retain exclusive responsibility for determining to what extent it should be determined according to, or governed by, common action. The new treaty seems to be designed to enhance the possibilities of defining common positions, and of adopting "joint actions" to execute them. It envisages the possibility of using the Community's own powers for this purpose.

The states' governments would manage their cooperation, and define common positions when necessary, in the Council, which could also decide in the future to execute some aspects of joint action by a qualified majority. The new treaty also amends the EEC treaty explicitly to empower Council, acting by a qualified majority on a proposal of the Commission, "to interrupt or to reduce, in part or completely, economic relations with one or more third countries" when the common foreign and security policy (CFSP) so requires (article 228a EC).

The CFSP is intended to include "the eventual framing of a common defence policy, which might in time lead to a common defence" (article J.4). The Union would not yet be endowed with a military capacity of its own, but it would be able to request the existing WEU to carry out decisions with "defence implications." The nine member states that already belong to WEU (shortly to be increased to eleven) have agreed to develop that organization's decisionmaking procedures and "operational role." Significantly, WEU is not required to confine its operations to the sphere defined for NATO.

The new treaty obliges the Council's presidency to "consult the European Parliament on the main aspects and the basic choices of the common foreign and security policy" and to "ensure that the views of the European Parliament are duly taken into consideration" (article J6). Both presidency and Commission are obliged to keep the Parliament informed. Parliament is empowered to ask questions of Council and make recommendations to it, and is obliged to hold an annual debate on the implementation of CFSP.

These provisions do little more than give the force of treaty to procedures that have already, as we have seen, been in place for some time, and Parliament is given no additional rights in relation to the common foreign and security policy. Indeed, by amending article 228 of the EEC treaty, the new treaty would define more narrowly the Parliament's power of assent in relation to international agreements made by the Community (and it does not give Parliament powers in relation to article 113 EEC or the new article 228a EC).

However, "administrative expenditure" incurred by the Community's institutions as a result of the new provisions on common foreign and security policy would be charged to the Community's budget, and Council may decide also to charge "operational expenditure" (such as that required for joint actions) to the budget. In this respect, Parliament would have the power to influence the governments' decisions indirectly, if only by threatening to refuse or amend the appropriations required to carry them out. The Commission, too, must exercise crucial executive functions in relation to the budget, while continuing to be a full participant in the decisionmaking procedures of EPC with its own right of initiative.

It is, of course, too soon to know whether, and if so how, any of these facilities and powers will be used to influence democracy, or any other aspect of the internal politics of nonmember states, especially beyond the territorial space defined as European. The "principles and general guidelines" of the new policy will continue to be defined by the heads of government and foreign ministers meeting as the European Council, which still has overriding powers of initiative and ultimate control. Significant differences between the attitudes and policies of member states remain, and will continue to restrict both the general scope of their common responsibilities in external affairs beyond the Community and their capacity to take effective common action.

In spite of those differences, both the Community and its member states had been obliged by events leading up to the Maastricht agreement to broaden and intensify their collective response to external affairs, including the sphere of military action. However, neither in their response to the Gulf crisis in 1990 nor in their policies for reacting to events in Central and Eastern Europe did the Community give sufficient reassurance that it was yet capable of being a coherent and effective independent actor in foreign and security policy. With respect to both economic and military means, it is ultimately dependent on international action of wider territorial scope as well as the national policies of its own member states, especially those with a sufficient economic or military capacity of their own.

Was the premature recognition of the republics seceding from the federation of Yugoslavia, which was largely forced on the Community by one of its own members, justified as a way of defending or promoting democracy in a neighboring region? That action was, indeed, explained as a necessary defense of the right of political communities to self-determination and followed a due process of popular election in the communities concerned. It did not, however, await a similar process of consultation and deliberation involving the Yugoslav federation as a whole; perhaps it could not have done so. Ironically, a group of states presumed to aspire toward federalism thus helped to preside over the dissolution of an existing federation on its immediate borders (albeit one deviating from federalism in crucial respects in practice).

The consequences have in any event proved to be tragic and damaging for rights and freedoms more basic than those associated with popular participation in government. They have also exposed the Community's own shortcomings as an international actor, even in a region adjacent to the Community itself and qualifying as European geographically and historically. This particular failure of policy in the eastern Mediterranean can only confirm the suspicion that the Community is, presently and in the foreseeable future, unable to back up any claim to assume responsibility for public affairs beyond its own existing jurisdiction.

Summary and Conclusions

Over the past 20 years the European Community has progressively enlarged both its scope and its capacity as an independent power in international affairs. It justified its previous territorial expansion in the Mediterranean region partly as a means of defending and promoting pluralist democracy as well as of realizing its members' own economic and strategic objectives. It has now had to assume, unexpectedly, a major share of the responsibility for managing a transition toward increased economic and political freedom by states in Central and Eastern Europe. All these developments have obliged the Community's own institutions and its member governments to decide far more comprehensively than before what their own interests and obligations require in terms of constitutional and political issues.

Nevertheless, the Community's attitude toward distinctively political values outside its own borders remains both equivocal and incoherent. Its member states' common declarations invariably promise more than is either genuinely intended or realistically possible. So far its policy regarding the accession of new members, and, therefore, also toward developments in southeastern Europe, seems to be determined mainly by economic and strategic considerations, and the commitment to democracy must be understood in that light.

It must also be interpreted in conjunction with the now explicit ideological commitment to the principles of an open market economy, emphasized in various instances throughout the new Treaty on European Union. To extend the operation of those principles is the primary common objective of external relations to which all the existing members of European Union are able to agree. But the freedom of movement envisaged both for a widening economic union itself and for that union's relations with the rest of the world is likely to affect goods, services, and capital rather than labor and still seems unlikely to lead within the union itself to common guarantees of human and civic rights. So long as democracy remains an essentially secondary concern within its external frontiers, it would be unwise to expect the European Union to be effective as a positive influence in favor of democracy elsewhere.

The existing members, or at least a substantial majority of them, might conceivably yet insist on a revival and reinforcement of the federalist principles on which the Community was originally founded. Since such a course would entail both the limitation of states' powers by constituting representative institutions for the union as a whole and the investment of the union's own government with powers of economic intervention adequate to deal with problems of spatial and social disparities, it would also greatly simplify the issue of future membership, including that of states in the eastern Mediterranean region. If acceding to such a union required states to limit sovereignty in favor of common institutions founded on democracy, then no new member could or would want to qualify for membership without a genuine commitment to democracy. If the common institutions were able to deal effectively with regional economic divergence and market failure, it would also make membership freely available to states regardless of their current economic capacity or past performance. The constitution of a federal union would also go a long way to remedy the deficit of democracy that has so far made the price of integration too high for some of the existing members and undermined the credibility of European Union as a force for democracy in neighboring regions or the wider world.

However, the prevailing trend seems to favor a system in which a core of mainly larger states, with substantial military capacity and relative economic strength, in effect determine the welfare and security both of a number of smaller powers in the core itself and of a wider periphery of satellite dependencies, including possibly some existing members, restricted to a qualified form of membership or association. The criteria for admission to the core would be mainly military and economic. Beyond the union's immediate sphere of total or partial jurisdiction, there would be a more widespread and miscellaneous series of client states, bound to the union by economic need and for purposes of security. States outside the core would share with those within it a right guaranteed by international law to separate sovereignty, though this freedom would be qualified in practice by the exigencies of conforming to an open market economy and by reliance on the core states of the European Union and respect for these states' own alliances for purposes of security within their own region.

This prognosis must be considered all the more plausible in view of the decision to enlarge membership selectively before reconstituting European Union according to Maastricht. The alternative to a federal Europe thus projected would be in many essentials a revival of what used to be called imperialism. In any circumstances the further development of relations between European states on those lines cannot bode well for democracy in any part of the world; in the newly unstable conditions of world politics today it is most unlikely, on the other hand, to restore significant power of independent action to European states, acting individually or collectively. The prospect of a European superpower, which both the grandiloquence and the substance of the Maastricht agreement seem to suggest, is still unlikely in practice. But so long as it continues to consume the energies and excite the ambitions of so many of those engaged in public affairs in Europe itself, it will impede rather than assist those who pursue economic, social, and political development elsewhere.

Contributors

EPHRAIM AHIRAM is senior researcher at the Leonard Davis Institute for International Relations and at the Harry S. Truman Institute for the Advancement of Peace, both of The Hebrew University of Jerusalem. He is also a research fellow of the Center for Middle Eastern Studies, Harvard University, and has held senior research and administrative positions at Tel Aviv University, the Israel Defense Forces, and the Bank of Israel.

TAMAR ALMOR lectures at the College of Management and teaches at the Faculty of Management, the Leon Recanati Graduate School of Business Administration, Tel Aviv University.

ABRAHAM ASHKENASI is professor of international politics and regional affairs at the Free University of Berlin. He has also taught at UCLA, Columbia University, Tel Aviv University, and others; a recent book is *Palestinian Identities and Preferences* (1992).

GIANNI BONVICINI is director of the Istituto Affari Internazionali (IAI), Rome, and editor of the *International Spectator*. He has contributed to scientific publications, professional journals, and newspapers, and was coeditor of *The Atlantic Alliance and the Middle East* (1989).

ELISE S. BREZIS is assistant professor of economics at Bar-Ilan University and coordinator of the Azrieli Institute for Research on the Israeli Economy. She has also taught at The Hebrew University of Jerusalem and at Brandeis University and was head of the Statistics Division, Research Department, at the Bank of Israel.

DAVID COOMBES is professor of European Studies at the University of Limerick in the Republic of Ireland and a member of visiting faculty and of the executive council of the European University Center of Peace Studies, Stadtschlaining, Austria. His most recent books are *Ireland and the European Communities* (1983) and *Representative Government and Economic Power* (1981).

VICTORIA CURZON PRICE is professor of economics at the University of Geneva and director of the university's European Institute. She has also taught at Colgate University and the University of Amsterdam.

EMILIO FONTELA is professor of applied economics at the University of Geneva and Autonoma of Madrid, former special advisor to the EC Commission, former president of the European Scientific Association of Applied Economics (ASEPELT), and coauthor of the Group of Lisbon "Limits to Competition" report (1995).

SEEV HIRSCH is Jaffee Professor of International Trade at the Leon Recanati Graduate School of Business Administration, Tel Aviv University. He is the author of *Location of Industry and International Competitiveness* and *The Export of Six Manufacturing Industries: A Comparative Study of Denmark, Holland, and Israel.*

ALEX KEYNAN is special advisor to the president of the Israel Academy of Sciences and Humanities and to the president of The Hebrew University of Jerusalem. He is a professor of microbiology and was vice-president for research and development at The Hebrew University of Jerusalem.

BEATE KOHLER KOCH is professor of political science at the University of Mannheim and director of the European Integration Department at the university's Centre for European Social Studies. She has also taught at the University of Darmstadt, the Johns Hopkins University School of Advanced International Studies at Bologna, and the European Institute of Public Administration at Maastricht, and is the author of *Political Forces in Spain, Greece and Portugal* (1982).

J. KOL is coordinator of the master's program on The Economics of European Integration at Erasmus University. He has published books and articles mainly on international trade and trade policy, and has been a consultant to the World Bank, the OECD, and the Commission of the European Union.

M. MACIOTI is chief advisor in the Directorate General for Science, Research and Development of the Commission of the European Community, Brussels. He has published widely in the international technical press.

ANKE MARTINY is representative of the Friedrich Ebert Foundation in Israel, and has been a member of the West German Parliament and senator for cultural affairs in Berlin. A recent publication is *Kühle Gefühle zur Lage der Nation* (1991).

LEORA MERIDOR is head of the research department of the Bank of Israel. She has published a number of studies of aspects of Israel's economic situation, and was coeditor of *Lessons of Economic Stabilization in Its Aftermath* (1991).

PAUL PASCH is project officer of the Friedrich Ebert Foundation in Israel. He has been a guest scholar of the Harry S. Truman Institute for the Advancement of Peace of The Hebrew University of Jerusalem, and affiliated with the Arab Thought Forum in East Jerusalem.

JOHN REDMOND is senior lecturer in European political economy and director of the Graduate School of International Studies at the University of Birmingham, England. His recent publications include *Prospective Europeans* (ed., 1994), *The Next Mediterranean Enlargement of the European Union* (1993), and *The External Relations of the European Community: The International Response to 1992* (ed., 1992).

EBERHARD RHEIN is director in the EC Commission (Mediterranean, Near and Middle East). He has also been Chef de Cabinet of the commissioner in charge of external affairs, EC Commission, along with other posts in the EC.

LUIS DE SEBASTIÁN has held different posts for the Interamerican Development Bank (Washington, D.C.) and has been professor of economics at Escuela Superior de Administracion y Direccion de Empresas (ESADE), Barcelona. His most recently published book is *El Mercado* (1994).

ALFRED TOVIAS is associate professor of international relations at The Hebrew University of Jerusalem, and currently visiting research fellow at the Centre for European Policy Studies. He is also chairman of the Israeli Association for the Study of European Integration (IASEI). His books include *Foreign Economic Relations of the European Community: The Impact of Spain and Portugal* (1990), and *The Economics of Peace-making: Focus on the Egyptian-Israeli Situation* (coauthor, 1983).

CHARALAMBOS TSARDANIDIS is coordinator of the Center for Islamic and Turkish Studies of the Hellenic Foundation for Defense and Foreign Policy. He is the author of *The Politics of the EC-Cyprus Association Agreement: 1972-1988* (1988).

ETHNIEN - REGIONEN - KONFLIKTE

Soziologische und politologische Untersuchungen

Herausgeber: Abraham Ashkenasi

Band 1 Klaus Gensicke: Der Mufti von Jerusalem, Amin el-Husseini, und die Nationalsozialisten. 1988

Band 2 Christa Klement: Gemeinwesenorientierte Erziehung und Bildung im Sinne von Community Education als Antwort auf gesellschaftspolitische Herausforderungen der Gegenwart. Eine Analyse des Bedarfs und der Implementationsmöglichkeiten unter Berücksichtigung der spezifischen Bedingungen in der Bundesrepublik Deutschland und in Berlin (West). 1990.

Band 3 Brigitte Mihok: Ethnostratifikation im Sozialismus, aufgezeigt an den Beispielländern Ungarn und Rumänien. 1990.

Band 4 Yousef Nashef: The Psycholocical Impact of the Intifada on Palestinian Children Living in Refugee Camps in the West Bank, as Reflected in their Dreams, Drawings and Behavior. 1992.

Band 5 Mehmet Ata Bakis: Türkische Nahostpolitik seit dem Zweiten Weltkrieg. Ein Beitrag zur türkischen Außenpolitik (1945-1991). 1993.

Band 6 Alfred Tovias and Ephraim Ahiram (Editors) with Paul Pasch in cooperation with the Leonard Davis Institute: Whither EU-Israeli Relations? Common and Divergent Interests. 1995.